NON SANZ DROICT.

New 06/07

822.33
S

Greatly reduced facsimile of the first page of the earliest publication of *The Two Gentlemen of Verona* in the First Folio, 1623.

William Shakespeare

The Two Gentlemen of Verona

With New and Updated Critical Essays and a Revised Bibliography

Edited by Bertrand Evans

THE SIGNET CLASSICS SHAKESPEARE
General Editor: Sylvan Barnet

SIGNET CLASSICS

MAY - 1 2007

SIGNET CLASSICS
Published by New American Library, a division of
Penguin Group (USA) Inc., 375 Hudson Street,
New York, New York 10014, USA
Penguin Group (Canada), 90 Eglinton Avenue East, Suite 700, Toronto,
Ontario M4P 2Y3, Canada (a division of Pearson Penguin Canada Inc.)
Penguin Books Ltd., 80 Strand, London WC2R 0RL, England
Penguin Ireland, 25 St. Stephen's Green, Dublin 2,
Ireland (a division of Penguin Books Ltd.)
Penguin Group (Australia), 250 Camberwell Road, Camberwell, Victoria 3124,
Australia (a division of Pearson Australia Group Pty. Ltd.)
Penguin Books India Pvt. Ltd., 11 Community Centre, Panchsheel Park,
New Delhi - 110 017, India
Penguin Group (NZ), 67 Apollo Drive, Mairangi Bay,
Auckland 1311, New Zealand (a division of Pearson New Zealand Ltd.)
Penguin Books (South Africa) (Pty.) Ltd., 24 Sturdee Avenue,
Rosebank, Johannesburg 2196, South Africa

Penguin Books Ltd., Registered Offices:
80 Strand, London WC2R 0RL, England

Published by Signet Classics, an imprint of New American Library,
a division of Penguin Group (USA) Inc.

First Signet Classics Printing (Second Revised Edition), May 2007
10 9 8 7 6 5 4 3 2 1

3 9082 10529 9419

Contents

Shakespeare: An Overview

Biographical Sketch

Between the record of his baptism in Stratford on 26 April 1564 and the record of his burial in Stratford on 25 April 1616, some forty official documents name Shakespeare, and many others name his parents, his children, and his grandchildren. Further, there are at least fifty literary references to him in the works of his contemporaries. More facts are known about William Shakespeare than about any other playwright of the period except Ben Jonson. The facts should, however, be distinguished from the legends. The latter, inevitably more engaging and better known, tell us that the Stratford boy killed a calf in high style, poached deer and rabbits, and was forced to flee to London, where he held horses outside a playhouse. These traditions are only traditions; they may be true, but no evidence supports them, and it is well to stick to the facts.

Mary Arden, the dramatist's mother, was the daughter of a substantial landowner; about 1557 she married John Shakespeare, a tanner, glove maker, and trader in wool, grain, and other farm commodities. In 1557 John Shakespeare was a member of the council (the governing body of Stratford), in 1558 a constable of the borough, in 1561 one of the two town chamberlains, in 1565 an alderman (entitling him to the appellation of "Mr."), in 1568 high bailiff—the town's highest political office, equivalent to mayor. After 1577, for an unknown reason he drops out of local politics. What *is* known is that he had to mortgage his wife's property, and that he was involved in serious litigation.

The birthday of William Shakespeare, the third child and the eldest son of this locally prominent man, is unrecorded, but the Stratford parish register records that the infant was baptized on 26 April 1564. (It is quite possible that he was born on 23 April, but this date has probably been assigned by tradition because it is the date on which, fifty-two years later, he died, and perhaps because it is the feast day of St. George, patron saint of England.) The attendance records of the Stratford grammar school of the period are not extant, but it is reasonable to assume that the son of a prominent local official attended the free school—it had been established for the purpose of educating males precisely of his class—and received substantial training in Latin. The masters of the school from Shakespeare's seventh to fifteenth years held Oxford degrees; the Elizabethan curriculum excluded mathematics and the natural sciences but taught a good deal of Latin rhetoric, logic, and literature, including plays by Plautus, Terence, and Seneca.

On 27 November 1582 a marriage license was issued for the marriage of Shakespeare and Anne Hathaway, eight years his senior. The couple had a daughter, Susanna, in May 1583. Perhaps the marriage was necessary, but perhaps the couple had earlier engaged, in the presence of witnesses, in a formal "troth plight," which would render their children legitimate even if no further ceremony were performed. In February 1585, Anne Hathaway bore Shakespeare twins, Hamnet and Judith.

That Shakespeare was born is excellent; that he married and had children is pleasant; but that we know nothing about his departure from Stratford to London or about the beginning of his theatrical career is lamentable and must be admitted. We would gladly sacrifice details about his children's baptism for details about his earliest days in the theater. Perhaps the poaching episode is true (but it is first reported almost a century after Shakespeare's death), or perhaps he left Stratford to be a schoolmaster, as another tradition holds; perhaps he was moved (like Petruchio in *The Taming of the Shrew*) by

> Such wind as scatters young men through the world,
> To seek their fortunes farther than at home
> Where small experience grows.   (1.2.49–51)

In 1592, thanks to the cantankerousness of Robert Greene, we have our first reference, a snarling one, to Shakespeare as an actor and playwright. Greene, a graduate of St. John's College, Cambridge, had become a playwright and a pamphleteer in London, and in one of his pamphlets he warns three university-educated playwrights against an actor who has presumed to turn playwright:

There is an upstart crow, beautified with our feathers, that with his *tiger's heart wrapped in a player's hide* supposes he is as well able to bombast out a blank verse as the best of you, and being an absolute Johannes-factotum [i.e., jack-of-all-trades] is in his own conceit the only Shake-scene in a country.

The reference to the player, as well as the allusion to Aesop's crow (who strutted in borrowed plumage, as an actor struts in fine words not his own), makes it clear that by this date Shakespeare had both acted and written. That Shakespeare is meant is indicated not only by *Shake-scene* but also by the parody of a line from one of Shakespeare's plays, *3 Henry VI*: "O, tiger's heart wrapped in a woman's hide" (1.4.137). If in 1592 Shakespeare was prominent enough to be attacked by an envious dramatist, he probably had served an apprenticeship in the theater for at least a few years.

In any case, although there are no extant references to Shakespeare between the record of the baptism of his twins in 1585 and Greene's hostile comment about "Shake-scene" in 1592, it is evident that during some of these "dark years" or "lost years" Shakespeare had acted and written. There are a number of subsequent references to him as an actor. Documents indicate that in 1598 he is a "principal comedian," in 1603 a "principal tragedian," in 1608 he is one of the "men players." (We do not have, however, any solid information about which roles he may have played; later traditions say he played Adam in *As You Like It* and the ghost in *Hamlet*, but nothing supports the assertions. Probably his role as dramatist came to supersede his role as actor.) The profession of actor was not for a gentleman, and it occasionally drew the scorn of university men like Greene, who resented writing speeches for persons less educated than themselves, but it was respectable enough; players, if prosperous, were in effect members of the bourgeoisie, and there is nothing to suggest that Stratford considered William Shakespeare less than a solid citizen. When, in 1596, the Shakespeares were granted a coat of arms—i.e., the right to be considered gentlemen—the grant was made to Shakespeare's father, but probably William Shakespeare had arranged the matter on his own behalf. In subsequent transactions he is occasionally styled a gentleman.

Although in 1593 and 1594 Shakespeare published two narrative poems dedicated to the Earl of Southampton, *Venus and Adonis* and *The Rape of Lucrece*, and may well have written most or all of his sonnets in the middle nineties, Shakespeare's literary activity seems to have been almost entirely devoted to the theater. (It may be significant that the two narrative poems were written in years when the plague closed the theaters for several months.) In 1594 he was a charter member of a theatrical company called the Chamberlain's Men, which in 1603 became the royal company, the King's Men, making Shakespeare the king's playwright. Until he retired to Stratford (about 1611, apparently), he was with this remarkably stable company. From 1599 the company acted primarily at the Globe theater, in which Shakespeare held a one-tenth interest. Other Elizabethan dramatists are known to have acted, but no other is known also to have been entitled to a share of the profits.

Shakespeare's first eight published plays did not have his name on them, but this is not remarkable; the most popular play of the period, Thomas Kyd's *The Spanish Tragedy*, went through many editions without naming Kyd, and Kyd's authorship is known only because a book on the profession of acting happens to quote (and attribute to Kyd) some lines on the interest of Roman emperors in the drama. What is remarkable is that after 1598 Shakespeare's name commonly appears on printed plays—some of which are not his. Presumably his name was a drawing card, and publishers used it to attract potential buyers. Another indication of his popularity comes from Francis Meres, author of *Palladis Tamia: Wit's Treasury* (1598). In this anthology of snippets accompanied by an essay on literature, many playwrights are mentioned, but Shakespeare's name occurs more often than any other, and Shakespeare is the only playwright whose plays are listed.

From his acting, his playwriting, and his share in a playhouse, Shakespeare seems to have made considerable money. He put it to work, making substantial investments in Stratford real estate. As early as 1597 he bought New Place, the second-largest house in Stratford. His family moved in soon afterward, and the house remained in the family until a granddaughter died in 1670. When Shakespeare made his will in 1616, less than a month before he died, he sought to leave his property intact to his descendants. Of small bequests to relatives and to friends (including three actors, Richard Burbage, John Heminges, and Henry Condell), that to his wife of the second-best bed has provoked the most comment. It has sometimes been taken as a sign of an unhappy marriage (other supposed signs are the apparently hasty marriage, his wife's seniority of eight years, and his residence in London without his family). Perhaps the second-best bed was the bed the couple had slept in, the best bed being reserved for visitors. In any case, had Shakespeare not excepted it, the bed would have gone (with the rest of his household possessions) to his daughter and her husband.

On 25 April 1616 Shakespeare was buried within the chancel of the church at Stratford. An unattractive monument to his memory, placed on a wall near the grave, says that he died on 23 April. Over the grave itself are the lines, perhaps by Shakespeare, that (more than his literary fame) have kept his bones undisturbed in the crowded burial ground, where old bones were often dislodged to make way for new:

Good friend, for Jesus' sake forbear
To dig the dust enclosed here.
Blessed be the man that spares these stones
And cursed be he that moves my bones.

A Note on the Anti-Stratfordians, Especially Baconians and Oxfordians

Not until 1769—more than a hundred and fifty years after Shakespeare's death—is there any record of anyone expressing doubt about Shakespeare's authorship of the plays and poems. In 1769, however, Herbert Lawrence nominated Francis Bacon (1561–1626) in *The Life and Adventures of Common Sense*. Since then, at least two dozen other nominees have been offered, including Christopher Marlowe, Sir Walter Raleigh, Queen Elizabeth I, and Edward de Vere, 17th earl of Oxford. The impulse behind all anti-Stratfordian movements is the scarcely concealed snobbish opinion that "the man from Stratford" simply could not have written the plays because he was a country fellow without a university education and without access to high society. Anyone, the argument goes, who used so many legal terms, medical terms, nautical terms, and so forth, and who showed some familiarity with classical writing, must have attended a university, and anyone who knew so much about courtly elegance and courtly deceit must himself have moved among courtiers. The plays do indeed reveal an author whose interests were exceptionally broad, but specialists in any given field—law, medicine, arms and armor, and so on—soon find that the plays do not reveal deep knowledge in specialized matters; indeed, the playwright often gets technical details wrong.

The claim on behalf of Bacon, forgotten almost as soon as it was put forth in 1769, was independently reasserted by Joseph C. Hart in 1848. In 1856 it was reaffirmed by W. H. Smith in a book, and also by Delia Bacon in an article; in 1857 Delia Bacon published a book, arguing that Francis Bacon had directed a group of intellectuals who wrote the plays.

Francis Bacon's claim has largely faded, perhaps because it was advanced with such evident craziness by Ignatius Donnelly, who in *The Great Cryptogram* (1888) claimed to break a code in the plays that proved Bacon had written not only the plays attributed to Shakespeare but also other Renaissance works, for instance the plays of Christopher Marlowe and the essays of Montaigne.

Consider the last two lines of the Epilogue in *The Tempest*:

As you from crimes would pardoned be,
Let your indulgence set me free.

What was Shakespeare—sorry, Francis Bacon, Baron Verulam—*really* saying in these two lines? According to Baconians, the lines are an anagram reading, "Tempest of Francis Bacon, Lord Verulam; do ye ne'er divulge me, ye words." Ingenious, and it is a pity that in the quotation the letter *a* appears only twice in the cryptogram, whereas in the deciphered message it appears three times. Oh, no problem; just alter "Verulam" to "Verul'm" and it works out very nicely.

Most people understand that with sufficient ingenuity one can torture any text and find in it what one wishes. For instance: Did Shakespeare have a hand in the King James Version of the Bible? It was nearing completion in 1610, when Shakespeare was forty-six years old. If you look at the 46th Psalm and count forward for forty-six words, you will find the word *shake*. Now if you go to the end of the psalm and count backward forty-six words, you will find the word *spear*. Clear evidence, according to some, that Shakespeare slyly left his mark in the book.

Bacon's candidacy has largely been replaced in the twentieth century by the candidacy of Edward de Vere (1550–1604), 17th earl of Oxford. The basic ideas behind the Oxford theory, advanced at greatest length by Dorothy and Charlton Ogburn in *This Star of England* (1952, rev. 1955), a book of 1297 pages, and by Charlton Ogburn in *The Mysterious William Shakespeare* (1984), a book of 892 pages, are these: (1) The man from Stratford could not possibly have had the mental equipment and the experience to have written the plays—only a courtier could have written them; (2) Oxford had the requisite background (social position, education, years at Queen Elizabeth's court); (3) Oxford did not wish his authorship to be known for two basic reasons: writing for the public theater was a vulgar pursuit, and the plays show so much courtly and royal disreputable behavior that they would have compromised Oxford's position at court. Oxfordians offer countless details to support the claim. For example, Hamlet's phrase "that ever I was born to set it right" (1.5.89) barely conceals "E. Ver, I was born to set it right," an unambiguous announcement of de Vere's authorship, according to *This Star of England* (p. 654). A second example: Consider Ben

Jonson's poem entitled "To the Memory of My Beloved Master William Shakespeare," prefixed to the first collected edition of Shakespeare's plays in 1623. According to Oxfordians, when Jonson in this poem speaks of the author of the plays as the "swan of Avon," he is alluding not to William Shakespeare, who was born and died in Stratford-on-Avon and who throughout his adult life owned property there; rather, he is alluding to Oxford, who, the Ogburns say, used "William Shakespeare" as his pen name, and whose manor at Bilton was on the Avon River. Oxfordians do not offer any evidence that Oxford took a pen name, and they do not care that Oxford had sold the manor in 1581, forty-two years before Jonson wrote his poem. Surely a reference to the Shakespeare who was born in Stratford, who had returned to Stratford, and who had died there only seven years before Jonson wrote the poem is more plausible. And exactly why Jonson, who elsewhere also spoke of Shakespeare as a playwright, and why Heminges and Condell, who had acted with Shakespeare for about twenty years, should speak of Shakespeare as the author in their dedication in the 1623 volume of collected plays is never adequately explained by Oxfordians. Either Jonson, Heminges and Condell, and numerous others were in on the conspiracy, or they were all duped—equally unlikely alternatives. Another difficulty in the Oxford theory is that Oxford died in 1604, and some of the plays are clearly indebted to works and events later than 1604. Among the Oxfordian responses are: At his death Oxford left some plays, and in later years these were touched up by hacks, who added the material that points to later dates. *The Tempest*, almost universally regarded as one of Shakespeare's greatest plays and pretty clearly dated to 1611, does indeed date from a period after the death of Oxford, but it is a crude piece of work that should not be included in the canon of works by Oxford.

The anti-Stratfordians, in addition to assuming that the author must have been a man of rank and a university man, usually assume two conspiracies: (1) a conspiracy in Elizabethan and Jacobean times, in which a surprisingly large number of persons connected with the theater knew that the actor Shakespeare did not write the plays attributed to him but for some reason or other pretended that he did; (2) a conspiracy of today's Stratfordians, the professors who teach Shakespeare in the colleges and universities, who are said to have a vested interest in preserving Shakespeare as the author of the plays they teach. In fact, (1) it is inconceivable that the secret of Shakespeare's nonauthorship could have been preserved by all of the people who supposedly were in on the conspiracy, and (2) academic fame awaits any scholar today who can disprove Shakespeare's authorship.

The Stratfordian case is convincing not only because hundreds or even thousands of anti-Stratford arguments—of the sort that say "ever I was born" has the secret double meaning "E. Ver, I was born"—add up to nothing at all but also because irrefutable evidence connects the man from Stratford with the London theater and with the authorship of particular plays. The anti-Stratfordians do not seem to understand that it is not enough to dismiss the Stratford case by saying that a fellow from the provinces simply couldn't have written the plays. Nor do they understand that it is not enough to dismiss all of the evidence connecting Shakespeare with the plays by asserting that it is perjured.

The Shakespeare Canon

We return to William Shakespeare. Thirty-seven plays as well as some nondramatic poems are generally held to constitute the Shakespeare canon, the body of authentic works. The exact dates of composition of most of the works are highly uncertain, but evidence of a starting point and/or of a final limiting point often provides a framework for informed guessing. For example, *Richard II* cannot be earlier than 1595, the publication date of some material to which it is indebted; *The Merchant of Venice* cannot be later than 1598, the year Francis Meres mentioned it. Sometimes arguments for a date hang on an alleged topical allusion, such as the lines about the unseasonable weather in *A Midsummer Night's Dream*, 2.1.81–117, but such an allusion, if indeed it is an allusion to an event in the real world, can be variously interpreted, and in any case there is always the possibility that a topical allusion was inserted years later, to bring the play up-to-date. (The issue of alterations in a text between the time that Shakespeare drafted it and the time that it was printed—alterations due to censorship or playhouse practice or Shakespeare's own second thoughts—will be discussed in "The Play Text as a Collaboration" later in this overview.) Dates are often attributed on the basis of style, and although conjectures about style usually rest on other conjectures (such as Shakespeare's development as a playwright, or the appropriateness of lines to character), sooner or later one must rely on one's literary sense. There is no documentary proof, for example, that *Othello* is not as early as *Romeo and Juliet*, but one feels that *Othello* is a later, more mature work, and because the first record of its performance is 1604, one is glad enough to set its composition at that date and not push it back into Shakespeare's early years. (*Romeo and Juliet* was first published in 1597, but evidence suggests that it was written a little earlier.) The following chronology, then, is indebted not only to facts but also to informed guesswork and sensitivity. The dates, necessarily imprecise for some works, indicate something like a scholarly consensus concerning the time of original composition. Some plays show evidence of later revision.

Plays. The first collected edition of Shakespeare, published in 1623, included thirty-six plays. These are all accepted as Shakespeare's, though for one of them, *Henry VIII*, he is thought to have had a collaborator. A thirty-seventh play, *Pericles*, published in 1609 and attributed to Shakespeare on the title page, is also widely accepted as being partly by Shakespeare even though it is not included in the 1623 volume. Still another play not in the 1623 volume, *The Two Noble Kinsmen*, was first published in 1634, with a title page attributing it to John Fletcher and Shakespeare. Probably most students of the subject now believe that Shakespeare did indeed have a hand in it. Of the remaining plays attributed at one time or another to Shakespeare, only one, *Edward III*, anonymously published in 1596, is now regarded by some scholars as a serious candidate. The prevailing opinion, however, is that this rather simple-minded play is not Shakespeare's; at most he may have revised some passages, chiefly scenes with the Countess of

Salisbury. We include *The Two Noble Kinsmen* but do not include *Edward III* in the following list.

1588–94	*The Comedy of Errors*
1588–94	*Love's Labor's Lost*
1589–91	*2 Henry VI*
1590–91	*3 Henry VI*
1589–92	*1 Henry VI*
1592–93	*Richard III*
1589–94	*Titus Andronicus*
1593–94	*The Taming of the Shrew*
1592–94	*The Two Gentlemen of Verona*
1594–96	*Romeo and Juliet*
1594–96	*The Merchant of Venice*
1595	*Richard II*
1595–96	*A Midsummer Night's Dream*
1596–97	*King John*
1596–97	*1 Henry IV*
1597	*The Merry Wives of Windsor*
1597–98	*2 Henry IV*
1598–99	*Much Ado About Nothing*
1598–99	*Henry V*
1599	*Julius Caesar*
1599–1600	*As You Like It*
1599–1600	*Twelfth Night*
1600–1601	*Hamlet*
1601–1602	*Troilus and Cressida*
1602–1604	*All's Well That Ends Well*
1603–1604	*Othello*
1604	*Measure for Measure*
1605–1606	*King Lear*
1605–1606	*Macbeth*
1606–1607	*Antony and Cleopatra*
1605–1608	*Timon of Athens*
1607–1608	*Coriolanus*
1607–1608	*Pericles*
1609–10	*Cymbeline*
1610–11	*The Winter's Tale*
1611	*The Tempest*

| 1612–13 | *Henry VIII* |
| 1613 | *The Two Noble Kinsmen* |

Poems. In 1989 Donald W. Foster published a book in which he argued that "A Funeral Elegy for Master William Peter," published in 1612, ascribed only to the initials W.S., *may* be by Shakespeare. Foster later published an article in a scholarly journal, *PMLA* 111 (1996), in which he asserted the claim more positively. The evidence begins with the initials, and includes the fact that the publisher and the printer of the elegy had published Shakespeare's *Sonnets* in 1609. But such facts add up to rather little, especially because no one has found any connection between Shakespeare and William Peter (an Oxford graduate about whom little is known, who was murdered at the age of twenty-nine). The argument is based chiefly on statistical examinations of word patterns, which are said to correlate with Shakespeare's known work. Despite such correlations, however, many readers feel that the poem does not sound like Shakespeare. True, Shakespeare has a great range of styles, but his work is consistently imaginative and interesting. Many readers find neither of these qualities in "A Funeral Elegy." The poem is now attributed to John Ford.

1592–93	*Venus and Adonis*
1593–94	*The Rape of Lucrece*
1593–1600	*Sonnets*
1600–1601	*The Phoenix and the Turtle*

Shakespeare's English

1. Spelling and Pronunciation. From the philologist's point of view, Shakespeare's English is modern English. It requires footnotes, but the inexperienced reader can comprehend substantial passages with very little help, whereas for the same reader Chaucer's Middle English is a foreign language. By the beginning of the fifteenth century the chief grammatical changes in English had taken place, and the final unaccented *-e* of Middle English had been lost (though it survives even today in spelling, as in *name*); during the fifteenth century the dialect of London, the commercial and political center, gradually displaced the provincial dialects, at least in writing; by the end of the century, printing had helped to regularize and stabilize the language, especially spelling. Elizabethan spelling may seem erratic to us (there were dozens of spellings of *Shakespeare*, and a simple word like *been* was also spelled *beene* and *bin*), but it had much in common with our spelling. Elizabethan spelling was conservative in that for the most part it reflected an older pronunciation (Middle English) rather than the sound of the language as it was then spoken, just as our spelling continues to reflect medieval pronunciation—most obviously in the now silent but formerly pronounced letters in a word such as *knight*. Elizabethan pronunciation, though not identical with ours, was much closer to ours than to that of the Middle Ages. Incidentally, though no one can be certain about what Elizabethan English sounded like, specialists tend to believe it was rather like the speech of a modern stage Irishman (*time* apparently was pronounced *toime*, *old* pronounced *awld*, *day* pronounced *die*, and *join* pronounced *jine*) and not at all like the Oxford speech that most of us think it was.

An awareness of the difference between our pronunciation and Shakespeare's is crucial in three areas—in accent, or number of syllables (many metrically regular lines may look irregular to us); in rhymes (which may not look like rhymes); and in puns (which may not look like puns). Examples will be useful. Some words that were at least on occasion stressed differently from today are *aspèct*, *còmplete*, *fòrlorn*, *revènue*, and *sepùlcher*. Words that sometimes had an additional syllable are *emp[e]ress*, *Hen[e]ry*, *mon[e]th*, and *villain* (three syllables, *vil-lay-in*). An additional syllable is often found in possessives, like *moon's* (pronounced *moones*), and in words ending in *-tion* or *-sion*. Words that had one less syllable than they now have are *needle* (pronounced *neel*) and *violet* (pronounced *vilet*). Among rhymes now lost are *one* with *loan*, *love* with *prove*, *beast* with *jest*, *eat* with *great*. (In reading, trust your sense of metrics and your ear, more than your eye.) An example of a pun that has become obliterated by a change in pronunciation is Falstaff's reply to Prince Hal's "Come, tell us your reason" in *1 Henry IV*: "Give you a reason on compulsion? If reasons were as plentiful as blackberries, I would give no man a reason upon compulsion, I" (2.4.237–40). The *ea* in *reason* was pronounced rather like a long *a,* like the *ai* in *raisin*, hence the comparison with blackberries.

Puns are not merely attempts to be funny; like metaphors they often involve bringing into a meaningful relationship areas of experience normally seen as remote. In *2 Henry IV,* when Feeble is conscripted, he stoically says, "I care not. A man can die but once. We owe God a death" (3.2.242–43), punning on *debt,* which was the way *death* was pronounced. Here an enormously significant fact of life is put into simple commercial imagery, suggesting its commonplace quality. Shakespeare used the same pun earlier in *1 Henry IV,* when Prince Hal says to Falstaff, "Why, thou owest God a death," and Falstaff replies, " 'Tis not due yet: I would be loath to pay him before his day. What need I be so forward with him that calls not on me?" (5.1.126–29).

Sometimes the puns reveal a delightful playfulness; sometimes they reveal aggressiveness, as when, replying to Claudius's "But now, my cousin Hamlet, and my son," Hamlet says, "A little more than kin, and less than kind!" (1.2.64–65). These are Hamlet's first words in the play, and we already hear him warring verbally against Claudius. Hamlet's "less than kind" probably means (1) Hamlet is not of Claudius's family or nature, *kind* having the sense it still has in our word *mankind*; (2) Hamlet is not kindly (affectionately) disposed toward Claudius; (3) Claudius is not naturally (but rather unnaturally, in a legal sense incestuously) Hamlet's father. The puns evidently were not put in as sops to the groundlings; they are an important way of communicating a complex meaning.

2. Vocabulary. A conspicuous difficulty in reading Shakespeare is rooted in the fact that some of his words are no longer in common use—for example, words concerned with armor, astrology, clothing, coinage, hawking, horsemanship, law, medicine, sailing, and war. Shakespeare had a large vocabulary—something near thirty thousand words—but it was not so much a vocabulary of big words as a vocabulary drawn from a wide range of life, and it is partly his ability to call upon a great body of concrete language that gives his plays the sense of being in close contact with life. When the right word did not already exist, he made it up. Among words thought to be his coinages are *accommodation, all-knowing, amazement, bare-faced, countless, dexterously, dislocate, dwindle, fancy-free, frugal, indistinguishable, lackluster, laughable, overawe, premeditated, sea change, star-crossed*. Among those that have not survived are the verb *convive*, meaning to feast together, and *smilet*, a little smile.

Less overtly troublesome than the technical words but more treacherous are the words that seem readily intelligible to us but whose Elizabethan meanings differ from their modern ones. When Horatio describes the Ghost as an "erring spirit," he is saying not that the ghost has sinned or made an error but that it is wandering. Here is a short list of some of the most common words in Shakespeare's plays that often (but not always) have a meaning other than their most usual modern meaning:

'a	he
abuse	deceive
accident	occurrence
advertise	inform
an, and	if
annoy	harm
appeal	accuse
artificial	skillful
brave	fine, splendid
censure	opinion
cheer	(1) face (2) frame of mind
chorus	a single person who comments on the events
closet	small private room
competitor	partner
conceit	idea, imagination
cousin	kinsman
cunning	skillful
disaster	evil astrological influence
doom	judgment
entertain	receive into service

envy	malice
event	outcome
excrement	outgrowth (of hair)
fact	evil deed
fancy	(1) love (2) imagination
fell	cruel
fellow	(1) companion (2) low person (often an insulting term if addressed to someone of approximately equal rank)
fond	foolish
free	(1) innocent (2) generous
glass	mirror
hap, haply	chance, by chance
head	army
humor	(1) mood (2) bodily fluid thought to control one's psychology
imp	child
intelligence	news
kind	natural, acting according to nature
let	hinder
lewd	base
mere(ly)	utter(ly)
modern	commonplace
natural	a fool, an idiot
naughty	(1) wicked (2) worthless
next	nearest
nice	(1) trivial (2) fussy
noise	music
policy	(1) prudence (2) stratagem
presently	immediately
prevent	anticipate
proper	handsome
prove	test
quick	alive
sad	serious
saw	proverb
secure	without care, incautious
silly	innocent

sensible	capable of being perceived by the senses
shrewd	sharp
so	provided that
starve	die
still	always
success	that which follows
tall	brave
tell	count
tonight	last night
wanton	playful, careless
watch	keep awake
will	lust
wink	close both eyes
wit	mind, intelligence

All glosses, of course, are mere approximations; sometimes one of Shakespeare's words may hover between an older meaning and a modern one, and as we have seen, his words often have multiple meanings.

3. Grammar. A few matters of grammar may be surveyed, though it should be noted at the outset that Shakespeare sometimes made up his own grammar. As E. A. Abbott says in *A Shakespearian Grammar,* "Almost any part of speech can be used as any other part of speech": a noun as a verb ("he childed as I fathered"); a verb as a noun ("She hath made compare"); or an adverb as an adjective ("a seldom pleasure"). There are hundreds, perhaps thousands, of such instances in the plays, many of which at first glance would not seem at all irregular and would trouble only a pedant. Here are a few broad matters.

Nouns: The Elizabethans thought the *-s* genitive ending for nouns (as in *man's*) derived from *his*; thus the line " 'gainst the count his galleys I did some service," for "the count's galleys."

Adjectives: By Shakespeare's time adjectives had lost the endings that once indicated gender, number, and case. About the only difference between Shakespeare's adjectives and ours is the use of the now redundant *more* or *most* with the comparative ("some more fitter place") or superlative

("This was the most unkindest cut of all"). Like double comparatives and double superlatives, double negatives were acceptable; Mercutio "will not budge for no man's pleasure."

Pronouns: The greatest change was in pronouns. In Middle English *thou, thy,* and *thee* were used among familiars and in speaking to children and inferiors; *ye, your,* and *you* were used in speaking to superiors (servants to masters, nobles to the king) or to equals with whom the speaker was not familiar. Increasingly the "polite" forms were used in all direct address, regardless of rank, and the accusative *you* displaced the nominative *ye.* Shakespeare sometimes uses *ye* instead of *you,* but even in Shakespeare's day *ye* was archaic, and it occurs mostly in rhetorical appeals.

Thou, thy, and *thee* were not completely displaced, however, and Shakespeare occasionally makes significant use of them, sometimes to connote familiarity or intimacy and sometimes to connote contempt. In *Twelfth Night* Sir Toby advises Sir Andrew to insult Cesario by addressing him as *thou:* "If thou thou'st him some thrice, it shall not be amiss" (3.2.46–47). In *Othello* when Brabantio is addressing an unidentified voice in the dark he says, "What are you?" (1.1.91), but when the voice identifies itself as the foolish suitor Roderigo, Brabantio uses the contemptuous form, saying, "I have charged thee not to haunt about my doors" (93). He uses this form for a while, but later in the scene, when he comes to regard Roderigo as an ally, he shifts back to the polite *you,* beginning in line 163, "What said she to you?" and on to the end of the scene. For reasons not yet satisfactorily explained, Elizabethans used *thou* in addresses to God—"O God, thy arm was here," the king says in *Henry V* (4.8.108)—and to supernatural characters such as ghosts and witches. A subtle variation occurs in *Hamlet.* When Hamlet first talks with the Ghost in 1.5, he uses *thou,* but when he sees the Ghost in his mother's room, in 3.4, he uses *you,* presumably because he is now convinced that the Ghost is not a counterfeit but is his father.

Perhaps the most unusual use of pronouns, from our point of view, is the neuter singular. In place of our *its, his* was often used, as in "How far that little candle throws *his* beams." But the use of a masculine pronoun for a neuter noun came to seem unnatural, and so *it* was used for the possessive as well as the nominative: "The hedge-sparrow fed the cuckoo so long / That it had it head bit off by it young." In the late sixteenth century the possessive form *its* developed, apparently by analogy with the *-s* ending used to indicate a genitive noun, as in *book*'s, but *its* was not yet common usage in Shakespeare's day. He seems to have used *its* only ten times, mostly in his later plays. Other usages, such as "you have seen Cassio and she together" or the substitution of *who* for *whom,* cause little problem even when noticed.

Verbs, Adverbs, and Prepositions: Verbs cause almost no difficulty: The third person singular present form commonly ends in *-s,* as in modern English (e.g., "He blesses"), but sometimes in *-eth* (Portia explains to Shylock that mercy "blesseth him that gives and him that takes"). Broadly speaking, the *-eth* ending was old-fashioned or dignified or "literary" rather than colloquial, except for the words *doth, hath,* and *saith.* The *-eth* ending (regularly used in the King James Bible, 1611) is very rare in Shakespeare's dramatic prose, though not surprisingly it occurs twice in the rather formal prose summary of the narrative poem *Lucrece.* Sometimes a plural subject, especially if it has collective force, takes a verb ending in *-s,* as in "My old bones aches." Some of our strong or irregular preterites (such as *broke*) have a different form in Shakespeare (*brake*); some verbs that now have a weak or regular preterite (such as *helped*) in Shakespeare have a strong or irregular preterite (*holp*). Some adverbs that today end in *-ly* were not inflected: "grievous sick," "wondrous strange." Finally, prepositions often are not the ones we expect: "We are such stuff as dreams are made on," "I have a king here to my flatterer."

Again, none of the differences (except meanings that have substantially changed or been lost) will cause much difficulty. But it must be confessed that for some elliptical passages there is no widespread agreement on meaning. Wise editors resist saying more than they know, and when they are uncertain they add a question mark to their gloss.

Shakespeare's Theater

In Shakespeare's infancy, Elizabethan actors performed wherever they could—in great halls, at court, in the courtyards of inns. These venues implied not only different audiences but also different playing conditions. The innyards must have made rather unsatisfactory theaters: on some days they were unavailable because carters bringing goods to London used them as depots; when available, they had to be rented from the innkeeper. In 1567, presumably to avoid such difficulties, and also to avoid regulation by the Common Council of London, which was not well disposed toward theatricals, one John Brayne, brother-in-law of the carpenter turned actor James Burbage, built the Red Lion in an eastern suburb of London. We know nothing about its shape or its capacity; we can say only that it may have been the first building in Europe constructed for the purpose of giving plays since the end of antiquity, a thousand years earlier. Even after the building of the Red Lion theatrical activity continued in London in makeshift circumstances, in marketplaces and inns, and always uneasily. In 1574 the Common Council required that plays and playing places in London be licensed because

> sundry great disorders and inconveniences have been found to ensue to this city by the inordinate haunting of great multitudes of people, specially youth, to plays, interludes, and shows, namely occasion of frays and quarrels, evil practices of incontinency in great inns having chambers and secret places adjoining to their open stages and galleries.

The Common Council ordered that innkeepers who wished licenses to hold performance put up a bond and make contributions to the poor.

The requirement that plays and innyard theaters be licensed, along with the other drawbacks of playing at inns and presumably along with the success of the Red Lion, led James Burbage to rent a plot of land northeast of the city walls, on property outside the jurisdiction of the city. Here he built England's second playhouse, called simply the Theatre. About all that is known of its construction is that it was wood. It soon had imitators, the most famous being the Globe (1599), essentially an amphitheater built across the Thames (again outside the city's jurisdiction), constructed with timbers of the Theatre, which had been dismantled when Burbage's lease ran out.

Admission to the theater was one penny, which allowed spectators to stand at the sides and front of the stage that jutted into the yard. An additional penny bought a seat in a covered part of the theater, and a third penny bought a more comfortable seat and a better location. It is notoriously difficult to translate prices into today's money, since some things that are inexpensive today would have been expensive in the past and vice versa—a pipeful of tobacco (imported, of course) cost a lot of money, about three pennies, and an orange (also imported) cost two or three times what a chicken cost—but perhaps we can get some idea of the low cost of the penny admission when we realize that a penny could also buy a pot of ale. An unskilled laborer made about five or sixpence a day, an artisan about twelve pence a day, and the hired actors (as opposed to the sharers in the company, such as Shakespeare) made about ten pence a performance. A printed play cost five or sixpence. Of course a visit to the theater (like a visit to a baseball game today) usually cost more than the admission since the spectator probably would also buy food and drink. Still, the low entrance fee meant that the theater was available to all except the very poorest people, rather as movies and most athletic events are today. Evidence indicates that the audience ranged from apprentices who somehow managed to scrape together the minimum entrance fee and to escape from their masters for a few hours, to prosperous members of the middle class and aristocrats who paid the additional fee for admission to the galleries. The exact proportion of men to women cannot be determined, but women of all classes certainly were present. Theaters were open every afternoon but Sundays for much of the year, except in times of plague, when they were closed because of fear of infection. By the way, no evidence suggests the presence of toilet facilities. Presumably the patrons relieved themselves by making a quick trip to the fields surrounding the playhouses.

There are four important sources of information about the

structure of Elizabethan public playhouses—drawings, a contract, recent excavations, and stage directions in the plays. Of drawings, only the so-called de Witt drawing (c. 1596) of the Swan—really his friend Aernout van Buchell's copy of Johannes de Witt's drawing—is of much significance. The drawing, the only extant representation of the interior of an Elizabethan theater, shows an amphitheater of three tiers, with a stage jutting from a wall into the yard or

Johannes de Witt, a Continental visitor to London, made a drawing of the Swan theater in about the year 1596. The original drawing is lost; this is Aernout van Buchell's copy of it.

center of the building. The tiers are roofed, and part of the stage is covered by a roof that projects from the rear and is supported at its front on two posts, but the groundlings, who paid a penny to stand in front of the stage or at its sides, were exposed to the sky. (Performances in such a playhouse were held only in the daytime; artificial illumination was not used.) At the rear of the stage are two massive doors; above the stage is a gallery.

The second major source of information, the contract for the Fortune (built in 1600), specifies that although the Globe (built in 1599) is to be the model, the Fortune is to be square, eighty feet outside and fifty-five inside. The stage is to be forty-three feet broad, and is to extend into the middle of the yard, i.e., it is twenty-seven and a half feet deep.

The third source of information, the 1989 excavations of the Rose (built in 1587), indicate that the Rose was fourteen-sided, about seventy-two feet in diameter with an inner yard almost fifty feet in diameter. The stage at the Rose was about sixteen feet deep, thirty-seven feet wide at the rear, and twenty-seven feet wide downstage. The relatively small dimensions and the tapering stage, in contrast to the rectangular stage in the Swan drawing, surprised theater historians and have made them more cautious in generalizing about the Elizabethan theater. Excavations at the Globe have not yielded much information, though some historians believe that the fragmentary evidence suggests a larger theater, perhaps one hundred feet in diameter.

From the fourth chief source, stage directions in the plays, one learns that entrance to the stage was by the doors at the rear (*"Enter one citizen at one door, and another at the other"*). A curtain hanging across the doorway—or a curtain hanging between the two doorways—could provide a place where a character could conceal himself, as Polonius does, when he wishes to overhear the conversation between Hamlet and Gertrude. Similarly, withdrawing a curtain from the doorway could "discover" (reveal) a character or two. Such discovery scenes are very rare in Elizabethan drama, but a good example occurs in *The Tempest* (5.1.171), where a stage direction tells us, *"Here Prospero discovers Ferdinand and Miranda playing at chess."* There was also some sort of playing space "aloft" or "above" to represent, for instance, the top of a city's walls or a room above the street. Doubtless each theater had its own peculiarities, but perhaps we can talk about a "typical" Elizabethan theater if we realize that no theater need exactly fit the description, just as no mother is the average mother with 2.7 children.

This hypothetical theater is wooden, round, or polygonal (in *Henry V* Shakespeare calls it a "wooden *O*"), capable of holding some eight hundred spectators who stood in the yard around the projecting elevated stage—these spectators were the "groundlings"—and some fifteen hundred additional spectators who sat in the three roofed galleries. The stage, protected by a "shadow" or "heavens" or roof, is entered from two doors; behind the doors is the "tiring house" (attiring house, i.e., dressing room), and above the stage is some sort of gallery that may sometimes hold spectators but can be used (for example) as the bedroom from which Romeo—according to a stage direction in one text—"goeth down." Some evidence suggests that a throne can be lowered onto the platform stage, perhaps from the "shadow"; certainly characters can descend from the stage through a trap or traps into the cellar or "hell." Sometimes this space beneath the stage accommodates a sound-effects man or musician (in *Antony and Cleopatra "music of the hautboys* [oboes] *is under the stage"*) or an actor (in *Hamlet* the *"Ghost cries under the stage"*). Most characters simply walk on and off through the doors, but because there is no curtain in front of the platform, corpses will have to be carried off (Hamlet obligingly clears the stage of Polonius's corpse, when he says, "I'll lug the guts into the neighbor room"). Other characters may have fallen at the rear, where a curtain on a doorway could be drawn to conceal them.

Such may have been the "public theater," so called because its inexpensive admission made it available to a wide range of the populace. Another kind of theater has been called the "private theater" because its much greater admission charge (sixpence versus the penny for general admission at the public theater) limited its audience to the wealthy or the prodigal. The private theater was basically a large room, entirely roofed and therefore artificially illuminated, with a stage at one end. The theaters thus were distinct in two ways: One was essentially an amphitheater that catered to the general public; the other was a hall that catered to the wealthy. In 1576 a hall theater was established in Blackfriars, a Dominican priory in London that had been suppressed in 1538 and confiscated by the Crown and thus was not under the city's jurisdiction. All the actors in this Blackfriars theater were boys about eight to thirteen years old (in the public theaters similar boys played female parts; a boy Lady Macbeth played to a man Macbeth). Near the end of this section on Shakespeare's theater we will talk at some length about possible implications in this convention of using boys to play female roles, but for the moment we should say that it doubtless accounts for the relative lack of female roles in Elizabethan drama. Thus, in *A Midsummer Night's Dream*, out of twenty-one named roles, only four are female; in *Hamlet*, out of twenty-four, only two (Gertrude and Ophelia) are female. Many of Shakespeare's characters have fathers but no mothers—for instance, King Lear's daughters. We need not bring in Freud to explain the disparity; a dramatic company had only a few boys in it.

To return to the private theaters, in some of which all of the performers were children—the "eyrie of . . . little eyases" (nest of unfledged hawks—2.2.347–48) which Rosencrantz mentions when he and Guildenstern talk with Hamlet. The theater in Blackfriars had a precarious existence, and ceased operations in 1584. In 1596 James Burbage, who had already made theatrical history by building the Theatre, began to construct a second Blackfriars theater. He died in 1597, and for several years this second Blackfriars theater was used by a troupe of boys, but in 1608 two of Burbage's sons and five other actors (including Shakespeare) became joint operators of the theater, using it in the winter when the open-air Globe was unsuitable. Perhaps such a smaller theater, roofed, artificially illuminated, and with a tradition of a wealthy audience, exerted an influence in Shakespeare's late plays.

Performances in the private theaters may well have had intermissions during which music was played, but in the public theaters the action was probably uninterrupted, flowing from scene to scene almost without a break. Actors would enter, speak, exit, and others would immediately enter and establish (if necessary) the new locale by a few properties and by words and gestures. To indicate that the scene took place at night, a player or two would carry a torch. Here are some samples of Shakespeare establishing the scene:

> This is Illyria, lady.   (*Twelfth Night*, 1.2.2)

> Well, this is the Forest of Arden.   (*As You Like It*, 2.4.14)

> This castle has a pleasant seat; the air
> Nimbly and sweetly recommends itself
> Unto our gentle senses.   (*Macbeth*, 1.6.1–3)

> The west yet glimmers with some streaks of day.
>   (*Macbeth*, 3.3.5)

Sometimes a speech will go far beyond evoking the minimal setting of place and time, and will, so to speak, evoke the social world in which the characters move. For instance, early in the first scene of *The Merchant of Venice* Salerio suggests an explanation for Antonio's melancholy. (In the following passage, *pageants* are decorated wagons, floats, and *cursy* is the verb "to curtsy," or "to bow.")

> Your mind is tossing on the ocean,
> There where your argosies with portly sail—
> Like signiors and rich burghers on the flood,
> Or as it were the pageants of the sea—
> Do overpeer the petty traffickers
> That cursy to them, do them reverence,
> As they fly by them with their woven wings.   (1.1.8–14)

Late in the nineteenth century, when Henry Irving produced the play with elaborate illusionistic sets, the first scene showed a ship moored in the harbor, with fruit vendors and dock laborers, in an effort to evoke the bustling and exotic life of Venice. But Shakespeare's words give us this exotic, rich world of commerce in his highly descriptive language when Salerio speaks of "argosies with portly sail" that fly with "woven wings"; equally important, through Salerio Shakespeare conveys a sense of the orderly, hierarchical society in which the lesser ships, "the petty traffickers," curtsy and thereby "do . . . reverence" to their superiors, the merchant prince's ships, which are "Like signiors and rich burghers."

On the other hand, it is a mistake to think that except for verbal pictures the Elizabethan stage was bare. Although Shakespeare's Chorus in *Henry V* calls the stage an "unworthy scaffold" (Prologue 1.10) and urges the spectators to "eke out our performance with your mind" (Prologue 3.35), there was considerable spectacle. The last act of *Macbeth*, for instance, has five stage directions calling for *"drum and colors,"* and another sort of appeal to the eye is indicated by the stage direction *"Enter Macduff, with Macbeth's head."* Some scenery and properties may have been substantial; doubtless a throne was used, but the pillars supporting the roof would have served for the trees on which Orlando pins his poems in *As You Like It*.

Having talked about the public theater—"this wooden *O*"—at some length, we should mention again that Shakespeare's plays were performed also in other locales. Alvin Kernan, in *Shakespeare, the King's Playwright: Theater in the Stuart Court 1603–1613* (1995), points out that "several of [Shakespeare's] plays contain brief theatrical performances, set always in a court or some noble house. When Shakespeare portrayed a theater, he did not, except for the choruses in *Henry V*, imagine a public theater" (p. 195). (Examples include episodes in *The Taming of the Shrew*, *A Midsummer Night's Dream*, *Hamlet*, and *The Tempest*.)

A Note on the Use of Boy Actors in Female Roles

Until fairly recently, scholars were content to mention that the convention existed; they sometimes also mentioned that it continued the medieval practice of using males in female roles, and that other theaters, notably in ancient Greece and in China and Japan, also used males in female roles. (In classical Noh drama in Japan, males still play the female roles.) Prudery may have been at the root of the academic failure to talk much about the use of boy actors, or maybe there really is not much more to say than that it was a convention of a male-centered culture (Stephen Greenblatt's view, in *Shakespearean Negotiations* [1988]). Further, the very nature of a convention is that it is not thought about: Hamlet is a Dane and Julius Caesar is a Roman, but in Shakespeare's plays they speak English, and we in the audience never give this odd fact a thought. Similarly, a character may speak in the presence of others and we understand, again without thinking about it, that he or she is not heard by the figures on the stage (the aside); a character alone on the stage may speak (the soliloquy), and we do not take the character to be unhinged; in a realistic (box) set, the fourth wall, which allows us to see what is going on, is miraculously missing. The no-nonsense view, then, is that the boy actor was an accepted convention, accepted unthinkingly—just as today we know that Kenneth Branagh is not Hamlet, Al Pacino is not Richard III, and Denzel Washington is not the Prince of Aragon. In this view, the audience takes the performer for the role, and that is that; such is the argument we now make for race-free casting, in which African-Americans and Asians can play roles of persons who lived in medieval Denmark and ancient Rome. But gender perhaps is different, at least today. It is a matter of abundant academic study: The Elizabethan theater is now sometimes called a transvestite theater, and we hear much about cross-dressing.

Shakespeare himself in a very few passages calls attention to the use of boys in female roles. At the end of *As You Like It* the boy who played Rosalind addresses the audience, and says, "O men, . . . if I were a woman, I would kiss as many of you as had beards that pleased me." But this is in the Epilogue; the plot is over, and the actor is stepping out of the play and into the audience's everyday world. A second reference to the practice of boys playing female roles occurs in *Antony and Cleopatra*, when Cleopatra imagines that she and Antony will be the subject of crude plays, her role being performed by a boy:

> The quick comedians
> Extemporally will stage us, and present
> Our Alexandrian revels: Antony
> Shall be brought drunken forth, and I shall see
> Some squeaking Cleopatra boy my greatness.   (5.2.216–20)

In a few other passages, Shakespeare is more indirect. For instance, in *Twelfth Night* Viola, played of course by a boy, disguises herself as a young man and seeks service in the house of a lord. She enlists the help of a Captain, and (by way of explaining away her voice and her beardlessness) says,

> I'll serve this duke
> Thou shalt present me as an eunuch to him. (1.2.55–56)

In *Hamlet*, when the players arrive in 2.2, Hamlet jokes with the boy who plays a female role. The boy has grown since Hamlet last saw him: "By'r Lady, your ladyship is nearer to heaven than when I saw you last by the altitude of a chopine" (a lady's thick-soled shoe). He goes on: "Pray God your voice . . . be not cracked" (434–38).

Exactly how sexual, how erotic, this material was and is, is now much disputed. Again, the use of boys may have been unnoticed, or rather not thought about—an unexamined convention—by most or all spectators most of the time, perhaps *all* of the time, except when Shakespeare calls the convention to the attention of the audience, as in the passages just quoted. Still, an occasional bit seems to invite erotic thoughts. The clearest example is the name that Rosalind takes in *As You Like It*, Ganymede—the beautiful youth whom Zeus abducted. Did boys dressed to play female roles carry homoerotic appeal for straight men (Lisa Jardine's view, in *Still Harping on Daughters* [1983]), or for gay men, or for some or all women in the audience? Further, when the boy actor played a woman who (for the purposes of the plot) disguised herself as a male, as Rosalind, Viola, and Portia do—so we get a boy playing a woman playing a man—what sort of appeal was generated, and for what sort of spectator?

Some scholars have argued that the convention empowered women by letting female characters display a freedom unavailable in Renaissance patriarchal society; the convention, it is said, undermined rigid gender distinctions. In this view, the convention (along with plots in which female characters for a while disguised themselves as young men) allowed Shakespeare to say what some modern gender critics say: Gender is a constructed role rather than a biological given, something we make, rather than a fixed binary opposition of male and female (see Juliet Dusinberre, in *Shakespeare and the Nature of Women* [1975]). On the other hand, some scholars have maintained that the male disguise assumed by some female characters serves only to reaffirm traditional social distinctions since female characters who don male garb (notably Portia in *The Merchant of Venice* and Rosalind in *As You Like It*) return to their female garb and at least implicitly (these critics say) reaffirm the status quo. (For this last view, see Clara Claiborne Park, in an essay in *The Woman's Part*, ed. Carolyn Ruth Swift Lenz et al. [1980].) Perhaps no one answer is right for all plays; in *As You Like It* cross-dressing empowers Rosalind, but in *Twelfth Night* cross-dressing comically traps Viola.

Shakespeare's Dramatic Language: Costumes, Gestures and Silences; Prose and Poetry

Because Shakespeare was a dramatist, not merely a poet, he worked not only with language but also with costume, sound effects, gestures, and even silences. We have already discussed some kinds of spectacle in the preceding section, and now we will begin with other aspects of visual language; a theater, after all, is literally a "place for seeing." Consider the opening stage direction in *The Tempest*, the first play in the first published collection of Shakespeare's plays: *"A tempestuous noise of thunder and Lightning heard: Enter a Ship-master, and a Boteswain."*

Costumes: What did that shipmaster and that boatswain wear? Doubtless they wore something that identified them as men of the sea. Not much is known about the costumes that Elizabethan actors wore, but at least three points are clear: (1) many of the costumes were splendid versions of contemporary Elizabethan dress; (2) some attempts were made to approximate the dress of certain occupations and of antique or exotic characters such as Romans, Turks, and Jews; (3) some costumes indicated that the wearer was supernatural. Evidence for elaborate Elizabethan clothing can be found in the plays themselves and in contemporary comments about the "sumptuous" players who wore the discarded clothing of noblemen, as well as in account books that itemize such things as "a scarlet cloak with two broad gold laces, with gold buttons down the sides."

The attempts at approximation of the dress of certain occupations and nationalities also can be documented from the plays themselves, and it derives additional confirmation from a drawing of the first scene of Shakespeare's *Titus Andronicus*—the only extant Elizabethan picture of an identifiable episode in a play. (See pp. xxxviii–xxxix.) The drawing, probably done in 1594 or 1595, shows Queen Tamora pleading for mercy. She wears a somewhat medieval-looking robe and a crown; Titus wears a toga and a wreath, but two soldiers behind him wear costumes fairly close to Elizabethan dress. We do not know, however, if the drawing represents an actual stage production in the public theater, or perhaps a private production, or maybe only a reader's visualization of an episode. Further, there is some conflicting evidence: In *Julius Caesar* a reference is made to Caesar's doublet (a close-fitting jacket), which, if taken literally, suggests that even the protagonist did not wear Roman clothing; and certainly the lesser characters, who are said to wear hats, did not wear Roman garb.

It should be mentioned, too, that even ordinary clothing can be symbolic: Hamlet's "inky cloak," for example, sets him apart from the brightly dressed members of Claudius's court and symbolizes his mourning; the fresh clothes that are put on King Lear partly symbolize his return to sanity. Consider, too, the removal of disguises near the end of some plays. For instance, Rosalind in *As You Like It* and Portia and Nerissa in *The Merchant of Venice* remove their male attire, thus again becoming fully themselves.

Gestures and Silences: Gestures are an important part of a dramatist's language. King Lear kneels before his daughter Cordelia for a benediction (4.7.57–59), an act of humility that contrasts with his earlier speeches banishing her and that contrasts also with a comparable gesture, his ironic

kneeling before Regan (2.4.153–55). Northumberland's failure to kneel before King Richard II (3.3.71–72) speaks volumes. As for silences, consider a moment in *Coriolanus*: Before the protagonist yields to his mother's entreaties (5.3.182), there is this stage direction: *"Holds her by the hand, silent."* Another example of "speech in dumbness" occurs in *Macbeth*, when Macduff learns that his wife and children have been murdered. He is silent at first, as Malcolm's speech indicates: "What, man! Ne'er pull your hat upon your brows. Give sorrow words" (4.3.208–9). (For a discussion of such moments, see Philip C. McGuire's *Speechless Dialect: Shakespeare's Open Silences* [1985].)

Of course when we think of Shakespeare's work, we think primarily of his language, both the poetry and the prose.

Prose: Although two of his plays (*Richard II* and *King John*) have no prose at all, about half the others have at least one quarter of the dialogue in prose, and some have notably more: *1 Henry IV* and *2 Henry IV*, about half; *As You Like It*

and *Twelfth Night*, a little more than half; *Much Ado About Nothing*, more than three quarters; and *The Merry Wives of Windsor*, a little more than five-sixths. We should remember that despite Molière's joke about M. Jourdain, who was amazed to learn that he spoke prose, most of us do not speak prose. Rather, we normally utter repetitive, shapeless, and often ungrammatical torrents; prose is something very different—a sort of literary imitation of speech at its most coherent.

Today we may think of prose as "natural" for drama; or even if we think that poetry is appropriate for high tragedy we may still think that prose is the right medium for comedy. Greek, Roman, and early English comedies, however, were written in verse. In fact, prose was not generally considered a literary medium in England until the late fifteenth century; Chaucer tells even his bawdy stories in verse. By the end of the 1580s, however, prose had established itself on the English comic stage. In tragedy, Marlowe made some use of prose, not simply in the speeches of clownish servants but even in the speech of a tragic hero, Doctor Faustus. Still, before Shakespeare, prose normally was used in the theater only for special circumstances: (1) letters and proclamations, to set them off from the poetic dialogue; (2) mad characters, to indicate that normal thinking has become disordered; and (3) low comedy, or speeches uttered by clowns even when they are not being comic. Shakespeare made use of these conventions, but he also went far beyond them. Sometimes he begins a scene in prose and then shifts into verse as the emotion is heightened; or conversely, he may shift from verse to prose when a speaker is lowering the emotional level, as when Brutus speaks in the Forum.

Shakespeare's prose usually is not prosaic. Hamlet's prose includes not only small talk with Rosencrantz and Guildenstern but also princely reflections on "What a piece of work is a man" (2.2.312). In conversation with Ophelia, he shifts from light talk in verse to a passionate prose denunciation of women (3.1.103), though the shift to prose here is perhaps also intended to suggest the possibility of madness. (Consult Brian Vickers, *The Artistry of Shakespeare's Prose* [1968].)

Poetry: Drama in rhyme in England goes back to the Middle Ages, but by Shakespeare's day rhyme no longer dominated poetic drama; a finer medium, blank verse (strictly speaking, unrhymed lines of ten syllables, with the stress on every second syllable) had been adopted. But before looking at unrhymed poetry, a few things should be said about the chief uses of rhyme in Shakespeare's plays. (1) A couplet (a pair of rhyming lines) is sometimes used to convey emotional heightening at the end of a blank verse speech; (2) characters sometimes speak a couplet as they leave the stage, suggesting closure; (3) except in the latest plays, scenes fairly often conclude with a couplet, and sometimes, as in *Richard II*, 2.1.145–46, the entrance of a new character within a scene is preceded by a couplet, which wraps up the earlier portion of that scene; (4) speeches of two characters occasionally are linked by rhyme, most notably in *Romeo and Juliet*, 1.5.95–108, where the lovers speak a sonnet between them; elsewhere a taunting reply occasionally rhymes with the previous speaker's last line; (5) speeches with sententious or gnomic remarks are sometimes in rhyme, as in the duke's speech in *Othello* (1.3.199–206); (6) speeches of sardonic mockery are sometimes in rhyme—for example, Iago's speech on women in *Othello* (2.1.146–58)—and they sometimes conclude with an emphatic couplet, as in Bolingbroke's speech on comforting words in *Richard II* (1.3.301–2); (7) some characters are associated with rhyme, such as the fairies in *A Midsummer Night's Dream*; (8) in the early plays, especially *The Comedy of Errors* and *The Taming of the Shrew*, comic scenes that in later plays would be in prose are in jingling rhymes; (9) prologues, choruses, plays-within-the-play, inscriptions, vows, epilogues, and so on are often in rhyme, and the songs in the plays are rhymed.

Neither prose nor rhyme immediately comes to mind when we first think of Shakespeare's medium: It is blank verse, unrhymed iambic pentameter. (In a mechanically exact line there are five iambic feet. An iambic foot consists of two syllables, the second accented, as in *away*; five feet make a pentameter line. Thus, a strict line of iambic pentameter contains ten syllables, the even syllables being stressed more heavily than the odd syllables. Fortunately, Shakespeare usually varies the line somewhat.) The first speech in *A Midsummer Night's Dream*, spoken by Duke Theseus to his betrothed, is an example of blank verse:

> Now, fair Hippolyta, our nuptial hour
> Draws on apace. Four happy days bring in
> Another moon; but, O, methinks, how slow
> This old moon wanes! She lingers my desires,
> Like to a stepdame, or a dowager,
> Long withering out a young man's revenue.   (1.1.1–6)

As this passage shows, Shakespeare's blank verse is not mechanically unvarying. Though the predominant foot is the iamb (as in *apace* or *desires*), there are numerous variations. In the first line the stress can be placed on "fair," as the regular metrical pattern suggests, but it is likely that "Now" gets almost as much emphasis; probably in the second line "Draws" is more heavily emphasized than "on," giving us a trochee (a stressed syllable followed by an unstressed one); and in the fourth line each word in the phrase "This old moon wanes" is probably stressed fairly heavily, conveying by two spondees (two feet, each of two stresses) the oppressive tedium that Theseus feels.

In Shakespeare's early plays much of the blank verse is end-stopped (that is, it has a heavy pause at the end of each line), but he later developed the ability to write iambic pentameter verse paragraphs (rather than lines) that give the illusion of speech. His chief techniques are (1) enjambing, i.e., running the thought beyond the single line, as in the first three lines of the speech just quoted; (2) occasionally replacing an iamb with another foot; (3) varying the position of the chief pause (the caesura) within a line; (4) adding an occasional unstressed syllable at the end of a line, traditionally called a feminine ending; and (5) beginning or ending a speech with a half line.

Shakespeare's mature blank verse has much of the rhythmic flexibility of his prose; both the language, though richly figurative and sometimes dense, and the syntax seem natural. It is also often highly appropriate to a particular character. Consider, for instance, this speech from *Hamlet*, in which Claudius, King of Denmark ("the Dane"), speaks to Laertes:

> And now, Laertes, what's the news with you?
> You told us of some suit. What is't, Laertes?
> You cannot speak of reason to the Dane
> And lose your voice. What wouldst thou beg, Laertes,
> That shall not be my offer, not thy asking?　　　(1.2.42–46)

Notice the short sentences and the repetition of the name "Laertes," to whom the speech is addressed. Notice, too, the shift from the royal "us" in the second line to the more intimate "my" in the last line, and from "you" in the first three lines to the more intimate "thou" and "thy" in the last two lines. Claudius knows how to ingratiate himself with Laertes.

For a second example of the flexibility of Shakespeare's blank verse, consider a passage from *Macbeth*. Distressed by the doctor's inability to cure Lady Macbeth and by the imminent battle, Macbeth addresses some of his remarks to the doctor and others to the servant who is arming him. The entire speech, with its pauses, interruptions, and irresolution (in "Pull't off, I say," Macbeth orders the servant to remove the armor that the servant has been putting on him), catches Macbeth's disintegration. (In the first line, *physic* means "medicine," and in the fourth and fifth lines, *cast the water* means "analyze the urine.")

> Throw physic to the dogs, I'll none of it.
> Come, put mine armor on. Give me my staff.
> Seyton, send out.—Doctor, the thanes fly from me.—
> Come, sir, dispatch. If thou couldst, doctor, cast
> The water of my land, find her disease
> And purge it to a sound and pristine health,
> I would applaud thee to the very echo,
> That should applaud again.—Pull't off, I say.—
> What rhubarb, senna, or what purgative drug,
> Would scour these English hence? Hear'st thou of them?
>
> (5.3.47–56)

Blank verse, then, can be much more than unrhymed iambic pentameter, and even within a single play Shakespeare's blank verse often consists of several styles, depending on the speaker and on the speaker's emotion at the moment.

The Play Text as a Collaboration

Shakespeare's fellow dramatist Ben Jonson reported that the actors said of Shakespeare, "In his writing, whatsoever he penned, he never blotted out line," i.e., never crossed out material and revised his work while composing. None of Shakespeare's plays survives in manuscript (with the possible exception of a scene in *Sir Thomas More*), so we cannot fully evaluate the comment, but in a few instances the published work clearly shows that he revised his manuscript. Consider the following passage (shown here in facsimile) from the best early text of *Romeo and Juliet*, the Second Quarto (1599):

Ro. Would I were sleepe and peace so sweet to rest
The grey eyde morne smiles on the frowning night,
Checkring the Easterne Clouds with streaks of light,
And darknesse fleckted like a drunkard reeles,
From forth daies pathway, made by *Tytans* wheeles.
Hence will I to my ghostly Friers close cell,
His helpe to craue, and my deare hap to tell.

                                                  Exit.

Enter Frier alone with a basket.   (night,
Fri. The grey-eyed morne smiles on the frowning
Checking the Easterne clowdes with streaks of light:
And fleckeld darknesse like a drunkard reeles,
From forth daies path, and *Titans* burning wheeles:
Now erethe sun aduance his burning eie,

Romeo rather elaborately tells us that the sun at dawn is dispelling the night (morning is smiling, the eastern clouds are checked with light, and the sun's chariot—Titan's wheels—advances), and he will seek out his spiritual father, the Friar. He exits and, oddly, the Friar enters and says pretty much the same thing about the sun. Both speakers say that "the gray-eyed morn smiles on the frowning night," but there are small differences, perhaps having more to do with the business of printing the book than with the author's composition: For Romeo's "checkring," "fleckted," and "pathway," we get the Friar's "checking," "fleckeld," and "path." (Notice, by the way, the inconsistency in Elizabethan spelling: Romeo's "clouds" become the Friar's "clowdes.")

Both versions must have been in the printer's copy, and it seems safe to assume that both were in Shakespeare's manuscript. He must have written one version—let's say he first wrote Romeo's closing lines for this scene—and then he decided, no, it's better to give this lyrical passage to the Friar, as the opening of a new scene, but he neglected to delete the first version. Editors must make a choice, and they may feel that the reasonable thing to do is to print the text as Shakespeare intended it. But how can we know what he intended? Almost all modern editors delete the lines from

Romeo's speech, and retain the Friar's lines. They don't do this because they know Shakespeare's intention, however. They give the lines to the Friar because the first published version (1597) of *Romeo and Juliet* gives only the Friar's version, and this text (though in many ways inferior to the 1599 text) is thought to derive from the memory of some actors, that is, it is thought to represent a performance, not just a script. Maybe during the course of rehearsals Shakespeare—an actor as well as an author—unilaterally decided that the Friar should speak the lines; if so (remember that we don't know this to be a fact) his final intention was to give the speech to the Friar. Maybe, however, the actors talked it over and settled on the Friar, with or without Shakespeare's approval. On the other hand, despite the 1597 version, one might argue (if only weakly) on behalf of giving the lines to Romeo rather than to the Friar, thus: (1) Romeo's comment on the coming of the daylight emphasizes his separation from Juliet, and (2) the figurative language seems more appropriate to Romeo than to the Friar. Having said this, in the Signet edition we have decided in this instance to draw on the evidence provided by earlier text and to give the lines to the Friar, on the grounds that since Q1 reflects a production, in the theater (at least on one occasion) the lines were spoken by the Friar.

A playwright sold a script to a theatrical company. The script thus belonged to the company, not the author, and author and company alike must have regarded this script not as a literary work but as the basis for a play that the actors would create on the stage. We speak of Shakespeare as the author of the plays, but readers should bear in mind that the texts they read, even when derived from a single text, such as the First Folio (1623), are inevitably the collaborative work not simply of Shakespeare with his company—doubtless during rehearsals the actors would suggest alterations—but also with other forces of the age. One force was governmental censorship. In 1606 parliament passed "an Act to restrain abuses of players," prohibiting the utterance of oaths and the name of God. So where the earliest text of *Othello* gives us "By heaven" (3.3.106), the first Folio gives "Alas," presumably reflecting the compliance of stage practice with the law. Similarly, the 1623 version of *King Lear* omits the oath "Fut" (probably from "By God's foot") at 1.2.142, again presumably reflecting the line as it was spoken on the stage. Editors who seek to give the reader the play that Shakespeare initially conceived—the "authentic" play conceived by the solitary Shakespeare— probably will restore the missing oaths and references to God. Other editors, who see the play as a collaborative work, a construction made not only by Shakespeare but also by actors and compositors and even government censors, may claim that what counts is the play as it was actually performed. Such editors regard the censored text as legitimate, since it is the play that was (presumably) finally put on. A performed text, they argue, has more historical reality than a text produced by an editor who has sought to get at what Shakespeare initially wrote. In this view, the text of a play is rather like the script of a film; the script is not the film, and the play text is not the performed play. Even if we want to talk about the play that Shakespeare "intended," we will find ourselves talking about a script that he handed over to a company with the intention that it be implemented by actors. The "intended" play is the one that the actors—we might almost say "society"—would help to construct.

Further, it is now widely held that a play is also the work of readers and spectators, who do not simply receive meaning, but who create it when they respond to the play. This idea is fully in accord with contemporary poststructuralist critical thinking, notably Roland Barthes's "The Death of the Author," in *Image-Music-Text* (1977), and Michel Foucault's "What Is an Author?", in *The Foucault Reader* (1984). The gist of the idea is that an author is not an isolated genius; rather, authors are subject to the politics and other social structures of their age. A dramatist especially is a worker in a collaborative project, working most obviously with actors—parts may be written for particular actors—but working also with the audience. Consider the words of Samuel Johnson, written to be spoken by the actor David Garrick at the opening of a theater in 1747:

> The stage but echoes back the public voice;
> The drama's laws, the drama's patrons give,
> For we that live to please, must please to live.

The audience—the public taste as understood by the playwright—helps to determine what the play is. Moreover, even members of the public who are not part of the playwright's immediate audience may exert an influence through censorship. We have already glanced at governmental censorship, but there are also other kinds. Take one of Shakespeare's most beloved characters, Falstaff, who appears in three of Shakespeare's plays, the two parts of *Henry IV* and *The Merry Wives of Windsor*. He appears with this name in the earliest printed version of the first of these plays, *1 Henry IV*, but we know that Shakespeare originally called him (after an historical figure) Sir John Oldcastle. Oldcastle appears in Shakespeare's source (partly reprinted in the Signet edition of *1 Henry IV*), and a trace of the name survives in Shakespeare's play, 1.2.43–44, where Prince Hal punningly addresses Falstaff as "my old lad of the castle." But for some reason—perhaps because the family of the historical Oldcastle complained—Shakespeare had to change the name. In short, the play as we have it was (at least in this detail) subject to some sort of censorship. If we think that a text should present what we take to be the author's intention, we probably will want to replace *Falstaff* with *Oldcastle*. But if we recognize that a play is a collaboration, we may welcome the change, even if it was forced on Shakespeare. Somehow *Falstaff*, with its hint of *false-staff*, i.e., inadequate prop, seems just right for this fat knight who, to our delight, entertains the young prince with untruths. We can go as far as saying that, at least so far as a play is concerned, an insistence on the author's original intention (even if we could know it) can sometimes impoverish the text.

The tiny example of Falstaff's name illustrates the point that the text we read is inevitably only a version—something in effect produced by the collaboration of the playwright with his actors, audiences, compositors, and editors—of a fluid text that Shakespeare once wrote, just as the *Hamlet* that we see on the screen starring Kenneth Branagh is not the *Hamlet* that Shakespeare saw in an open-air playhouse starring Richard Burbage. *Hamlet* itself, as we shall note in a moment, also exists in several versions. It is not surprising that there is now much talk about the *instability* of Shakespeare's texts.

Because he was not only a playwright but was also an actor and a shareholder in a theatrical company, Shakespeare probably was much involved with the translation of the play from a manuscript to a stage production. He may or may not have done some rewriting during rehearsals, and he may or may not have been happy with cuts that were made. Some plays, notably *Hamlet* and *King Lear*, are so long that it is most unlikely that the texts we read were acted in their entirety. Further, for both of these plays we have more than one early text that demands consideration. In *Hamlet*, the Second Quarto (1604) includes some two hundred lines not found in the Folio (1623). Among the passages missing from the Folio are two of Hamlet's reflective speeches, the "dram of evil" speech (1.4.13–38) and "How all occasions do inform against me" (4.4.32–66). Since the Folio has more numerous and often fuller stage directions, it certainly looks as though in the Folio we get a theatrical version of the play, a text whose cuts were probably made—this is only a hunch, of course—not because Shakespeare was changing his conception of Hamlet but because the playhouse demanded a modified play. (The problem is complicated, since the Folio not only cuts some of the Quarto but adds some material. Various explanations have been offered.)

Or take an example from *King Lear*. In the First and Second Quarto (1608, 1619), the final speech of the play is given to Albany, Lear's surviving son-in-law, but in the First Folio version (1623), the speech is given to Edgar. The Quarto version is in accord with tradition—usually the highest-ranking character in a tragedy speaks the final words. Why does the Folio give the speech to Edgar? One possible answer is this: The Folio version omits some of Albany's speeches in earlier scenes, so perhaps it was decided (by Shakespeare? by the players?) not to give the final lines to so pale a character. In fact, the discrepancies are so many between the two texts, that some scholars argue we do not simply have texts showing different theatrical productions. Rather, these scholars say, Shakespeare substantially revised the play, and we really have two versions of *King Lear* (and of *Othello* also, say some)—two different plays—not simply two texts, each of which is in some ways imperfect.

In this view, the 1608 version of *Lear* may derive from Shakespeare's manuscript, and the 1623 version may derive from his later revision. The Quartos have almost three hundred lines not in the Folio, and the Folio has about a hundred lines not in the Quartos. It used to be held that all the texts were imperfect in various ways and from various causes— some passages in the Quartos were thought to have been set from a manuscript that was not entirely legible, other passages were thought to have been set by a compositor who was new to setting plays, and still other passages were thought to have been provided by an actor who misremembered some of the lines. This traditional view held that an editor must draw on the Quartos and the Folio in order to get Shakespeare's "real" play. The new argument holds (although not without considerable strain) that we have two authentic plays, Shakespeare's early version (in the Quarto) and Shakespeare's—or his theatrical company's—revised version (in the Folio). Not only theatrical demands but also Shakespeare's own artistic sense, it is argued, called for extensive revisions. Even the titles vary: Q1 is called *True Chronicle Historie of the life and death of King Lear and his three Daughters*, whereas the Folio text is called *The Tragedie of King Lear*. To combine the two texts in order to produce what the editor thinks is the play that Shakespeare intended to write is, according to this view, to produce a text that is false to the history of the play. If the new view is correct, and we do have texts of two distinct versions of *Lear* rather than two imperfect versions of one play, it supports in a textual way the poststructuralist view that we cannot possibly have an unmediated vision of (in this case) a play by Shakespeare; we can only recognize a plurality of visions.

Editing Texts

Though eighteen of his plays were published during his lifetime, Shakespeare seems never to have supervised their publication. There is nothing unusual here; when a playwright sold a play to a theatrical company he surrendered his ownership to it. Normally a company would not publish the play, because to publish it meant to allow competitors to acquire the piece. Some plays did get published: Apparently hard-up actors sometimes pieced together a play for a publisher; sometimes a company in need of money sold a play; and sometimes a company allowed publication of a play that no longer drew audiences. That Shakespeare did not concern himself with publication is not remarkable; of his contemporaries, only Ben Jonson carefully supervised the publication of his own plays.

In 1623, seven years after Shakespeare's death, John Heminges and Henry Condell (two senior members of Shakespeare's company, who had worked with him for about twenty years) collected his plays—published and unpublished—into a large volume, of a kind called a folio. (A folio is a volume consisting of large sheets that have been folded once, each sheet thus making two leaves, or four pages. The size of the page of course depends on the size of the sheet—a folio can range in height from twelve to sixteen inches, and in width from eight to eleven; the pages in the 1623 edition of Shakespeare, commonly called the First Folio, are approximately thirteen inches tall and eight inches wide.) The eighteen plays published during Shakespeare's lifetime had been issued one play per volume in small formats called quartos. (Each sheet in a quarto has been folded twice, making four leaves, or eight pages, each page being about nine inches tall and seven inches wide, roughly the size of a large paperback.)

Heminges and Condell suggest in an address "To the great variety of readers" that the republished plays are presented in better form than in the quartos:

> Before you were abused with diverse stolen and surreptitious copies, maimed and deformed by the frauds and stealths of injurious impostors that exposed them; even those, are now offered to your view cured and perfect of their limbs, and all the rest absolute in their numbers, as he [i.e., Shakespeare] conceived them.

There is a good deal of truth to this statement, but some of the quarto versions are better than others; some are in fact preferable to the Folio text.

Whoever was assigned to prepare the texts for publication in the first Folio seems to have taken the job seriously and yet not to have performed it with uniform care. The sources of the texts seem to have been, in general, good unpublished copies or the best published copies. The first play in the collection, *The Tempest*, is divided into acts and scenes, has unusually full stage directions and descriptions of spectacle, and concludes with a list of the characters, but the editor was not able (or willing) to present all of the succeeding texts so fully dressed. Later texts occasionally show signs of carelessness: in one scene of *Much Ado About Nothing* the names of actors, instead of characters, appear as speech prefixes, as they had in the Quarto, which the Folio reprints; proofreading throughout the Folio is spotty and apparently was done without reference to the printer's copy; the pagination of *Hamlet* jumps from 156 to 257. Further, the proofreading was done while the presses continued to print, so that each play in each volume contains a mix of corrected and uncorrected pages.

Modern editors of Shakespeare must first select their copy; no problem if the play exists only in the Folio, but a considerable problem if the relationship between a Quarto and the Folio—or an early Quarto and a later one—is unclear. In the case of *Romeo and Juliet*, the First Quarto (Q1), published in 1597, is vastly inferior to the Second (Q2), published in 1599. The basis of Q1 apparently is a version put together from memory by some actors. Not surprisingly, it garbles many passages and is much shorter than Q2. On the other hand, occasionally Q1 makes better sense than Q2. For instance, near the end of the play, when the parents have assembled and learned of the deaths of Romeo and Juliet, in Q2 the Prince says (5.3.208–9),

Come, *Montague;* for thou art early vp
To see thy sonne and heire, now earling downe.

The last three words of this speech surely do not make sense, and many editors turn to Q1, which instead of "now earling downe" has "more early downe." Some modern editors take only "early" from Q1, and print "now early down"; others take "more early," and print "more early down." Further, Q1 (though, again, quite clearly a garbled and abbreviated text) includes some stage directions that are not found in Q2, and today many editors who base their text on Q2 are glad to add these stage directions, because the directions help to give us a sense of what the play looked like on Shakespeare's stage. Thus, in 4.3.58, after Juliet drinks the potion, Q1 gives us this stage direction, not in Q2: *"She falls upon her bed within the curtains."*

In short, an editor's decisions do not end with the choice of a single copy text. First of all, editors must reckon with Elizabethan spelling. If they are not producing a facsimile, they probably modernize the spelling, but ought they to preserve the old forms of words that apparently were pronounced quite unlike their modern forms—*lanthorn, alablaster*? If they preserve these forms are they really preserving Shakespeare's forms or perhaps those of a compositor in the printing house? What is one to do when one finds *lanthorn* and *lantern* in adjacent lines? (The editors of this series in general, but not invariably, assume that words should be spelled in their modern form, unless, for instance, a rhyme is involved.) Elizabethan punctuation, too, presents problems. For example, in the First Folio, the only text for the play, Macbeth rejects his wife's idea that he can wash the blood from his hand (2.2.60–62):

No: this my Hand will rather
The multitudinous Seas incarnardine,
Making the Greene one, Red.

Obviously an editor will remove the superfluous capitals, and will probably alter the spelling to "incarnadine," but what about the comma before "Red"? If we retain the comma, Macbeth is calling the sea "the green one." If we drop the comma, Macbeth is saying that his bloody hand will make the sea ("the Green") *uniformly* red.

An editor will sometimes have to change more than spelling and punctuation. Macbeth says to his wife (1.7.46–47):

I dare do all that may become a man,
Who dares no more, is none.

For two centuries editors have agreed that the second line is unsatisfactory, and have emended "no" to "do": "Who dares do more is none." But when in the same play (4.2.21–22) Ross says that fearful persons

Floate vpon a wilde and violent Sea
Each way, and moue,

need we emend the passage? On the assumption that the compositor misread the manuscript, some editors emend "each way, and move" to "and move each way"; others emend "move" to "none" (i.e., "Each way and none"). Other editors, however, let the passage stand as in the original. The editors of the Signet Classics Shakespeare have restrained themselves from making abundant emendations. In their minds they hear Samuel Johnson on the dangers of emendation: "I have adopted the Roman sentiment, that it is more honorable to save a citizen than to kill an enemy." Some departures (in addition to spelling, punctuation, and lineation) from the copy text have of course been made, but the original readings are listed in a note following the play, so that readers can evaluate the changes for themselves.

Following tradition, the editors of the Signet Classics Shakespeare have prefaced each play with a list of characters, and throughout the play have regularized the names of the speakers. Thus, in our text of *Romeo and Juliet*, all speeches by Juliet's mother are prefixed "Lady Capulet," although the 1599 Quarto of the play, which provides our copy text, uses at various points seven speech tags for this one character: *Capu. Wi.* (i.e., Capulet's wife), *Ca. Wi., Wi., Wife, Old La.* (i.e., Old Lady), *La.,* and *Mo.* (i.e., Mother). Similarly, in *All's Well That Ends Well*, the character whom we regularly call "Countess" is in the Folio (the copy text) variously identified as *Mother, Countess, Old Countess, Lady,* and *Old Lady*. Admittedly there is some loss in regularizing, since the various prefixes may give us a hint of the way Shakespeare (or a scribe who copied Shakespeare's manuscript) was thinking of the character in a particular scene—for instance, as a mother, or as an old lady. But too much can be made of these differing prefixes, since the social relationships implied are *not* always relevant to the given scene.

We have also added line numbers and in many cases act and scene divisions as well as indications of locale at the beginning of scenes. The Folio divided most of the plays into acts and some into scenes. Early eighteenth-century editors increased the divisions. These divisions, which provide a convenient way of referring to passages in the plays, have been retained, but when not in the text chosen as the basis for the Signet Classics text they are enclosed within square brackets, [ ], to indicate that they are editorial additions. Similarly, though no play of Shakespeare's was equipped with indications of the locale at the heads of scene divisions, locales have here been added in square brackets for the convenience of readers, who lack the information that costumes, properties, gestures, and scenery afford to spectators. Spectators can tell at a glance they are in the throne room, but without an editorial indication the reader may be puzzled for a while. It should be mentioned, incidentally, that there are a few authentic stage directions—perhaps Shakespeare's, perhaps a prompter's—that suggest locales, such as *"Enter Brutus in his orchard,"* and *"They go up into the Senate house."* It is hoped that the bracketed additions in the Signet text will provide readers with the sort of help provided by these two authentic directions, but it is equally hoped that the reader will remember that the stage was not loaded with scenery.

Shakespeare on the Stage

Each volume in the Signet Classics Shakespeare includes a brief stage (and sometimes film) history of the play. When we read about earlier productions, we are likely to find them eccentric, obviously wrongheaded—for instance, Nahum Tate's version of *King Lear*, with a happy ending, which held the stage for about a century and a half, from the late seventeenth century until the end of the first quarter of the nineteenth. We see engravings of David Garrick, the greatest actor of the eighteenth century, in eighteenth-century garb as King Lear, and we smile, thinking how absurd the production must have been. If we are more thoughtful, we say, with the English novelist L. P. Hartley, "The past is a foreign country: they do things differently there." But if the eighteenth-century staging is a foreign country, what of the plays of the late sixteenth and seventeenth centuries? A foreign language, a foreign theater, a foreign audience. Probably all viewers of Shakespeare's plays, beginning with Shakespeare himself, at times have been unhappy with the plays on the stage. Consider three comments about production that we find in the plays themselves, which suggest Shakespeare's concerns. The Chorus in *Henry V* complains that the heroic story cannot possibly be adequately staged:

> But pardon, gentles all,
> The flat unraisèd spirits that hath dared
> On this unworthy scaffold to bring forth
> So great an object. Can this cockpit hold
> The vasty fields of France? Or may we cram
> Within this wooden *O* the very casques
> That did affright the air at Agincourt?
> . . . .
> Piece out our imperfections with your thoughts.
>
> (Prologue 1.8–14, 23)

Second, here are a few sentences (which may or may not represent Shakespeare's own views) from Hamlet's longish lecture to the players:

> Speak the speech, I pray you, as I pronounced it to you, trippingly on the tongue. But if you mouth it, as many of our players do, I had as lief the town crier spoke my lines. . . . O, it offends me to the soul to hear a robustious periwig-pated fellow tear a passion to tatters, to very rags, to split the ears of the groundlings. . . . And let those that play your clowns speak no more than is set down for them, for there be of them that will themselves laugh, to set on some quantity of barren spectators to laugh too, though in the meantime some necessary question of the play be then to be considered. That's villainous and shows a most pitiful ambition in the fool that uses it. (3.2.1–47)

Finally, we can quote again from the passage cited earlier in this introduction, concerning the boy actors who played the female roles. Cleopatra imagines with horror a theatrical version of her activities with Antony:

> The quick comedians
> Extemporally will stage us, and present
> Our Alexandrian revels: Antony
> Shall be brought drunken forth, and I shall see

Some squeaking Cleopatra boy my greatness
I' th' posture of a whore.   (5.2.216–21)

It is impossible to know how much weight to put on such passages—perhaps Shakespeare was just being modest about his theater's abilities—but it is easy enough to think that he was unhappy with some aspects of Elizabethan production. Probably no production can fully satisfy a playwright, and for that matter, few productions can fully satisfy *us;* we regret this or that cut, this or that way of costuming the play, this or that bit of business.

One's first thought may be this: Why don't they just do "authentic" Shakespeare, "straight" Shakespeare, the play as Shakespeare wrote it? But as we read the plays—words written to be performed—it sometimes becomes clear that we do not know *how* to perform them. For instance, in *Antony and Cleopatra* Antony, the Roman general who has succumbed to Cleopatra and to Egyptian ways, says, "The nobleness of life / Is to do thus" (1.1.36–37). But what is "thus"? Does Antony at this point embrace Cleopatra? Does he embrace and kiss her? (There are, by the way, very few scenes of kissing on Shakespeare's stage, possibly because boys played the female roles.) Or does he make a sweeping gesture, indicating the Egyptian way of life?

This is not an isolated example; the plays are filled with lines that call for gestures, but we are not sure what the gestures should be. *Interpretation* is inevitable. Consider a passage in *Hamlet.* In 3.1, Polonius persuades his daughter, Ophelia, to talk to Hamlet while Polonius and Claudius eavesdrop. The two men conceal themselves, and Hamlet encounters Ophelia. At 3.1.131 Hamlet suddenly says to her, "Where's your father?" Why does Hamlet, apparently out of nowhere—they have not been talking about Polonius—ask this question? Is this an example of the "antic disposition" (fantastic behavior) that Hamlet earlier (1.5.172) had told Horatio and others—including us—he would display? That is, is the question about the whereabouts of her father a seemingly irrational one, like his earlier question (3.1.103) to Ophelia, "Ha, ha! Are you honest?" Or, on the other hand, has Hamlet (as in many productions) suddenly glimpsed Polonius's foot protruding from beneath a drapery at the rear? That is, does Hamlet ask the question because he has suddenly seen something suspicious and now is testing Ophelia? (By the way, in productions that do give Hamlet a physical cue, it is almost always Polonius rather than Claudius who provides the clue. This itself is an act of interpretation on the part of the director.) Or (a third possibility) does Hamlet get a clue from Ophelia, who inadvertently betrays the spies by nervously glancing at their place of hiding? This is the interpretation used in the BBC television version, where Ophelia glances in fear toward the hiding place just after Hamlet says "Why wouldst thou be a breeder of sinners?" (121–22). Hamlet, realizing that he is being observed, glances here and there *before* he asks "Where's your father?" The question thus is a climax to what he has been doing while speaking the preceding lines. Or (a fourth interpretation) does Hamlet suddenly, without the aid of any clue whatsoever, intuitively (insightfully, mysteriously, wonderfully) sense that someone is spying? Directors must decide, of course—and so must readers.

Recall, too, the preceding discussion of the texts of the plays, which argued that the texts—though they seem to be before us in permanent black on white—are unstable. The Signet text of *Hamlet*, which draws on the Second Quarto (1604) and the First Folio (1623) is considerably longer than any version staged in Shakespeare's time. Our version, even if spoken very briskly and played without any intermission, would take close to four hours, far beyond "the two hours' traffic of our stage" mentioned in the Prologue to *Romeo and Juliet*. (There are a few contemporary references to the duration of a play, but none mentions more than three hours.) Of Shakespeare's plays, only *The Comedy of Errors*, *Macbeth*, and *The Tempest* can be done in less than three hours without cutting. And even if we take a play that exists only in a short text, *Macbeth*, we cannot claim that we are experiencing the very play that Shakespeare conceived, partly because some of the Witches' songs almost surely are non-Shakespearean additions, and partly because we are not willing to watch the play performed without an intermission and with boys in the female roles.

Further, as the earlier discussion of costumes mentioned, the plays apparently were given chiefly in contemporary, that is, in Elizabethan dress. If today we give them in the costumes that Shakespeare probably saw, the plays seem not contemporary but curiously dated. Yet if we use our own dress, we find lines of dialogue that are at odds with what we see; we may feel that the language, so clearly not our own, is inappropriate coming out of people in today's dress. A common solution, incidentally, has been to set the plays in the nineteenth century, on the grounds that this attractively distances the plays (gives them a degree of foreignness, allowing for interesting costumes) and yet doesn't put them into a museum world of Elizabethan England.

Inevitably our productions are adaptations, *our* adaptations, and inevitably they will look dated, not in a century but in twenty years, or perhaps even in a decade. Still, we cannot escape from our own conceptions. As the director Peter Brook has said, in *The Empty Space* (1968):

> It is not only the hair-styles, costumes and make-ups that look dated. All the different elements of staging—the shorthands of behavior that stand for emotions; gestures, gesticulations and tones of voice—are all fluctuating on an invisible stock exchange all the time. . . . A living theatre that thinks it can stand aloof from anything as trivial as fashion will wilt. (p. 16)

As Brook indicates, it is through today's hairstyles, costumes, makeup, gestures, gesticulations, tones of voice—this includes our *conception* of earlier hairstyles, costumes, and so forth if we stage the play in a period other than our own—that we inevitably stage the plays.

It is a truism that every age invents its own Shakespeare, just as, for instance, every age has invented its own classical world. Our view of ancient Greece, a slave-holding society in which even free Athenian women were severely circumscribed, does not much resemble the Victorians' view of ancient Greece as a glorious democracy, just as, perhaps, our view of Victorianism itself does not much resemble theirs. We cannot claim that the Shakespeare on our stage is the true Shakespeare, but in our stage productions we find a Shakespeare that speaks to us, a Shakespeare that our ancestors doubtless did not know but one that seems to us to be the true Shakespeare—at least for a while.

Our age is remarkable for the wide variety of kinds of staging that it uses for Shakespeare, but one development deserves special mention. This is the now common practice of race-blind or color-blind or nontraditional casting, which allows persons who are not white to play in Shakespeare. Previously blacks performing in Shakespeare were limited to a mere three roles, Othello, Aaron (in *Titus Andronicus*), and the Prince of Morocco (in *The Merchant of Venice*), and there were no roles at all for Asians. Indeed, African-Americans rarely could play even one of these three roles, since they were not welcome in white companies. Ira Aldridge (c.1806–1867), a black actor of undoubted talent, was forced to make his living by performing Shakespeare in England and in Europe, where he could play not only Othello but also—in whiteface—other tragic roles such as King Lear. Paul Robeson (1898–1976) made theatrical history when he played Othello in London in 1930, and there was some talk about bringing the production to the United States, but there was more talk about whether American audiences would tolerate the sight of a black man—a real black man, not a white man in blackface—kissing and then killing a white woman. The idea was tried out in summer stock in 1942, the reviews were enthusiastic, and in the following year Robeson opened on Broadway in a production that ran an astounding 296 performances. An occasional all-black company sometimes performed Shakespeare's plays, but otherwise blacks (and other minority members) were in effect shut out from performing Shakespeare. Only since about 1970 has it been common for nonwhites to play major roles along with whites. Thus, in a 1996–97 production of *Antony and Cleopatra,* a white Cleopatra, Vanessa Redgrave, played opposite a black Antony, David Harewood. Multiracial casting is now especially common at the New York Shakespeare Festival, founded in 1954 by Joseph Papp, and in England, where even siblings such as Claudio and Isabella in *Measure for Measure* or Lear's three daughters may be of different races. Probably most viewers today soon stop worrying about the lack of realism, and move beyond the color of the performers' skin to the quality of the performance.

Nontraditional casting is not only a matter of color or race; it includes sex. In the past, occasionally a distinguished woman of the theater has taken on a male role—Sarah Bernhardt (1844–1923) as Hamlet is perhaps the most famous example—but such performances were widely regarded as eccentric. Although today there have been some performances involving cross-dressing (a drag *As You Like It* staged by the National Theatre in England in 1966 and in the United States in 1974 has achieved considerable fame in the annals of stage history), what is more interesting is the casting of women in roles that traditionally are male but that need not be. Thus, a 1993–94 English production of *Henry V* used a woman—*not* cross-dressed—in the role of the governor of Harfleur. According to Peter Holland, who reviewed the production in *Shakespeare Survey* 48 (1995), "having a female Governor of Harfleur feminized the city and provided a direct response to the horrendous threat of rape and murder that Henry had offered, his language and her body in direct connection and opposition" (p. 210). Ten years from now the device may not play so effectively, but today it speaks to us. Shakespeare, born in the Elizabethan Age, has been dead nearly four hundred years, yet he is, as Ben Jonson said, "not of an age but for all time." We must understand, however, that he is "for all time" precisely because each age finds in his abundance something for itself and something of itself.

And here we come back to two issues discussed earlier in this introduction—the instability of the text and, curiously, the Bacon/Oxford heresy concerning the authorship of the plays. *Of course* Shakespeare wrote the plays, and we should daily fall on our knees to thank him for them—and yet there is something to the idea that he is not their only author. Every editor, every director and actor, and every reader to some degree shapes them, too, for when we edit, direct, act, or read, we inevitably become Shakespeare's collaborator and re-create the plays. The plays, one might say, are so cunningly contrived that they guide our responses, tell us how we ought to feel, and make a mark on us, but (for better or for worse) we also make a mark on them.

—SYLVAN BARNET
Tufts University

Introduction

Perhaps more than any other work of Shakespeare's, *The Two Gentlemen of Verona* needs to be taken for what it is: a product of its time written by a young poet-dramatist seeking his way in what was for him a new genre. So understood, it requires no defense and no apology.

The genre was romantic comedy, in the sense we mean when we mention the masterpieces that would follow in quick succession—*The Merchant of Venice, Much Ado About Nothing, As You Like It,* and *Twelfth Night.* The date of *The Two Gentlemen of Verona* is uncertain; the play may have been written as early as 1590–91, or as late as 1594–95. Most likely it was written in about 1592–93. But however late or early, within these extremes, it was for Shakespeare the first of a kind. Probably the only comedy he had written before it was *The Comedy of Errors,* a generally more satisfactory work than this, but one of an essentially different species, which gave him little practice toward the new kind that he was attempting. For the *Errors* he had a model, a good one, made by a master craftsman of Latin comedy, Plautus. Though Shakespeare injected certain romantic elements into this model, or grafted them onto it, the finished work remained rather more Plautine than Shakespearean, more a succession of farcical incidents than a pattern woven of romance elements.

And in the unlikely event that *The Two Gentlemen of Verona* followed rather than preceded *Love's Labor's Lost**and *The Taming of the Shrew,* it must yet be said that Shakespeare gained from these very little practice toward his new genre. *Love's Labor's Lost* was aimed satirically at fashionable but outlandish excesses in courtly language, manners, and ideas, and to the exploitation of these excesses the elements of romance were only incidental. The main plot of the *Shrew,* that of the taming, had no place at all for romance, in either atmosphere or action; it was hilarious farce, done in burlesque proportions. Nor did the secondary plot, that of the competition for Bianca, offer happy accommodation to the spirit and mood of romance; it turned upon a game of "supposes," in which only the attitudes of farce could be at home.

Whether before or after *Love's Labor's Lost* and *The Taming of the Shrew,* then, it was with *The Two Gentlemen of Verona* that Shakespeare found the way that led to the ultimate *Twelfth Night.* The basic stuff of romance, of course, lay around him everywhere, in prose and verse, in English, French, Spanish, and Italian, in medieval and in contemporary tellings and retellings. Long before *The Two Gentlemen of Verona* was written, the materials of romance had grown enamored of specific themes and encrusted with specific conventions. The theme of conflict between friendship and love was one that Chaucer had used and that was used again and again, in various forms of romantic tale and in various countries; indeed, Shakespeare's own sonnets play variations upon this theme, in the shadowy outline of a story that they tell of friendship between young men, of jealousy and separation occasioned by love of a third person, and finally of reconciliation. Lyly in his *Euphues,* Sidney in his *Arcadia,* less well-known contemporary romancers and translators all contributed to make the matters of romance,

* For an argument to the contrary, suggesting that *Love's Labors Lost* may be as early as 1588, see Alfred Harbage, "*Love's Labor's Lost* and the Early Shakespeare," *Philological Quarterly* XLI (1962): 18–36.

their themes and conventions, familiar to everyone who read or listened, familiar enough, indeed, that in any "new" romance, how a friend or lover, hero or heroine would behave in a given situation might be foretold with considerable accuracy.

What Shakespeare undertook in *The Two Gentlemen of Verona* was the experimental task of adapting the materials, themes, and conventions of meandering narrative romance (or of lyric verse) to dramatic form—to create action that might be contained in two hours, characters sufficiently credible that they might be represented by corporeal actors on a stage, a "world" of sufficient density to sustain both the action and the characters. For what he attempted there was nothing like a satisfactory precedent. For *The Comedy of Errors* he had had Plautus' *Menaechmi;* for the new genre of romantic comedy, he had nothing more suitable than, say, Lyly's *Endimion,* which was useful in every way except the one way that was needed; instead of being dramatically solid, *Endimion* was as watery as the moon.

For his principal story he turned to the tale of her life told by the shepherdess Felismena, in the *Diana Enamorada* of Jorge de Montemayor, of which the relevant portions are reprinted after the text in this edition of the play. But in fact the whole reservoir of romance served him, inevitably, whether he would or no. Its conventions, intruding, have made three centuries of critics of *The Two Gentlemen* wince: How could Proteus have been so dastardly as to betray, in an instant, his beloved, his friend, and his royal host—not to mention his own honor? How could Valentine so abruptly forgive his disloyal friend all his trespasses? How could he as quickly proffer his beloved Silvia to the miscreant Proteus who only a moment before threatened to rape her? How could Silvia—the daughter of a duke—stand by without a word during this base interchange? How could Julia, after this exhibition of general dastardliness, on the second or third bounce, welcome back her errant lover?

Indeed, very nearly the sole good thing that critics have found it appropriate to say about *The Two Gentlemen of Verona* is that it was a kind of "dry run" for its great successors, anticipating in many of its details the incidents, persons, and relationships the more masterful delineation of which distinguishes the later romantic comedies. It is impossible to do other than concur—in part—with this view of the play as proving ground for the later, greater works; in fact, we have already gone somewhat beyond concurrence by flatly stating that in this play Shakespeare found the way to *Twelfth Night.* That alone should be praise enough, for it allows to *The Two Gentlemen* the same kind and degree of significance that we allow to *Julius Caesar* when we say that in it Shakespeare first worked out the basic pattern of order and relationships that we have in mind when we speak of "Shakespearean" tragedy.

It is appropriate, therefore, that we review some of the ways in which this first of the romantic comedies prepared for those to come. Perhaps it is just to say that in most cases it furnished no more than an artist's preliminary sketches for the fuller, finished portraits of character, incident, and "world" that would come after. But at the same time that we review these, we should consider whether anything contains merit and deserves praise for itself, aside from being a "first."

A good place to begin is with the heroine. Shakespeare did not invent the bright, daring girl of the comedies who, for one reason or another, casts off the outward signs of her sex and personal identity and goes a-masquerading in the world as a man; she existed already in the romances, both in those on which he directly drew for plot and in others which exercised a pervasive influence merely by existing. But in the romances she is a shadowy, pale, and bloodless abstraction that does not come alive enough to be visualized; she would never do on any stage. Shakespeare's creation, in Julia, of the flesh-and-blood heroine who set a great line going was a tremendous achievement. The world of the romantic comedies is a woman's world, and it is dominated by this recurrent figure who masquerades as a man while all of her womanliness is apparent to the audience, which is always aware of her secret. While each belongs to the line, each superlative heroine also has a life that is peculiarly her own. Portia of *The Merchant of Venice,* Rosalind of *As You Like It,* Viola of *Twelfth Night*—these can properly be likened to one another only in the common role they play, in specific recurrent situations in which they take part, and in a kind of brilliance they share that marks them as extraordinary human beings: yet this very brilliance varies markedly in its quality, showing in one as a grand and dignified capability, in another as a mischievous brightness, and in another as a gently feminine and utterly disarming subtlety.

No doubt each of these represents as much of an improvement on Julia as Julia does upon the nebulous female of the prose romances. Nearly every incident in which Julia takes part will be repeated in richer detail by one or more of the later heroines, and just because we are so busy noting the resemblances of the first version to the later ones, and mentally comparing the earlier—to its disadvantage, of course—with the later, we may overlook the peculiar charm of this first heroine herself as she plays her part. Thus in 1.2, Julia's review of the "fair resort of gentlemen" who "every day with parle encounter me" appears a puny forerunner of Portia's review, with Nerissa, of her suitors at Belmont; for one reason, in the latter version Shakespeare knew to give the witty descriptive lines to Portia, not Nerissa, whereas in this first sketch Julia merely asks the questions and it is Lucetta who furnishes the witty replies. But it is in the incident of the letter—an incident that is *not* repeated and thereby shamed by later versions—that we come suddenly upon the fresh and ingratiating charm by which Julia bursts out of the conventions among which the insipid heroines of prose romance move, and comes quite alive; no doubt, this was the first glimpse afforded by the English stage of a new and magnificent creature, the heroine of romantic comedy. The incident immediately follows the review of potential suitors. Lucetta presents a letter from Proteus, and Julia stretches to the tiptoes of indignation in upbraiding her:

> Now, by my modesty, a goodly broker!
> Dare you presume to harbor wanton lines?
> To whisper and conspire against my youth?
> Now, trust me, 'tis an office of great worth,
> And you an officer fit for the place.
> There, take the paper; see it be returned,
> Or else return no more into my sight.

(41–47)

This show of spunk is itself worth a good deal; the pale heroine of romance could never have risen to it. Yet the heroine of Shakespearean romantic comedy is not truly born until the next instant, after Lucetta has left the stage; then, thus she speaks:

> And yet I would I had o'erlooked the letter.
> It were a shame to call her back again,
> And pray her to a fault for which I chid her.
> What fool is she, that knows I am a maid,
> And would not force the letter to my view!

(50–54)

Shakespeare could definitely have stopped the incident at this; it would have been enough to establish a new institution. But he goes on: Julia calls back Lucetta, takes the letter from her, and, in a simply superb demonstration of the chastity of mind appropriate to highborn ladies in the presence of their lessers, tears it all to bits. Shakespeare could have stopped here, too; it would have been more than enough. But once more he goes on: Lucetta is again dismissed—and in an instant Julia is down on the floor, scrambling to reassemble the pieces:

Be calm, good wind, blow not a word away
Till I have found each letter in the letter,
Except mine own name: that some whirlwind bear
Unto a ragged, fearful-hanging rock,
And throw it thence into the raging sea!

(118–22)

In later scenes Julia repeatedly breaks the way for her great successors. In 2.7, she takes the plunge for all of them: she decides to go to Milan, to check on her—of course!—completely faithful Proteus; but not in her own identity:

Not like a woman, for I would prevent
The loose encounters of lascivious men.
Gentle Lucetta, fit me with such weeds
As may beseem some well-reputed page.

(40–43)

This was a fateful step. Soon Portia would say to Nerissa,

I'll hold thee any wager,
When we are both accoutred like young men,
I'll prove the prettier fellow of the two . . .
(*Merchant of Venice,* 3.4.62–64)

Rosalind would say to Celia,

Were it not better,
Because that I am more than common tall,
That I did suit me all points like a man?
A gallant curtle-ax upon my thigh,
A boar-spear in my hand . . .
(*As You Like It,* 1.3.112–16)

And Viola would say to the Captain, who fished her out of the deep,

> Conceal me what I am, and be my aid
> For such disguise as haply shall become
> The form of my intent. I'll serve this duke . . .
>
> *(Twelfth Night,* 1.2.53–55)

The parallels of this kind are numerous. Like all three of her famed successors, Julia talks with her loved one, who knows her not. Like Viola, she is sent as an envoy of love by her truelove to *his* love. Like Portia, she receives from his finger the ring that she gave him. Like Rosalind, she all but gives away her sex by swooning at a crucial time. And like all the others, she gets her love at last on terms of uncompromising surrender:

> What is in Silvia's face, but I may spy
> More fresh in Julia's with a constant eye?
> . . . .
> Bear witness, Heaven, I have my wish forever.
>
> (5.4.114–15, 119)

In every parallel incident, she suffers from the inevitable comparison, and it is only in the rare moments when we catch her, so to speak, alone, doing something uniquely hers, not "trying out" something that her successors would perfect, that she has a chance to shine. So she does in the incident of the letter, and so, for example, she does in 4.2, when, wearing boy's clothes and accompanied by the Host, she eavesdrops on Proteus' serenade of Silvia. Here, though the song is all Silvia's, the dramatic center is all Julia's:

Host. How do you, man? The music likes you not.

Julia. You mistake; the musician likes me not.

Host. Why, my pretty youth?

Julia. He plays false, father.

(54–57)

She is great here not merely for the emotional impact of her moment of heartbreak, but for her resilience. The pallid heroine of prose romance would have crawled away to bleed in secret; but Julia asks of the Host, "Where lies Sir Proteus?" Her mind has already conceived a device by which she can keep an eye on him until such time as she can capture him for once and all.

It is almost certain that Proteus and Valentine suffer less by comparison with their successors than does Julia. This will appear a startling statement, particularly with reference to Proteus, who has a long and virtually undeviating history of being abominated by critics. It is nevertheless essentially true, and the reason it is so is not hard to find. The fact is that the heroes of the romantic comedies—unlike the heroines, whose power to dazzle the eye and the imagination makes a beginning with Julia and at once thereafter becomes blinding—never do come to amount to very much. Proteus and Valentine, therefore, look about as good as any.

Between them, these two gentlemen define both of the emphases of which the one or the other dominates the later heroes. It is not strictly accurate to classify Shakespeare's romantic young males in two "types"—one wicked, the other stupid—but it is fair to say that each of them evinces a *tendency* in one or the other direction, and that two of them even tend toward both directions at the same time. To say that they exhibit a tendency toward wickedness or toward stupidity is not to say that they are wicked or stupid, but is to suggest that if they went somewhat farther along the road their qualities point them in, they would indeed be downright wicked or downright stupid. It should be added at once that though this view of the heroes is hardly flattering, surely none of us could seriously wish any one of the heroes changed in the slightest; each is perfect for the thing he is, perfect for the particular dramatic "world" of which he is part—and, what is most important, in each case the brilliant heroine loves the fellow either just as he stands or just as she has made him be by the end of the play.

Valentine is the simpler case, in more ways than one, and we should look at him before we deal with Proteus. Valentine looks ahead to the hero who is best represented by Orlando of *As You Like It.* The main thing to be said of this kind of hero is that there is nothing in the least "wrong" with him. He has nothing but virtues—all the virtues that anyone can name, except brilliance. He is kind, brave, loyal, generous, modest, forgiving—anything and everything as you like it; but any passing remark can make him look like a wonderful simpleton in an instant: "I found him under a tree," says Celia of Orlando, "like a dropped acorn." If Valentine is not quite up to Orlando in the kind that he is, he is nevertheless very nearly his equal, both in the sterling qualities of romantic young manhood that his kind of hero stands for and in the lack of intellectual keenness (especially around heroines) that he also stands for. Valentine is the perfect exemplar of friendship; he would never violate friendship even for love—and he is entirely true to his kind when, in the end, without needing to go through the painful process of thinking about it, he cheerfully offers Silvia—for whom he would just as cheerfully die—to Proteus. He could not do otherwise and be what he is; and because Shakespeare has been entirely clear in showing us what he is, it is we who are at fault if we so much as imagine that he should do otherwise. Valentine shares with Orlando, and not particularly with any of Shakespeare's other heroes of romantic comedy, a certain exaggeratedly heroic valor. Orlando hurls a professional wrestler to the ground, breaking his bones, and deals just as directly, and with no sweat, with a "sucked and hungry" lioness. But he best sums up all the qualities of his kind of romantic hero in a single incident and a single posture when, seeking food for old Adam, he pops into the clearing where the exiled Duke and his followers are at table, and mistaking them all for savages who have never been out of the woods, demands with drawn sword that they "Forbear, and eat no more" until his needs are served. Here, in a stroke, he is heroic on the grand scale, greathearted, nobly unselfish for his old servant—and, quite unconsciously, just a little ludicrous for having so much misjudged the situation.

With such a stroke, Shakespeare imparted a kind of flavor that transformed the romance hero, somewhat as he transformed the vapid romance heroine by adding some special feminine touches, including spunk. Bassanio of *The Merchant of Venice* exhibits the added quality very well when—of all people—he, the golden-fleece hunter, coolly reasons his way past the gold casket and the silver casket and takes the lead one; and he exhibits it again when, in the court scene, after Portia has pinned Shylock to the wall and has him quite at her mercy, he fails to perceive how completely the tables have turned and continues to rush forward, nobly generous, with bags of ducats—Portia's own—to buy off his friend. And this very way of surrounding his hero's grimly stalwart attitude with a tongue-in-cheek attitude Shakespeare first explored in Valentine, notably at his first encounter with the outlaws, upon whom he makes such a favorable impression that they invite him to be "king for our wild faction" after two minutes of conversation. Surely, this is an incident to the abruptness of which critics should take no such exception as some have; like Orlando's heroic-ludicrous posture at the Duke's banquet, and like Valentine's own quick offer to surrender Silvia to Proteus, and like Bassanio's straight-faced choice of the leaden casket, it hints of what Shakespeare did to romance to make it romantic *comedy*.

Thus the attitude of comedy within which the actions of the Valentine-Orlando kind of hero are framed is not limited to the more obvious situations in which the comic potentialities of the hero's intellectual equipment are exploited—as in the case of Valentine's penning a love note for Silvia and not understanding, while the simple Speed is appalled by his obtuseness, that her "secret nameless friend" is himself—but extends to his most heroic and high-minded moments. On both counts, Valentine is more nearly a finished portrait than a first sketch.

At least as much may be said of Proteus, first of those who represent a contrary emphasis in the heroic character. Valentine, Bassanio, Orlando are innocent and goodhearted; none of them could ever be imagined as "going bad" under any circumstances. Proteus not only could but temporarily does go bad, and so do those who follow in his line, namely, Claudio of *Much Ado About Nothing* and—stepping just over the boundary into the "dark comedies"—Bertram of *All's Well That Ends Well.*

These heroes are clearly not so much like one another as are those of the other line, who might almost be said to be interchangeable. Claudio, in particular, shares with the Valentine-Orlando hero a certain congenital unawareness of situation; but, curiously, while this appears a lovable fault in the others and endears them to us as well as to the heroines, in Claudio it is odious. A callow princox of a youth, Claudio looks from the outset like one who could mistake a situation and become nasty about it, as indeed he does. If he is "cured" in the end, when the truth of the situation has been made apparent, yet he remains the same callow princox still, and one supposes that he would be capable of dastardly conduct again tomorrow or the next day if the right set of circumstances invited him. Bertram and Claudio differ most notably in that, while each is capable of dastardly conduct, Claudio's worst exhibition of contemptible qualities is based on his initial misunderstanding of situation, whereas Bertram's involvement in such unheroic activities as illicit pursuits and outright lying is quite deliberate. If Claudio is capable of contemptible behavior only when he misunderstands, Bertram is most capable of it when he understands very well.

As a hero of his kind, therefore, not being in competition with the Valentine-Orlando kind, but compared with Claudio and Bertram, Proteus looks remarkably good. As a dramatic character he is certainly as well drawn as they are, and as a man he is hardly worse than they. Proteus is like Bertram in needing no misunderstanding of situation to start him on a wayward course. It has been remarked of Macbeth that of all Shakespeare's tragic heroes he alone knowingly embraces evil as his good, and it may as well be said of Proteus and Bertram that they alone of the comic heroes knowingly take to the crooked paths of dishonor. Bertram rejects the wife of inferior birth who was forced on him; lies to her; pursues, with the intention of corrupting, for no reason but lust, a virgin of Florence; is prevented from committing adultery only by his wife's shrewd intervention; and thereafter, confronted with his deeds, lies, slanders others, and abandons all dignity and honor in an exhibition of squirming and twisting; and after his disgraceful wallowing, he is abruptly forgiven all his trespasses and welcomed home as a worthy subject, son, and husband.

Against Bertram's record as a hero, Proteus' fairly shines. He does not choose to leave his Julia, but is sent away by his father. Neither does he choose to fall in love with Silvia, any more than Romeo chooses to fall in love with Juliet (and many details of the play prove that Shakespeare had Brooke's *Romeus and Juliet* in mind as he wrote). Here, in reducing the odium of Proteus' initial fault, Shakespeare has been characteristically shrewd, for he has made Silvia irresistible, with both an inward and an outward beauty. If, lest she put Julia in the shade, he had made her only an ordinary beauty, Proteus' "threefold perjury" committed in pursuit of her would have been difficult to understand and all but impossible to forgive. But on Silvia he has lavished all his superlatives, made her dazzling, wholly worthy of the song with which she is serenaded in Act 4 and which is itself incomparable. All things considered, Silvia being as she is and what she is, who can blame Proteus?

In two other ways, also, Shakespeare goes farther toward explaining and extenuating Proteus' fault than he was to do with the faults of Claudio and Bertram. In the first scene of the play, Proteus is shown to be both a faithful friend and a faithful lover; but also the point is made evident that in a crisis of conflict between friendship and love, love would claim him:

> He after honor hunts, I after love.
> He leaves his friends to dignify them more,
> I leave myself, my friends, and all, for love.
>
> (1.1.63–65)

He is love's votary; as it has been with Julia, so will it be with Silvia when the time comes: he will leave himself, his true friend, and all else, for love. Second, as he does not do for Claudio and Bertram, Shakespeare does Proteus the credit of allowing him to debate the right and wrong of his multiple perjury before he commits it, to debate the question, in fact, twice, in 2.4.191–213, and in 2.6.1–43. Claudio and Bertram, one notes, engage in no self-debate; they directly announce their bad intentions without troubling with any such preliminaries. Even though his decision is "wrong," Proteus at least undergoes the formality of weighing right and wrong. It is true that his self-debate involves no agonizing soul struggle such as Angelo of *Measure for Measure* undergoes in a roughly comparable situation, when flesh and the spirit are at war in him; Shakespeare quite rightly keeps Proteus' "struggle" light, superficial, artificial, well within the tone and the terms appropriate to romantic comedy:

> And ev'n that pow'r which gave me first my oath
> Provokes me to this threefold perjury:
> Love bade me swear, and Love bids me forswear.
>
> (2.6.4–6)

Surely, this is as far as a proper hero of romantic comedy dare go in soul struggle, and critics who deplore the too-easy entrance of Proteus into treachery—even as they deplore his too-easy return from it—would do well to remember that the moral ponderings of a Hamlet, an Angelo, or a Macbeth at this point would crash out of and destroy the very genre that this particular romantic hero helped to create.

But all this is not to suggest that Proteus is a blameless hero; if he were so, he would not belong with Claudio and Bertram, but with Valentine and Orlando. It is rather to insist that of the specific kind he represents, he runs true to form and measures up extremely well. Launce identifies him and his kind clearly enough: "I am but a fool, look you, and yet I have the wit to think my master is a kind of a knave." Is he any worse than that? For only a moment he seems to be, when he threatens Silvia with violence in the forest, and here perhaps Shakespeare did indeed go too far. But whether he would actually attack Silvia we neither know nor need to know; the fact is that he does not attack her, and we are quite aware that, with Valentine at hand, watching every move, there never was any real danger in the situation. He is guilty of nothing more than a thoroughly wicked intent, which is thwarted while it is only an impulse. A wicked impulse is not punishable, and in the world of romantic comedy is not even to be thought on too seriously.

Julia and Silvia, Valentine and Proteus are the most notable human fixtures in the special world of romantic comedy that was born with *The Two Gentlemen of Verona*. They are light but durable fixtures, as that world requires. If they are not wholly credible, yet they are more credible than were their forbears in the romances, and they are credible enough, palpable enough, one may say, for the world of romantic comedy, the nature of which would be altered if it were made to sustain creatures more solid. They are of a kind with this special world.

The world of romantic comedy, both as it was first drawn

in this play and as it was re-created in each of the master-pieces that followed, of course includes other features besides the heroes and the heroines who invariably inhabit it. It includes, for example, clowns and fools. Speed and Launce stand rather uncertainly between the twin Dromios, the bewildered but witty slaves of *The Comedy of Errors,* before them, and the magnificent creations that came after, like Launcelot Gobbo of *The Merchant of Venice* and Touchstone of *As You Like It.* They are not as gifted as these—if Launcelot Gobbo, a great dunce, may be said to be gifted—and they talk too long with one another and with their masters. With the exception of Launce's long exhortation to his dog to be a better dog, their appearances are likely to be found tedious in both the theater and the study. But if they are not at all well and functionally fitted into the plot of the play—and the fact is that they are almost always purely interruptive—yet Shakespeare's introduction of them into romance helped to bring romantic comedy into being: the oozy world of romance needed their dryness. Their presence does not particularly help to make this incredible world more credible; but it does what is just as good—namely, helps to make the point that this world does not *have* to be perfectly credible, helps to render its very incredibility acceptable. In such a world as they inhabit, how can we reasonably balk at such a turn as the sudden redemption of Proteus or Valentine's magnanimous offer of Silvia? They are reminders that we are to keep our perspective and not consider things too seriously; annoying as they have proved for many critics, with their dreary stretches of low-grade quibbles and mental horseplay, they nevertheless serve the important perspective-giving function implied by Feste's refrain at the end of *Twelfth Night:* ". . . the rain it raineth every day."

Like the heroes and the heroines, the clowns and fools, and the incidents that take extravagant turns, the dramatic verse of *The Two Gentlemen of Verona* needs also to be taken for what it is and does within the world of romantic comedy. No passages and almost no single lines in this play (setting aside the whole of the song to Silvia) are particularly memorable. If one sets, for instance, the poetic language of Julia's interviews (in disguise) with Proteus and with Silvia beside that of Viola-Cesario's interviews with Orsino and Olivia in *Twelfth Night*—a fair comparison, involving similar characters in virtually identical situations—the contrast is obvious enough; yet it is not shocking. Here is Julia-Sebastian speaking to Silvia:

> She hath been fairer, madam, than she is.
> When she did think my master loved her well,
> She, in my judgment, was as fair as you.
> But since she did neglect her looking glass,
> And threw her sun-expelling mask away,
> The air hath starved the roses in her cheeks
> And pinched the lily-tincture of her face,
> That now she is become as black as I.

(4.4.149–56)

And here is Viola-Cesario, telling how she-he would woo Olivia:

> Make me a willow cabin at your gate,
> And call upon my soul within the house;
> Write loyal cantons of contemnèd love
> And sing them loud even in the dead of night;
> Halloo your name to the reverberate hills
> And make the babbling gossip of the air
> Cry out "Olivia!"

(*Twelfth Night*, 1.5.254–60)

There is a resonance, a throaty vibrance in the music of the great poetic passages of *Twelfth Night*—

> She never told her love,
> But let concealment, like a worm i' th' bud,
> Feed on her damask cheek. She pined in thought,
> And with a green and yellow melancholy
> She sat, like Patience on a monument,
> Smiling at grief.

(2.4.109–14)

—to which at best *The Two Gentlemen of Verona* never once attains, unless in the single line so much praised by Logan Pearsall Smith (*Shakespeare*, p. 74): ". . . but it is only in the *Two Gentlemen of Verona,* with the song 'Who is Silvia,' with the line:

> The uncertain glory of an April day,

and the passage about the brook that makes sweet music as it strays, that his power over words becomes a magic power, and his golden mastery of speech begins to almost blind us with its beauty."

Though it is easy to assent to the glory of this single line, no one would be likely to claim particular distinction for all the poetry of the play. What is here asserted, instead, is that the poetic language is "right" for the play, that it helps in the same way that the heroes and heroines and the extravagant incidents do to create the "world" of romantic comedy. This poetry has a good deal of chaff in it; it is sometimes glittering chaff, but chaff it is. It is light and usually frivolous; even when deep ideas are asserted, they are not asserted profoundly. The speakers habitually play along the surface of things:

Proteus. So, by your circumstance, you call me fool.

Valentine. So, by your circumstance, I fear you'll prove.

Proteus. 'Tis love you cavil at. I am not Love.

Valentine. Love is your master, for he masters you;

And he that is so yokèd by a fool,
Methinks, should not be chronicled for wise.

Proteus. Yet writers say, as in the sweetest bud
The eating canker dwells, so eating love
Inhabits in the finest wits of all.

Valentine. And writers say . . .

(1.1.36–45)

This is as typical an example as any of the poetic talk that fills the play, and in filling it defines its kind. It is both superficial and artificial, if one will, but "right" for the kind of world in which it is spoken and which it creates in being spoken, just as, for the same reason, the principal characters and incidents are also "right." There is an attitude of frivolity about this world which is figured forth in language, character, and incident.

Viewed thus, for what it is in part and whole, the play needs no apology, and certainly it does not deserve the harsh criticism that it has received from many who have not been content to take it for what it is. It transformed romance to romantic comedy, and it founded a great line. But, viewed as we have viewed it, it need not depend for its whole credit upon the fact that it was an important "first." It would be what it is if there were no *Twelfth Night*—indeed, it would no doubt look much better if there were no *Twelfth Night*.

—BERTRAND EVANS

The Two Gentlemen of Verona

The Names of All the Actors

Duke [of Milan], father to Silvia
Valentine ⎫
Proteus ⎭ the two gentlemen
Antonio, father to Proteus
Thurio, a foolish rival to Valentine
Eglamour, agent for Silvia in her escape
Host, where Julia lodges
Outlaws, with Valentine
Speed, a clownish servant to Valentine
Launce, the like to Proteus
Panthino, servant to Antonio
Julia, beloved of Proteus
Silvia, beloved of Valentine
Lucetta, waiting woman to Julia
[Servants, Musicians

Scene: Verona; Milan; a forest]

The Two Gentlemen of Verona

ACT 1

Scene 1. [*Verona. An open place.*]

[Enter] Valentine [and] Proteus.

Valentine. Cease to persuade, my loving Proteus:
  Home-keeping youth have ever homely wits.
  Were't not affection chains thy tender days
  To the sweet glances of thy honored love,
  I rather would entreat thy company   5
  To see the wonders of the world abroad,
  Than, living dully sluggardized at home,
  Wear out thy youth with shapeless idleness.
  But since thou lov'st, love still, and thrive therein,
  Even as I would, when I to love begin.   10

Proteus. Wilt thou be gone? Sweet Valentine, adieu!
  Think on thy Proteus when thou haply°[1] seest
  Some rare noteworthy object in thy travel:
  Wish me partaker in thy happiness
  When thou dost meet good hap;° and in thy danger,   15

---

[1] The degree sign (°) indicates a footnote, which is keyed to the text by line number. Text references are printed in **boldface**; the annotation follows in roman type. 1.1.12 **haply** by chance 15 **hap** luck

If ever danger do environ thee,
Commend thy grievance to my holy prayers,
For I will be thy beadsman,° Valentine.

Valentine. And on a love-book° pray for my success?

20 *Proteus.* Upon some book I love I'll pray for thee.

Valentine. That's on some shallow story of deep love:
How young Leander° crossed the Hellespont.

Proteus. That's a deep story of a deeper love,
For he was more than over shoes in love.

25 *Valentine.* 'Tis true, for you are over boots in love,
And yet you never swum the Hellespont.

Proteus. Over the boots? Nay, give me not the boots.°

Valentine. No, I will not, for it boots° thee not.

Proteus.   What?

Valentine. To be in love—where scorn is bought with
groans,
Coy looks with heartsore sighs, one fading mo-
30 ment's mirth
With twenty watchful, weary, tedious nights;
If haply won, perhaps a hapless° gain;
If lost, why then a grievous labor won;
However,° but a folly bought with wit,
35 Or else a wit by folly vanquishèd.

Proteus. So, by your circumstance,° you call me fool.

Valentine. So, by your circumstance, I fear you'll
prove.

Proteus. 'Tis love you cavil at. I am not Love.

Valentine. Love is your master, for he masters you;

18 **beadsman** one who contracts to pray in behalf of another   19 **love-book** i.e., instead of a prayer book   22 **Leander** (legendary Greek youth who nightly swam the Hellespont to visit his beloved Hero and, one night, was drowned)   27 **give me not the boots** i.e., don't jest with me   28 **boots** benefits (with pun on preceding line)   32 **hapless** luckless   34 **However** in either case   36 **by your circumstance** i.e., by your argument (in the next line the same phrase means "in your condition [of love]")

And he that is so yokèd by a fool,   40
Methinks, should not be chronicled° for wise.

Proteus. Yet writers say, as in the sweetest bud
   The eating canker° dwells, so eating love
   Inhabits in the finest wits of all.

Valentine. And writers say, as the most forward° bud   45
   Is eaten by the canker ere it blow,°
   Even so by love the young and tender wit
   Is turned to folly, blasting° in the bud,
   Losing his verdure even in the prime,°
   And all the fair effects of future hopes.   50
   But wherefore waste I time to counsel thee,
   That art a votary to fond desire?
   Once more adieu! My father at the road°
   Expects my coming, there to see me shipped.

Proteus. And thither will I bring° thee, Valentine.   55

Valentine. Sweet Proteus, no; now let us take our
      leave.
   To Milan let me hear from thee by letters
   Of thy success° in love, and what news else
   Betideth here in absence of thy friend,
   And I likewise will visit thee with mine.   60

Proteus. All happiness bechance to thee in Milan!

Valentine. As much to you at home! And so, farewell.
                                             Exit.

Proteus. He after honor hunts, I after love.
   He leaves his friends to dignify them more,
   I leave myself, my friends, and all, for love.   65
   Thou, Julia, thou hast metamorphized me,
   Made me neglect my studies, lose my time,
   War with good counsel, set the world at nought,
   Made wit with musing weak, heart sick with
      thought.

41 **chronicled** written down   43 **canker** cankerworm   45 **most forward** earliest   46 **blow** bloom   48 **blasting** withering   49 **prime**
spring   53 **road** harbor   55 **bring** accompany   58 **success** fortune
(good or bad)

[*Enter Speed.*]

70 *Speed.* Sir Proteus, save you!° Saw you my master?

Proteus. But now he parted hence, to embark for Milan.

Speed. Twenty to one, then, he is shipped already,
And I have played the sheep° in losing him.

Proteus. Indeed, a sheep doth very often stray,
75 And if° the shepherd be awhile away.

Speed. You conclude that my master is a shepherd, then, and I a sheep?

Proteus. I do.

Speed. Why then, my horns are his horns,° whether I
80 wake or sleep.

Proteus. A silly answer, and fitting well a sheep.

Speed. This proves me still a sheep.

Proteus. True, and thy master a shepherd.

Speed. Nay, that I can deny by a circumstance.°

85 *Proteus.* It shall go hard but I'll prove it by another.

Speed. The shepherd seeks the sheep, and not the sheep the shepherd; but I seek my master, and my master seeks not me. Therefore I am no sheep.

Proteus. The sheep for fodder follow the shepherd;
90 the shepherd for food follows not the sheep; thou for wages followest thy master, thy master for wages follows not thee. Therefore thou art a sheep.

Speed. Such another proof will make me cry "baa."

Proteus. But, dost thou hear? Gav'st thou my letter to
95 Julia?

---

70 **save you** (a greeting) 73 **sheep** (pun on "ship") 75 **And if** if 79 **my horns are his horns** i.e., my (sheep's) horns belong to him (making him a cuckold) 84 **circumstance** logical proof

Speed. Ay, sir: I, a lost mutton, gave your letter to her, a laced mutton,° and she, a laced mutton, gave me, a lost mutton, nothing for my labor.

Proteus. Here's too small a pasture for such store of muttons.   *100*

Speed. If the ground be overcharged,° you were best stick° her.

Proteus. Nay, in that you are astray; 'twere best pound° you.

Speed. Nay, sir, less than a pound shall serve me for   *105* carrying your letter.

Proteus. You mistake. I mean the pound—a pinfold.

Speed. From a pound to a pin? Fold it over and over, 'Tis threefold too little for carrying a letter to your lover.

Proteus. But what said she?   *110*

Speed. [*Nodding*] Ay.

Proteus. Nod—ay. Why, that's noddy.°

Speed. You mistook, sir. I say she did nod; and you ask me if she did nod, and I say, "Ay."

Proteus. And that set together is noddy.   *115*

Speed. Now you have taken the pains to set it together, take it for your pains.

Proteus. No, no. You shall have it for bearing the letter.

Speed. Well, I perceive I must be fain to bear with   *120* you.

Proteus. Why, sir, how do you bear with me?

96–97 **lost mutton . . . laced mutton** i.e., lost sheep and laced courtesan (probably "lost" and "laced" were similarly pronounced) 101 **overcharged** overgrazed 102 **stick** stab (slaughter) 104 **pound** impound (with pun) 112 **noddy** fool

Speed. Marry,° sir, the letter, very orderly; having
nothing but the word "noddy" for my pains.

125 *Proteus.* Beshrew° me, but you have a quick wit.

Speed. And yet it cannot overtake your slow purse.

Proteus. Come, come, open the matter in brief. What
said she?

Speed. Open your purse, that the money and the mat-
130 ter may be both at once delivered.

Proteus. Well, sir, here is for your pains. What said
she?

Speed. Truly, sir, I think you'll hardly win her.

Proteus. Why, couldst thou perceive so much from
135 her?

Speed. Sir, I could perceive nothing at all from her;
no, not so much as a ducat for delivering your letter.
And being so hard to me that brought your mind,
I fear she'll prove as hard to you in telling your
140 mind. Give her no token but stones;° for she's as
hard as steel.

Proteus. What said she? Nothing?

Speed. No, not so much as "Take this for thy pains."
To testify your bounty, I thank you, you have tes-
145 terned me;° in requital whereof, henceforth carry
your letters yourself. And so, sir, I'll commend you
to my master.

Proteus. Go, go, be gone, to save your ship from wrack,
Which cannot perish, having thee aboard,
150 Being destined to a drier death on shore.°

[*Exit Speed.*]

---

123 **Marry** by the Virgin Mary (a casual oath)   125 **Beshrew** curse
(used casually)   140 **stones** (in addition to punning on its meanings of
"jewels" and "worthless gifts," Speed may be punning on another
meaning, "testicles")   144–45 **testerned me** i.e., given me a testern (sixpence) 150 **Being destined . . . shore** i.e., being destined to hang

I must go send some better messenger;
I fear my Julia would not deign my lines,
Receiving them from such a worthless post.°   *Exit.*

Scene 2. [*Verona. Julia's house.*]

Enter Julia and Lucetta.

Julia. But say, Lucetta, now we are alone,
  Wouldst thou, then, counsel me to fall in love?

Lucetta. Ay, madam; so you stumble not unheedfully.

Julia. Of all the fair resort of gentlemen°
  That every day with parle° encounter me,   5
  In thy opinion which is worthiest love?

Lucetta. Please you repeat their names, I'll show my
    mind
  According to my shallow simple skill.

Julia. What think'st thou of the fair Sir Eglamour?

Lucetta. As of a knight well-spoken, neat, and fine;   10
  But, were I you, he never should be mine.

Julia. What think'st thou of the rich Mercatio?

Lucetta. Well of his wealth; but of himself, so so.

Julia. What think'st thou of the gentle Proteus?

Lucetta. Lord, Lord! To see what folly reigns in us!   15

Julia. How now! What means this passion° at his
    name?

Lucetta. Pardon, dear madam; 'tis a passing° shame
  That I, unworthy body as I am,
  Should censure° thus on lovely gentlemen.

---

153 **post** messenger   1.2.4 **resort of gentlemen** crowd of suitors   5
parle parley   16 **passion** emotion   17 **passing** surpassing   19 **censure**
pass judgment

20   *Julia.* Why not on Proteus, as of all the rest?

Lucetta. Then thus: of many good I think him best.

Julia. Your reason?

Lucetta. I have no other but a woman's reason:
   I think him so because I think him so.

25   *Julia.* And wouldst thou have me cast my love on him?

Lucetta. Ay, if you thought your love not cast away.

Julia. Why, he, of all the rest, hath never moved° me.

Lucetta. Yet he, of all the rest, I think, best loves ye.

Julia. His little speaking shows his love but small.

30   *Lucetta.* Fire that's closest kept burns most of all.

Julia. They do not love that do not show their love.

Lucetta. O, they love least that let men know their love.

Julia. I would I knew his mind.

Lucetta. Peruse this paper, madam.

35   *Julia.* "To Julia."—Say, from whom?

Lucetta. That the contents will show.

Julia. Say, say, who gave it thee?

Lucetta. Sir Valentine's page; and sent, I think, from
      Proteus.
   He would have given it you; but I, being in the way,
40   Did in your name receive it. Pardon the fault, I pray.

Julia. Now, by my modesty, a goodly broker!°
   Dare you presume to harbor wanton lines?
   To whisper and conspire against my youth?
   Now, trust me, 'tis an office of great worth,
45   And you an officer fit for the place.
   There, take the paper; see it be returned,
   Or else return no more into my sight.

27 **moved** i.e., proposed to   41 **broker** go-between

Lucetta. To plead for love deserves more fee than hate.

Julia. Will ye be gone?

Lucetta.   That you may ruminate.   *Exit.*

Julia. And yet I would I had o'erlooked° the letter.   50
It were a shame to call her back again,
And pray her to° a fault for which I chid her.
What fool is she, that knows I am a maid,
And would not force the letter to my view!
Since maids, in modesty, say "no" to that   55
Which they would have the profferer construe "ay."
Fie, fie, how wayward is this foolish love,
That, like a testy° babe, will scratch the nurse,
And presently,° all humbled, kiss the rod!
How churlishly I chid Lucetta hence,   60
When willingly I would have had her here!
How angerly I taught my brow to frown,
When inward joy enforced my heart to smile!
My penance is to call Lucetta back
And ask remission for my folly past.   65
What, ho! Lucetta!

[*Enter Lucetta.*]

Lucetta.   What would your ladyship?

Julia. Is't near dinnertime?

Lucetta.   I would it were;
That you might kill your stomach° on your meat,
And not upon your maid.°

Julia. What is't that you took up so gingerly?   70

Lucetta. Nothing.

Julia. Why didst thou stoop, then?

Lucetta. To take a paper up that I let fall.

---

50 **o'erlooked** perused   52 **pray her to** apologize to her for   58 **testy**
irritable   59 **presently** immediately   68 **kill your stomach** (1) allay
your vexation (2) appease your hunger   68–69 **meat . . . maid** (pun on
"mate")

Julia. And is that paper nothing?

75 *Lucetta.* Nothing concerning me.

Julia. Then let it lie for those that it concerns.

Lucetta. Madam, it will not lie where it concerns,°
Unless it have a false interpreter.

Julia. Some love of yours hath writ to you in rhyme.

80 *Lucetta.* That I might sing it, madam, to a tune.
Give me a note: your ladyship can set.°

Julia. As little by such toys° as may be possible.
Best sing it to the tune of "Light o' love."°

Lucetta. It is too heavy for so light a tune.

85 *Julia.* Heavy! Belike it hath some burden,° then?

Lucetta. Ay, and melodious were it, would you sing it.

Julia. And why not you?

Lucetta.   I cannot reach so high.

Julia. Let's see your song. [*Takes the letter.*] How now,
minion!

Lucetta. Keep tune there still, so you will sing it out:
90 And yet methinks I do not like this tune.

Julia. You do not?

Lucetta.   No, madam; 'tis too sharp.

Julia. You, minion, are too saucy.

Lucetta. Nay, now you are too flat,
And mar the concord with too harsh a descant.°
95 There wanteth but a mean° to fill your song.

Julia. The mean is drowned with your unruly bass.

---

77 **lie where it concerns** i.e., express its content falsely (with quibble on
preceding line)   81 **set** set to music   82 **toys** trifles   83 **Light o' love** a
contemporary popular ditty   85 **burden** bass refrain (with pun)   94
descant improvised harmony   95 **wanteth but a mean** lacks a tenor
part (Proteus?)

Lucetta. Indeed, I bid the base° for Proteus.

Julia. This babble shall not henceforth trouble me.
    Here is a coil with protestation!°   [*Tears the letter.*]
    Go get you gone, and let the papers lie;   *100*
    You would be fing'ring them, to anger me.

Lucetta. She makes it strange;° but she would be best
    pleased
    To be so ang'red with another letter.   [*Exit.*]

Julia. Nay, would I were so ang'red with the same!
    O hateful hands, to tear such loving words!   *105*
    Injurious wasps, to feed on such sweet honey,
    And kill the bees, that yield it, with your stings!
    I'll kiss each several° paper for amends.
    Look, here is writ "kind Julia." Unkind Julia!
    As in revenge of thy ingratitude,   *110*
    I throw thy name against the bruising stones,
    Trampling contemptuously on thy disdain.
    And here is writ "love-wounded Proteus."
    Poor wounded name! My bosom, as a bed,
    Shall lodge thee, till thy wound be throughly°
      healed;   *115*
    And thus I search° it with a sovereign kiss.
    But twice or thrice was "Proteus" written down.
    Be calm, good wind, blow not a word away
    Till I have found each letter in the letter,
    Except mine own name: that some whirlwind bear *120*
    Unto a ragged, fearful-hanging rock,
    And throw it thence into the raging sea!
    Lo, here in one line is his name twice writ,
    "Poor forlorn Proteus, passionate Proteus,
    To the sweet Julia." That I'll tear away.—   *125*
    And yet I will not, sith° so prettily
    He couples it to his complaining names.

---

97 **bid the base** (in the game of Prisoner's Base, a challenge to a test of speed [with pun])   99 **coil with protestation** much ado made up of lover's protestations   102 **makes it strange** i.e., pretends that it is nothing to her   108 **several** separate   115 **throughly** thoroughly   116 **search** probe (as in cleaning a wound)   126 **sith** since

Thus will I fold them one upon another.
Now kiss, embrace, contend, do what you will.

[*Enter Lucetta.*]

130 *Lucetta.* Madam,
     Dinner is ready, and your father stays.

Julia. Well, let us go.

Lucetta. What, shall these papers lie like telltales here?

Julia. If you respect them, best to take them up.

135 *Lucetta.* Nay, I was taken up for laying them down;
     Yet here they shall not lie, for catching cold.

Julia. I see you have a month's mind° to them.

Lucetta. Ay, madam, you may say what sights you see;
     I see things too, although you judge I wink.°

140 *Julia.* Come, come; will't please you go?   *Exeunt.*

Scene 3. [*Verona. Antonio's house.*]

Enter Antonio and Panthino.

Antonio. Tell me, Panthino, what sad° talk was that
     Wherewith my brother held you in the cloister?

Panthino. 'Twas of his nephew Proteus, your son.

Antonio. Why, what of him?

Panthino.   He wond'red that your lordship
5   Would suffer him to spend his youth at home,
     While other men, of slender reputation,°
     Put forth their sons to seek preferment out:

137 **month's mind** i.e., lasting desire   139 **wink** have my eyes shut, see nothing   1.3.1 **sad** serious   6 **slender reputation** unimportant place

Some to the wars, to try their fortune there,
Some to discover islands far away,
Some to the studious universities.   *10*
For any, or for all these exercises,
He said that Proteus your son was meet,°
And did request me to importune you
To let him spend his time no more at home,
Which would be great impeachment° to his age,   *15*
In having known no travel in his youth.

Antonio. Nor need'st thou much importune me to that
  Whereon this month I have been hammering.°
  I have considered well his loss of time,
  And how he cannot be a perfect man,   *20*
  Not being tried and tutored in the world.
  Experience is by industry achieved,
  And perfected° by the swift course of time.
  Then, tell me, whither were I best to send him?

Panthino. I think your lordship is not ignorant   *25*
  How his companion, youthful Valentine,
  Attends the Emperor° in his royal court.

Antonio. I know it well.

Panthino. 'Twere good, I think, your lordship sent him
    thither.
  There shall he practice tilts and tournaments,   *30*
  Hear sweet discourse, converse with noblemen,
  And be in eye of° every exercise
  Worthy his youth and nobleness of birth.

Antonio. I like thy counsel; well hast thou advised.
  And that thou mayst perceive how well I like it,   *35*
  The execution of it shall make known.
  Even with the speediest expedition°
  I will dispatch him to the Emperor's court.

Panthino. Tomorrow, may it please you, Don Al-
    phonso,

12 **meet** fitted   15 **impeachment** detriment   18 **hammering** i.e., pondering   23 **perfected** (accent on first syllable)   27 **Emperor** i.e., Duke (of Milan)   32 **be in eye of** have sight of   37 **expedition** haste

40   With other gentlemen of good esteem,
       Are journeying to salute the Emperor,
       And to commend their service to his will.

       Antonio. Good company; with them shall Proteus go.
       And—in good time! Now will we break with° him.

                    [*Enter Proteus.*]

45   *Proteus.* Sweet love! Sweet lines! Sweet life!
       Here is her hand, the agent of her heart.
       Here is her oath for love, her honor's pawn.°
       O, that our fathers would applaud our loves,
       To seal our happiness with their consents!
50   O heavenly Julia!

       Antonio. How now! What letter are you reading there?

       Proteus. May't please your lordship, 'tis a word or two
       Of commendations° sent from Valentine,
       Delivered by a friend that came from him.

55   *Antonio.* Lend me the letter; let me see what news.

       Proteus. There is no news, my lord, but that he writes
       How happily he lives, how well beloved
       And daily gracèd by the Emperor,
       Wishing me with him, partner of his fortune.

60   *Antonio.* And how stand you affected to his wish?

       Proteus. As one relying on your lordship's will,
       And not depending on his friendly wish.

       Antonio. My will is something sorted° with his wish.
       Muse not that I thus suddenly proceed,
65   For what I will, I will, and there an end.
       I am resolved that thou shalt spend some time
       With Valentinus in the Emperor's court.
       What maintenance he from his friends receives,
       Like exhibition° thou shalt have from me.
70   Tomorrow be in readiness to go.

44 **break with** break the news to   47 **pawn** pledge   53 **commenda-tions** greetings   63 **something sorted** somewhat in accord   69 **exhibi-tion** allowance

Excuse it not,° for I am peremptory.°

Proteus. My lord, I cannot be so soon provided.
Please you, deliberate a day or two.

Antonio. Look what° thou want'st shall be sent after
thee.
No more of stay! Tomorrow thou must go.   75
Come on, Panthino; you shall be employed
To hasten on his expedition.
                    [*Exeunt Antonio and Panthino.*]

Proteus. Thus have I shunned the fire for fear of
burning,
And drenched me in the sea, where I am drowned.
I feared to show my father Julia's letter,   80
Lest he should take exceptions to my love;
And with the vantage of mine own excuse
Hath he excepted most against my love.°
O, how this spring of love resembleth
The uncertain glory of an April day,   85
Which now shows all the beauty of the sun,
And by and by a cloud takes all away!

                    [*Enter Panthino.*]

Panthino. Sir Proteus, your father calls for you.
He is in haste; therefore, I pray you, go.

Proteus. Why, this it is: my heart accords thereto,   90
And yet a thousand times it answers "no."   *Exeunt.*

---

71 **Excuse it not** offer no excuses   71 **peremptory** determined   74
Look what whatever   82–83 **with the vantage . . . my love** i.e., he took
advantage of my own device (the pretended letter from Valentine) to
strike the heaviest blow to my affair of love (with Julia)

ACT 2

Scene 1. [*Milan. The Duke's palace.*]

Enter Valentine [and] Speed.

Speed. Sir, your glove.

Valentine.   Not mine; my gloves are on.

Speed. Why, then, this may be yours, for this is but one.°

Valentine. Ha, let me see. Ay, give it me, it's mine.
Sweet ornament that decks a thing divine!
5   Ah, Silvia, Silvia!

Speed. Madam Silvia! Madam Silvia!

Valentine. How now, sirrah?°

Speed. She is not within hearing, sir.

Valentine. Why, sir, who bade you call her?

10 *Speed.* Your worship, sir, or else I mistook.

Valentine. Well, you'll still° be too forward.

Speed. And yet I was last chidden for being too slow.

Valentine. Go to, sir. Tell me, do you know Madam
Silvia?

2.1.1–2 **on . . . one** (a pun in Elizabethan speech)   7 **sirrah** (common
form of address to inferiors)   11 **still** always

18

Speed. She that your worship loves?   15

Valentine. Why, how know you that I am in love?

Speed. Marry, by these special marks: first, you have learned, like Sir Proteus, to wreathe your arms, like a malcontent; to relish a love song, like a robin redbreast; to walk alone, like one that had the pestilence; to sigh, like a schoolboy that had lost his A B C; to weep, like a young wench that had buried her grandam; to fast, like one that takes diet; to watch,° like one that fears robbing; to speak puling,° like a beggar at Hallowmas.° You were wont, when you laughed, to crow like a cock; when you walked, to walk like one of the lions; when you fasted, it was presently after dinner; when you looked sadly, it was for want of money. And now you are metamorphized with a mistress, that,° when I look on you, I can hardly think you my master.   20   25   30

Valentine. Are all these things perceived in me?

Speed. They are all perceived without ye.°

Valentine. Without me? They cannot.

Speed. Without you? Nay, that's certain, for, without° you were so simple, none else would. But you are so without these follies, that these follies are within you, and shine through you like the water in an urinal, that not an eye that sees you but is a physician to comment on your malady.   35   40

Valentine. But tell me, dost thou know my lady Silvia?

Speed. She that you gaze on so as she sits at supper?

Valentine. Hast thou observed that? Even she, I mean.

Speed. Why, sir, I know her not.

24 **watch** lie awake   24 **puling** whiningly   25 **at Hallowmas** on All Saints' Day (when beggars vied for special treats)   30 **that** so that   33 **without ye** i.e., by external signs (here begins a series of quibbles)   35 **without** unless

45 *Valentine.* Dost thou know her by my gazing on her, and yet know'st her not?

Speed. Is she not hard-favored,° sir?

Valentine. Not so fair, boy, as well-favored.

Speed. Sir, I know that well enough.

50 *Valentine.* What dost thou know?

Speed. That she is not so fair as, of you, well-favored.

Valentine. I mean that her beauty is exquisite, but her favor° infinite.

Speed. That's because the one is painted, and the other
55 out of all count.°

Valentine. How painted? And how out of count?

Speed. Marry, sir, so painted, to make her fair, that no man counts of° her beauty.

Valentine. How esteem'st thou me? I account of her
60 beauty.

Speed. You never saw her since she was deformed.°

Valentine. How long hath she been deformed?

Speed. Ever since you loved her.

Valentine. I have loved her ever since I saw her; and
65 still I see her beautiful.

Speed. If you love her, you cannot see her.

Valentine. Why?

Speed. Because Love is blind. O, that you had mine eyes; or your own eyes had the lights they were wont
70 to have when you chid at Sir Proteus for going ungartered!°

---

47 **hard-favored** homely   53 **favor** charm, graciousness   55 **out of all count** beyond counting   58 **counts of** takes account of   61 **deformed** i.e., distorted by your lover's view   70–71 **going ungartered** (a sure sign that one is in love; see *As You Like It,* 3.2.371)

Valentine. What should I see then?

Speed. Your own present folly, and her passing° deformity. For he, being in love, could not see to garter his hose; and you, being in love, cannot see to put on your hose. 75

Valentine. Belike, boy, then, you are in love; for last morning you could not see to wipe my shoes.

Speed. True, sir; I was in love with my bed. I thank you, you swinged° me for my love, which makes me the bolder to chide you for yours. 80

Valentine. In conclusion, I stand affected to her.

Speed. I would you were set,° so your affection would cease.

Valentine. Last night she enjoined me to write some lines to one she loves. 85

Speed. And have you?

Valentine. I have.

Speed. Are they not lamely writ?

Valentine. No, boy, but as well as I can do them. Peace! Here she comes. 90

Speed. [*Aside*] O excellent motion! O exceeding puppet! Now will he interpret° to her.

[*Enter Silvia.*]

Valentine. Madam and mistress, a thousand good morrows. 95

Speed. [*Aside*] O, give ye good ev'n! Here's a million of manners.

Silvia. Sir Valentine and servant,° to you two thousand.

73 **passing** surpassing, extreme   80 **swinged** beat   83 **set** seated (quibble on "stand")   92–93 **motion . . . puppet . . . interpret** (the puppeteer's voice "interprets" for the figures in the puppet play, or "motion")   98 **servant** gallant lover (i.e., alludes not to Speed but to Valentine)

Speed. [*Aside*] He should give her interest, and she
100   gives it him.

Valentine. As you enjoined me, I have writ your letter
Unto the secret nameless friend of yours,
Which I was much unwilling to proceed in,
But for my duty to your ladyship.

Silvia. I thank you, gentle servant; 'tis very clerkly°
105   done.

Valentine. Now trust me, madam, it came hardly off;
For, being ignorant to whom it goes,
I writ at random, very doubtfully.

Silvia. Perchance you think too much of so much
pains?

110 *Valentine.* No, madam; so it stead° you, I will write,
Please you command, a thousand times as much.
And yet—

Silvia. A pretty period!° Well, I guess the sequel;
And yet I will not name it; and yet I care not;
115   And yet take this again; and yet I thank you,
Meaning henceforth to trouble you no more.

Speed. [*Aside*] And yet you will; and yet another "yet."

Valentine. What means your ladyship? Do you not
like it?

Silvia. Yes, yes: the lines are very quaintly° writ;
120   But since unwillingly, take them again.
Nay, take them.

Valentine. Madam, they are for you.

Silvia. Ay, ay. You writ them, sir, at my request;
But I will none of them; they are for you;
125   I would have had them writ more movingly.

Valentine. Please you, I'll write your ladyship another.

Silvia. And when it's writ, for my sake read it over,

105 **clerkly** scholarly 110 **stead** be useful to 113 **period** full
stop 119 **quaintly** ingeniously

And if it please you, so; if not, why, so.

Valentine. If it please me, madam, what then?

Silvia. Why, if it please you, take it for your labor;   *130*
And so, good morrow, servant.   *Exit Silvia.*

Speed. O jest unseen, inscrutable, invisible,
As a nose on a man's face, or a weathercock on a
steeple!
My master sues to her, and she hath taught her
suitor,
He being her pupil, to become her tutor.   *135*
O excellent device! Was there ever heard a better,
That my master, being scribe, to himself should
write the letter?

Valentine. How now, sir? What are you reasoning with
yourself?

Speed. Nay, I was rhyming; 'tis you that have the   *140*
reason.

Valentine. To do what?

Speed. To be a spokesman from Madam Silvia.

Valentine. To whom?

Speed. To yourself. Why, she woos you by a figure.°   *145*

Valentine. What figure?

Speed. By a letter, I should say.

Valentine. Why, she hath not writ to me?

Speed. What need she, when she hath made you write
to yourself? Why, do you not perceive the jest?   *150*

Valentine. No, believe me.

Speed. No believing you, indeed, sir. But did you
perceive her earnest?°

Valentine. She gave me none, except an angry word.

145 **by a figure** by indirect means   153 **earnest** (1) seriousness
(2) token payment

155 *Speed.* Why, she hath given you a letter.

Valentine. That's the letter I writ to her friend.

Speed. And that letter hath she delivered, and there an end.

Valentine. I would it were no worse.

160 *Speed.* I'll warrant you, 'tis as well;
For often have you writ to her, and she, in modesty,
Or else for want of idle time, could not again reply;
Or fearing else some messenger that might her mind
discover,°
Herself hath taught her love himself to write unto
her lover.

165 All this I speak in print,° for in print I found it.
Why muse you, sir? 'Tis dinnertime.

Valentine. I have dined.

Speed. Ay, but hearken, sir; though the chameleon
Love can feed on the air,° I am one that am nour-
170 ished by my victuals, and would fain have meat. O,
be not like your mistress; be moved, be moved.

Exeunt.

Scene 2. [*Verona. Julia's house.*]

Enter Proteus [*and*] *Julia.*

Proteus. Have patience, gentle Julia.

Julia. I must, where is no remedy.

Proteus. When possibly I can, I will return.

163 **discover** reveal 165 **speak in print** i.e., quote 168–69
chameleon . . . the air (the chameleon was thought to eat nothing but air;
see also 2.4.24–27 and *Hamlet* 3.2.95)

Julia. If you turn° not, you will return the sooner.
  Keep this remembrance for thy Julia's sake.   5
                                        [*Giving a ring.*]

Proteus. Why, then, we'll make exchange; here, take
  you this.

Julia. And seal the bargain with a holy kiss.

Proteus. Here is my hand for my true constancy;
  And when that hour o'erslips me in the day
  Wherein I sigh not, Julia, for thy sake,   10
  The next ensuing hour some foul mischance
  Torment me for my love's forgetfulness!
  My father stays° my coming; answer not;
  The tide is now:—nay, not thy tide of tears;
  That tide will stay me longer than I should.   15
  Julia, farewell!   [*Exit Julia.*]
            What, gone without a word?
  Ay, so true love should do: it cannot speak;
  For truth hath better deeds than words to grace it.

                [*Enter Panthino.*]

Panthino. Sir Proteus, you are stayed for.

Proteus. Go; I come, I come.   20
  Alas! This parting strikes poor lovers dumb.   *Exeunt.*

                Scene 3. [*Verona. A street.*]

                Enter Launce [, *leading a dog*].

Launce. Nay, 'twill be this hour ere I have done weeping; all the kind of the Launces have this very fault.
  I have received my proportion,° like the prodigious°

2.2.4 **turn** i.e., change your affection (perhaps with the additional
meaning of "engage in sexual acts")   13 **stays** waits for   2.3.3 **proportion** (Launce's blunder for "portion")   3 **prodigious** (blunder for
"prodigal")

son, and am going with Sir Proteus to the Imperial's
5   court. I think Crab my dog be the sourest-natured
dog that lives. My mother weeping, my father wailing, my sister crying, our maid howling, our cat
wringing her hands, and all our house in a great
perplexity, yet did not this cruel-hearted cur shed
10   one tear. He is a stone, a very pebble stone, and
has no more pity in him than a dog. A Jew would
have wept to have seen our parting. Why, my
grandam, having no eyes, look you, wept herself
blind at my parting. Nay, I'll show you the manner
15   of it. This shoe is my father; no, this left shoe is
my father. No, no, this left shoe is my mother; nay,
that cannot be so neither. Yes, it is so, it is so, it
hath the worser sole. This shoe, with the hole in it,
is my mother, and this my father; a vengeance on't!
20   There 'tis. Now, sir, this staff is my sister, for, look
you, she is as white as a lily, and as small as a
wand. This hat is Nan, our maid. I am the dog. No,
the dog is himself, and I am the dog. Oh! The dog
is me, and I am myself; ay, so, so. Now come I to
25   my father: Father, your blessing. Now should not
the shoe speak a word for weeping: now should I
kiss my father: well, he weeps on. Now come I to
my mother. Oh, that she could speak now like a
wood woman!° Well, I kiss her; why, there 'tis.
30   Here's my mother's breath up and down.° Now
come I to my sister; mark the moan she makes.
Now the dog all this while sheds not a tear, nor
speaks a word; but see how I lay the dust with my
tears.

[Enter Panthino.]

35 *Panthino.* Launce, away, away, aboard! Thy master is
shipped, and thou art to post after with oars. What's
the matter? Why weep'st thou, man? Away, ass!
You'll lose the tide, if you tarry any longer.

28–29 **Oh, that . . . wood woman** (Launce laments that his [wooden]
shoe is not really his mother, madly distressed [wood] as she was at
parting) 30 **up and down** identically

Launce. It is no matter if the tied were lost; for it is the unkindest tied that ever any man tied. 40

Panthino. What's the unkindest tide?

Launce. Why, he that's tied here, Crab, my dog.

Panthino. Tut, man, I mean thou'lt lose the flood,° and, in losing the flood, lose thy voyage, and, in losing thy voyage, lose thy master, and, in losing 45 thy master, lose thy service, and, in losing thy service— Why dost thou stop my mouth?

Launce. For fear thou shouldst lose thy tongue.

Panthino. Where should I lose my tongue?

Launce. In thy tale. 50

Panthino. In thy tail!

Launce. Lose the tide, and the voyage, and the master, and the service, and the tied! Why, man, if the river were dry, I am able to fill it with my tears; if the wind were down, I could drive the boat with my 55 sighs.

Panthino. Come, come away, man; I was sent to call thee.

Launce. Sir, call me what thou dar'st.

Panthino. Wilt thou go? 60

Launce. Well, I will go. *Exeunt.*

Scene 4. [*Milan. The Duke's palace.*]

Enter Valentine, Silvia, Thurio, [and] Speed.

Silvia. Servant!

Valentine. Mistress?

43 **flood** full tide

Speed. Master, Sir Thurio frowns on you.

Valentine. Ay, boy, it's for love.

5   *Speed.* Not of you.

Valentine. Of my mistress, then.

Speed. 'Twere good you knocked him.   [*Exit.*]

Silvia. Servant, you are sad.

Valentine. Indeed, madam, I seem so.

10   *Thurio.* Seem you that you are not?

Valentine. Haply I do.

Thurio. So do counterfeits.

Valentine. So do you.

Thurio. What seem I that I am not?

15   *Valentine.* Wise.

Thurio. What instance of the contrary?

Valentine. Your folly.

Thurio. And how quote° you my folly?

Valentine. I quote it in your jerkin.

20   *Thurio.* My jerkin is a doublet.°

Valentine. Well, then, I'll double your folly.

Thurio. How?

Silvia. What, angry, Sir Thurio! Do you change color?

Valentine. Give him leave, madam; he is a kind of
25   chameleon.

Thurio. That hath more mind to feed on your blood
than live in your air.

Valentine. You have said, sir.

2.4.18 **quote** observe (pronounced "coat") 20 **doublet** close-fitting
jacket

Thurio. Ay, sir, and done too, for this time.

Valentine. I know it well, sir; you always end ere you   *30*
  begin.

Silvia. A fine volley of words, gentlemen, and quickly
  shot off.

Valentine. 'Tis indeed, madam; we thank the giver.

Silvia. Who is that, servant?   *35*

Valentine. Yourself, sweet lady; for you gave the fire.
  Sir Thurio borrows his wit from your ladyship's
  looks, and spends what he borrows kindly in your
  company.

Thurio. Sir, if you spend word for word with me, I   *40*
  shall make your wit bankrupt.

Valentine. I know it well, sir. You have an exchequer
  of words, and, I think, no other treasure to give
  your followers, for it appears by their bare° liveries
  that they live by your bare words.   *45*

Silvia. No more, gentlemen, no more—here comes my
  father.

[Enter Duke.]

Duke. Now, daughter Silvia, you are hard beset.
  Sir Valentine, your father's in good health.
  What say you to a letter from your friends   *50*
  Of much good news?

Valentine.   My lord, I will be thankful
  To any happy messenger° from thence.

Duke. Know ye Don Antonio, your countryman?

Valentine. Ay, my good lord, I know the gentleman
  To be of worth, and worthy estimation,   *55*
  And not without desert so well reputed.

Duke. Hath he not a son?

---

44 **bare** threadbare   52 **happy messenger** i.e., bringer of good news

Valentine. Ay, my good lord, a son that well deserves
The honor and regard of such a father.

60 *Duke.* You know him well?

Valentine. I knew him as myself; for from our infancy
We have conversed and spent our hours together;
And though myself have been an idle truant,
Omitting the sweet benefit of time
65 To clothe mine age with angel-like perfection,
Yet hath Sir Proteus, for that's his name,
Made use and fair advantage of his days;
His years but young, but his experience old;
His head unmellowed, but his judgment ripe.
70 And, in a word, for far behind his worth
Comes all the praises that I now bestow,
He is complete in feature and in mind
With all good grace to grace a gentleman.

Duke. Beshrew me, sir, but if he make this good,
75 He is as worthy for an empress' love
As meet° to be an emperor's counselor.
Well, sir, this gentleman is come to me
With commendation from great potentates,
And here he means to spend his time awhile.
80 I think 'tis no unwelcome news to you.

Valentine. Should I have wished a thing, it had been he.

Duke. Welcome him, then, according to his worth.
Silvia, I speak to you, and you, Sir Thurio;
For Valentine, I need not cite° him to it.
85 I will send him hither to you presently.   [*Exit.*]

Valentine. This is the gentleman I told your ladyship
Had come along with me, but that his mistress
Did hold his eyes locked in her crystal looks.

Silvia. Belike that now she hath enfranchised them,
90 Upon some other pawn for fealty.°

---

76 **meet** fitted   84 **cite** incite, urge   90 **pawn for fealty** pledge for loyalty

Valentine. Nay, sure, I think she holds them prisoners
   still.

Silvia. Nay, then, he should be blind; and, being blind,
   How could he see his way to seek out you?

Valentine. Why, lady, Love hath twenty pair of eyes.

Thurio. They say that Love hath not an eye at all.   95

Valentine. To see such lovers, Thurio, as yourself.
   Upon a homely object Love can wink. [*Exit Thurio.*]

Silvia. Have done, have done; here comes the gentleman.

[*Enter Proteus.*]

Valentine. Welcome, dear Proteus! Mistress, I beseech
   you,
   Confirm his welcome with some special favor.   100

Silvia. His worth is warrant for his welcome hither,
   If this be he you oft have wished to hear from.

Valentine. Mistress, it is. Sweet lady, entertain° him
   To be my fellow servant to your ladyship.

Silvia. Too low a mistress for so high a servant.   105

Proteus. Not so, sweet lady, but too mean° a servant
   To have a look of such a worthy mistress.

Valentine. Leave off discourse of disability.°
   Sweet lady, entertain him for your servant.

Proteus. My duty will I boast of, nothing else.   110

Silvia. And duty never yet did want his meed.°
   Servant, you are welcome to a worthless mistress.

Proteus. I'll die on° him that says so but yourself.

Silvia. That you are welcome?

---

103 **entertain** welcome   106 **mean** low, humble   108 **Leave ... disability** i.e., cease this modest talk   111 **want his meed** lack its
reward   113 **die on** fight to the death

Proteus.   That you are worthless.

                    [*Enter Thurio.*]

Servant. Madam, my lord your father would speak
115   with you.

   Silvia. I wait upon his pleasure. [*Exit Servant.*] Come,
     Sir Thurio,
     Go with me. Once more, new servant, welcome.
     I'll leave you to confer of home affairs.
     When you have done, we look to hear from you.

120 *Proteus.* We'll both attend upon your ladyship.
                    [*Exeunt Silvia and Thurio.*]

   Valentine. Now, tell me, how do all from whence you
     came?

   Proteus. Your friends are well, and have them much
     commended.°

   Valentine. And how do yours?

   Proteus.   I left them all in health.

   Valentine. How does your lady? And how thrives your
     love?

125 *Proteus.* My tales of love were wont to weary you;
     I know you joy not in a love discourse.

   Valentine. Ay, Proteus, but that life is altered now.
     I have done penance for contemning Love,
     Whose high imperious thoughts have punished me
130   With bitter fasts, with penitential groans,
     With nightly tears, and daily heartsore sighs;
     For, in revenge of my contempt of love,
     Love hath chased sleep from my enthrallèd eyes,
     And made them watchers of mine own heart's sor-
     row.
135   O gentle Proteus, Love's a mighty lord,
     And hath so humbled me, as° I confess

___

122 **have them much commended** i.e., themselves to you   136 **as** that

There is no woe to° his correction,
Nor to his service no such joy on earth.
Now no discourse, except it be of love;
Now can I break my fast, dine, sup, and sleep   *140*
Upon the very naked name of love.

Proteus. Enough; I read your fortune in your eye.
  Was this the idol that you worship so?

Valentine. Even she; and is she not a heavenly saint?

Proteus. No; but she is an earthly paragon.   *145*

Valentine. Call her divine.

Proteus.   I will not flatter her.

Valentine. O, flatter me, for love delights in praises.

Proteus. When I was sick, you gave me bitter pills,
  And I must minister the like to you.

Valentine. Then speak the truth by her; if not divine, *150*
  Yet let her be a principality,
  Sovereign to all the creatures on the earth.

Proteus. Except my mistress.

Valentine.   Sweet, except not any,
  Except thou wilt except against° my love.

Proteus. Have I not reason to prefer mine own?   *155*

Valentine. And I will help thee to prefer° her too.
  She shall be dignified with this high honor—
  To bear my lady's train, lest the base earth
  Should from her vesture chance to steal a kiss,
  And, of so great a favor growing proud,   *160*
  Disdain to root the summer-swelling flow'r,
  And make rough winter everlastingly.

Proteus. Why, Valentine, what braggardism is this?

Valentine. Pardon me, Proteus. All I can is nothing

---

137 **to** like unto   154 **Except thou wilt except against** unless you will
take exception to   156 **prefer** advance

165 To her, whose worth makes other worthies nothing;
   She is alone.

   Proteus.   Then let her alone.

   Valentine. Not for the world. Why, man, she is mine
      own,
      And I as rich in having such a jewel
      As twenty seas, if all their sand were pearl,
170   The water nectar, and the rocks pure gold.
      Forgive me that I do not dream on° thee,
      Because thou see'st me dote upon my love.
      My foolish rival, that her father likes
      Only for his possessions are so huge,
175   Is gone with her along; and I must after,
      For love, thou know'st, is full of jealousy.

   Proteus. But she loves you?

   Valentine. Ay, and we are betrothed; nay, more, our
      marriage hour,
      With all the cunning manner of our flight,
180   Determined of: how I must climb her window,
      The ladder made of cords, and all the means
      Plotted and 'greed on for my happiness.
      Good Proteus, go with me to my chamber,
      In these affairs to aid me with thy counsel.

185 *Proteus.* Go on before; I shall inquire you forth.
      I must unto the road, to disembark
      Some necessaries that I needs must use,
      And then I'll presently attend you.

   Valentine. Will you make haste?

190 *Proteus.* I will.   *Exit [Valentine].*
      Even as one heat another heat expels,
      Or as one nail by strength drives out another,
      So the remembrance of my former love
      Is by a newer object quite forgotten.
195   Is it mine eye, or Valentine's praise,
      Her true perfection, or my false transgression,
      That makes me reasonless° to reason thus?

171 **on** of   197 **reasonless** without justification

She is fair; and so is Julia, that I love—
That I did love, for now my love is thawed,
Which, like a waxen image 'gainst a fire,   *200*
Bears no impression of the thing it was.
Methinks my zeal to Valentine is cold,
And that I love him not as I was wont.
O, but I love his lady too too much!
And that's the reason I love him so little.   *205*
How shall I dote on her with more advice,°
That thus without advice begin to love her!
'Tis but her picture° I have yet beheld,
And that hath dazzled my reason's light;
But when I look on her perfections,   *210*
There is no reason° but I shall be blind.
If I can check my erring love, I will;
If not, to compass° her I'll use my skill.   *Exit.*

Scene 5. [*Milan. A street.*]

Enter Speed and Launce [meeting].

Speed. Launce! By mine honesty, welcome to Padua!°

Launce. Forswear° not thyself, sweet youth; for I am
not welcome. I reckon this always—that a man is
never undone till he be hanged, nor never welcome
to a place till some certain shot° be paid, and the   *5*
hostess say "Welcome!"

Speed. Come on, you madcap, I'll to the alehouse with
you presently, where, for one shot of five pence,
thou shalt have five thousand welcomes. But, sirrah,
how did thy master part with Madam Julia?   *10*

206 **advice** careful thought   208 **picture** i.e., her visible being, outward
appearance   211 **reason** question   213 **compass** get, achieve   2.5.1
Padua (apparently Shakespeare forgot that his characters are in Milan)
2 **Forswear** perjure   5 **shot** alehouse bill

Launce. Marry, after they closed in earnest,° they parted very fairly in jest.

Speed. But shall she marry him?

Launce. No.

15 *Speed.* How, then? Shall he marry her?

Launce. No, neither.

Speed. What, are they broken?

Launce. No, they are both as whole as a fish.

Speed. Why, then, how stands the matter with them?

20 *Launce.* Marry, thus: when it stands well with him, it stands well with her.

Speed. What an ass art thou! I understand thee not.

Launce. What a block art thou, that thou canst not! My staff understands me.

25 *Speed.* What thou sayest?

Launce. Ay, and what I do too. Look thee, I'll but lean, and my staff understands me.

Speed. It stands under thee, indeed.

Launce. Why, stand-under and under-stand is all one.

30 *Speed.* But tell me true, will't be a match?

Launce. Ask my dog. If he say ay, it will; if he say, no, it will; if he shake his tail and say nothing, it will.

Speed. The conclusion is, then, that it will.

35 *Launce.* Thou shalt never get such a secret from me but by a parable.°

Speed. 'Tis well that I get it so. But, Launce, how say-

---

11 **closed in earnest** (1) formally agreed (2) embraced   36 **by a parable** i.e., by indirect affirmation

est thou,° that my master is become a notable
lover?

Launce. I never knew him otherwise.   *40*

Speed. Than how?

Launce. A notable lubber, as thou reportest him to be.

Speed. Why, thou whoreson ass, thou mistak'st me.

Launce. Why fool, I meant not thee; I meant thy
master.   *45*

Speed. I tell thee, my master is become a hot lover.

Launce. Why, I tell thee, I care not though he burn
himself in love. If thou wilt, go with me to the alehouse; if not, thou art an Hebrew, a Jew, and not
worth the name of a Christian.   *50*

Speed. Why?

Launce. Because thou hast not so much charity in
thee as to go to the ale with a Christian.° Wilt thou
go?

Speed. At thy service.   *Exeunt.*   *55*

Scene 6. [*Milan. The Duke's palace.*]

Enter Proteus solus.°

Proteus. To leave my Julia shall I be forsworn;
   To love fair Silvia shall I be forsworn;
   To wrong my friend, I shall be much forsworn;
   And ev'n that pow'r which gave me first my oath
   Provokes me to this threefold perjury: *5*

37–38 **how sayest thou** what do you think about this   53 **go to the ale
with a Christian** i.e., attend a church-benefit festivity   2.6.s.d **solus**
alone (Latin)

Love bade me swear, and Love bids me forswear.
O sweet-suggesting Love, if thou hast sinned,
Teach me, thy tempted subject, to excuse it!
At first I did adore a twinkling star,
10 But now I worship a celestial sun.
Unheedful vows may heedfully be broken;
And he wants° wit that wants resolvèd will
To learn° his wit t' exchange the bad for better.
Fie, fie, unreverend tongue! To call her bad,
15 Whose sovereignty so oft thou hast preferred
With twenty thousand soul-confirming oaths.
I cannot leave to love, and yet I do;
But there I leave to love where I should love.
Julia I lose, and Valentine I lose.
20 If I keep them, I needs must lose myself;
If I lose them, thus find I by their loss
For Valentine, myself, for Julia, Silvia.
I to myself am dearer than a friend,
For love is still most precious in itself;
25 And Silvia—witness Heaven, that made her fair!—
Shows Julia but a swarthy Ethiope.
I will forget that Julia is alive,
Rememb'ring that my love to her is dead;
And Valentine I'll hold an enemy,
30 Aiming at Silvia as a sweeter friend.
I cannot now prove constant to myself,
Without some treachery used to Valentine.
This night he meaneth with a corded ladder
To climb celestial Silvia's chamber window,
35 Myself in counsel, his competitor.°
Now presently I'll give her father notice
Of their disguising and pretended° flight;
Who, all enraged, will banish Valentine;
For Thurio, he intends, shall wed his daughter.
40 But, Valentine being gone, I'll quickly cross
By some sly trick blunt Thurio's dull proceeding.
Love, lend me wings to make my purpose swift,
As thou hast lent me wit to plot this drift!°   *Exit.*

12 **wants** lacks   13 **learn** teach   35 **competitor** accomplice   37 **pretended** intended   43 **drift** device

Scene 7. [*Verona. Julia's house.*]

Enter Julia and Lucetta.

Julia. Counsel, Lucetta; gentle girl, assist me;
   And, ev'n in kind love, I do conjure thee,
   Who art the table° wherein all my thoughts
   Are visibly charactered and engraved,
   To lesson me, and tell me some good mean,   5
   How, with my honor,° I may undertake
   A journey to my loving Proteus.

Lucetta. Alas, the way is wearisome and long!

Julia. A true-devoted pilgrim is not weary
   To measure kingdoms with his feeble steps;   10
   Much less shall she that hath Love's wings to fly—
   And when the flight is made to one so dear,
   Of such divine perfection, as Sir Proteus.

Lucetta. Better forbear till Proteus make return.

Julia. O, know'st thou not his looks are my soul's
      food?   15
   Pity the dearth that I have pinèd in
   By longing for that food so long a time.
   Didst thou but know the inly° touch of love,
   Thou wouldst as soon go kindle fire with snow
   As seek to quench the fire of love with words.   20

Lucetta. I do not seek to quench your love's hot fire,
   But qualify° the fire's extreme rage,
   Lest it should burn above the bounds of reason.

Julia. The more thou damm'st it up, the more it burns.
   The current that with gentle murmur glides,   25
   Thou know'st, being stopped, impatiently doth rage;
   But when his fair course is not hinderèd,
   He makes sweet music with th' enameled° stones,

2.7.3 **table** tablet   6 **with my honor** preserving my honor   18 **inly**
inward   22 **qualify** mitigate   28 **enameled** shiny

Giving a gentle kiss to every sedge
30   He overtaketh in his pilgrimage;
And so by many winding nooks he strays,
With willing sport, to the wild ocean.
Then let me go, and hinder not my course.
I'll be as patient as a gentle stream,
35   And make a pastime of each weary step,
Till the last step have brought me to my love;
And there I'll rest, as after much turmoil
A blessèd soul doth in Elysium.

Lucetta. But in what habit° will you go along?

40   *Julia.* Not like a woman, for I would prevent
The loose encounters of lascivious men.
Gentle Lucetta, fit me with such weeds°
As may beseem some well-reputed page.

Lucetta. Why, then, your ladyship must cut your hair.

45   *Julia.* No, girl; I'll knit it up in silken strings
With twenty odd-conceited° truelove knots.
To be fantastic may become a youth
Of greater time° than I shall show to be.

Lucetta. What fashion, madam, shall I make your
breeches?

50   *Julia.* That fits as well as, "Tell me, good my lord,
What compass° will you wear your farthingale?"°
Why, ev'n what fashion thou best likes, Lucetta.

Lucetta. You must needs have them with a codpiece,°
madam.

Julia. Out, out,° Lucetta! That will be ill-favored.

55   *Lucetta.* A round hose, madam, now's not worth a pin,
Unless you have a codpiece to stick pins on.

Julia. Lucetta, as thou lov'st me, let me have

39 **habit** costume   42 **weeds** garments   46 **odd-conceited** ingeniously
devised   48 **Of greater time** i.e., older   51 **compass** circumfer-
ence   51 **farthingale** hooped petticoat   53 **codpiece** pocket or bag at
front of men's breeches (**round hose,** line 55), often fashionably exag-
gerated   54 **Out, out** fie, fie

What thou think'st meet, and is most mannerly.
But tell me, wench, how will the world repute me
For undertaking so unstaid° a journey?   *60*
I fear me, it will make me scandalized.

Lucetta. If you think so, then stay at home, and go not.

Julia. Nay, that I will not.

Lucetta. Then never dream on infamy, but go.
If Proteus like your journey when you come,   *65*
No matter who's displeased when you are gone:
I fear me, he will scarce be pleased withal.°

Julia. That is the least, Lucetta, of my fears.
A thousand oaths, an ocean of his tears,
And instances of infinite° of love   *70*
Warrant me welcome to my Proteus.

Lucetta. All these are servants to deceitful men.

Julia. Base men, that use them to so base effect!
But truer stars did govern Proteus' birth.
His words are bonds, his oaths are oracles;   *75*
His love sincere, his thoughts immaculate;
His tears pure messengers sent from his heart;
His heart as far from fraud as heaven from earth.

Lucetta. Pray heav'n he prove so, when you come to
him!

Julia. Now, as thou lov'st me, do him not that wrong,   *80*
To bear a hard opinion of his truth.
Only deserve my love by loving him,
And presently go with me to my chamber
To take a note of what I stand in need of
To furnish me upon my longing° journey.   *85*
All that is mine I leave at thy dispose,
My goods, my lands, my reputation;
Only, in lieu thereof, dispatch me hence.
Come, answer not, but to it presently!
I am impatient of my tarriance.   *Exeunt.*   *90*

60 **unstaid** unbecoming   67 **withal** with it   70 **infinite** infinity   85
longing i.e., occasioned by my longing

ACT 3

Scene 1. [*Milan. The Duke's palace.*]

Enter Duke, Thurio, [and] Proteus.

Duke. Sir Thurio, give us leave, I pray, awhile;
We have some secrets to confer about.
                                        [*Exit Thurio.*]
Now, tell me, Proteus, what's your will with me?

Proteus. My gracious lord, that which I would discover°
5   The law of friendship bids me to conceal;
But when I call to mind your gracious favors
Done to me, undeserving as I am,
My duty pricks me on to utter that
Which else no worldly good should draw from me.
10 Know, worthy prince, Sir Valentine, my friend,
This night intends to steal away your daughter.
Myself am one made privy to the plot.
I know you have determined to bestow her
On Thurio, whom your gentle daughter hates,
15 And should she thus be stol'n away from you,
It would be much vexation to your age.
Thus, for my duty's sake, I rather chose

3.1.4 **discover** disclose

42

To cross my friend in his intended drift
Than, by concealing it, heap on your head
A pack of sorrows which would press you down,   20
Being unprevented, to your timeless° grave.

Duke. Proteus, I thank thee for thine honest care,
Which to requite, command me while I live.
This love of theirs myself have often seen,
Haply when they have judged me fast asleep;   25
And oftentimes have purposed to forbid
Sir Valentine her company and my court.
But, fearing lest my jealous° aim might err,
And so, unworthily disgrace the man,
A rashness that I ever yet have shunned,   30
I gave him gentle looks; thereby to find
That which thyself hast now disclosed to me.
And, that thou mayst perceive my fear of this,
Knowing that tender youth is soon suggested,°
I nightly lodge her in an upper tow'r,   35
The key whereof myself have ever kept;
And thence she cannot be conveyed away.

Proteus. Know, noble lord, they have devised a mean
How he her chamber window will ascend,
And with a corded ladder fetch her down;   40
For which the youthful lover now is gone,
And this way comes he with it presently,
Where, if it please you, you may intercept him.
But, good my lord, do it so cunningly
That my discovery be not aimèd at;°   45
For love of you, not hate unto my friend,
Hath made me publisher of this pretense.°

Duke. Upon mine honor, he shall never know
That I had any light from thee of this.

Proteus. Adieu, my lord; Sir Valentine is coming.   50
                                                 [*Exit.*]

---

21 **timeless** untimely   28 **jealous** suspicious   34 **suggested** tempted,
prompted   45 **aimèd at** guessed   47 **pretense** intention

[*Enter Valentine.*]

Duke. Sir Valentine, whither away so fast?

Valentine. Please it your Grace, there is a messenger
That stays to bear my letters to my friends,
And I am going to deliver them.

55 *Duke.* Be they of much import?

Valentine. The tenor of them doth but signify
My health and happy being at your court.

Duke. Nay then, no matter; stay with me awhile.
I am to break with thee of some affairs
60 That touch me near, wherein thou must be secret.
'Tis not unknown to thee that I have sought
To match my friend Sir Thurio to my daughter.

Valentine. I know it well, my lord; and, sure, the
match
Were rich and honorable; besides, the gentleman
65 Is full of virtue, bounty, worth, and qualities
Beseeming such a wife as your fair daughter.
Cannot your Grace win her to fancy him?

Duke. No, trust me; she is peevish, sullen, froward,°
Proud, disobedient, stubborn, lacking duty,
70 Neither regarding that she is my child
Nor fearing me as if I were her father.
And, may I say to thee, this pride of hers,
Upon advice,° hath drawn° my love from her;
And, where I thought the remnant of mine age
75 Should have been cherished by her childlike duty,
I now am full resolved to take a wife,
And turn her out to who will take her in.
Then let her beauty be her wedding dow'r,
For me and my possessions she esteems not.

Valentine. What would your Grace have me to do in
80   this?

68 **peevish . . . froward** obstinate . . . willful   73 **advice** consideration
73 **drawn** withdrawn

Duke. There is a lady in Verona here°
  Whom I affect; but she is nice° and coy,
  And nought esteems my agèd eloquence.
  Now, therefore, would I have thee to my tutor—
  For long agone I have forgot to court; 85
  Besides, the fashion of the time is changed—
  How and which way I may bestow° myself,
  To be regarded in her sun-bright eye.

Valentine. Win her with gifts, if she respect not words.
  Dumb jewels often in their silent kind° 90
  More than quick words do move a woman's mind.

Duke. But she did scorn a present that I sent her.

Valentine. A woman sometime scorns what best con-
    tents her.
  Send her another; never give her o'er;
  For scorn at first makes after-love the more. 95
  If she do frown, 'tis not in hate of you,
  But rather to beget more love in you.
  If she do chide, 'tis not to have you gone;
  For why, the fools are mad, if left alone.
  Take no repulse, whatever she doth say; 100
  For "get you gone," she doth not mean "away!"
  Flatter and praise, commend, extol their graces;
  Though ne'er so black, say they have angels' faces.
  That man that hath a tongue, I say, is no man,
  If with his tongue he cannot win a woman. 105

Duke. But she I mean is promised by her friends
  Unto a youthful gentleman of worth,
  And kept severely from resort of men,
  That no man hath access by day to her.

Valentine. Why, then, I would resort to her by night. 110

Duke. Ay, but the doors be locked, and keys kept safe,
  That no man hath recourse to her by night.

81 **in Verona here** (some editors emend *in* to "of," but probably Shakespeare forgot his characters are now in Milan) 82 **nice** fastidious 87
bestow conduct 90 **kind** nature

Valentine. What lets° but one may enter at her window?

Duke. Her chamber is aloft, far from the ground,
115 And built so shelving° that one cannot climb it
Without apparent hazard of his life.

Valentine. Why, then, a ladder, quaintly made of cords,
To cast up, with a pair of anchoring hooks,
Would serve to scale another Hero's tow'r,
120 So bold Leander would adventure it.

Duke. Now, as thou art a gentleman of blood,°
Advise me where I may have such a ladder.

Valentine. When would you use it? Pray, sir, tell me that.

Duke. This very night; for Love is like a child,
125 That longs for everything that he can come by.

Valentine. By seven o'clock I'll get you such a ladder.

Duke. But, hark thee; I will go to her alone.
How shall I best convey the ladder thither?

Valentine. It will be light, my lord, that you may bear it
130 Under a cloak that is of any length.

Duke. A cloak as long as thine will serve the turn?

Valentine. Ay, my good lord.

Duke. Then let me see thy cloak.
I'll get me one of such another length.

Valentine. Why, any cloak will serve the turn, my lord.

135 *Duke.* How shall I fashion me to wear a cloak?
I pray thee, let me feel thy cloak upon me.
                    [*Opens Valentine's cloak.*]
What letter is this same? What's here? "To Silvia"—

113 **lets** prevents   115 **shelving** steeply sloping   121 **of blood** i.e., of noble blood

And here an engine° fit for my proceeding.
I'll be so bold to break the seal for once.   [*Reads.*]
"My thoughts do harbor with my Silvia nightly;   *140*
    And slaves they are to me, that send them flying.
O, could their master come and go as lightly,
    Himself would lodge where senseless they are
        lying!
My herald thoughts in thy pure bosom rest them,
    While I, their king, that thither them importune,   *145*
Do curse the grace that with such grace hath blessed
        them,
    Because myself do want my servants' fortune.
I curse myself, for they are sent by me,
That they should harbor where their lord should be."
What's here?   *150*
"Silvia, this night I will enfranchise thee."
'Tis so; and here's the ladder for the purpose.
Why, Phaethon—for thou art Merops' son—
Wilt thou aspire to guide the heavenly car,
And with thy daring folly burn the world?°   *155*
Wilt thou reach stars, because they shine on thee?
Go, base intruder! Overweening slave!
Bestow thy fawning smiles on equal mates,
And think my patience, more than thy desert,
Is privilege for thy departure hence.   *160*
Thank me for this more than for all the favors
Which all too much I have bestowed on thee.
But if thou linger in my territories
Longer than swiftest expedition°
Will give thee time to leave our royal court,   *165*
By heaven, my wrath shall far exceed the love
I ever bore my daughter or thyself.
Be gone! I will not hear thy vain excuse;
But, as thou lov'st thy life, make speed from hence.
                                                        [*Exit.*]

138 **engine** contrivance (here, the ladder)   153–55 **Phaethon . . . the world** (Phaethon's father, Phoebus—not Merops, who was his mother's husband—forbade the youth to drive the horses of the sun across the sky, but the youth disobeyed him, with dire results)   164 **expedition** speed

Valentine. And why not death rather than living tor-
170   ment?
        To die is to be banished from myself;
        And Silvia is myself. Banished from her
        Is self from self: a deadly banishment!
        What light is light, if Silvia be not seen?
175   What joy is joy, if Silvia be not by?—
        Unless it be to think that she is by,
        And feed upon the shadow° of perfection.
        Except I be by Silvia in the night,
        There is no music in the nightingale;
180   Unless I look on Silvia in the day,
        There is no day for me to look upon.
        She is my essence, and I leave° to be,
        If I be not by her fair influence°
        Fostered, illumined, cherished, kept alive.
185   I fly not death, to fly his deadly doom:
        Tarry I here, I but attend on death;
        But, fly I hence, I fly away from life.

            [*Enter Proteus and Launce.*]

Proteus. Run, boy, run, run, and seek him out.

Launce. Soho, soho!

190 *Proteus.* What seest thou?

Launce. Him we go to find. There's not a hair° on's
        head but 'tis a Valentine.°

Proteus. Valentine?

Valentine. No.

195 *Proteus.* Who then? His spirit?

Valentine. Neither.

Proteus. What then?

___

177 **shadow** mere image   182 **leave** cease   183 **influence** i.e., like that
of the stars (see especially Sonnet 15)   191 **hair** (with pun on "hare,"
prepared by preceding *Soho*, a hunting cry)   192 **Valentine** (with pun,
as in lines 210–14 below)

Valentine. Nothing.

Launce. Can nothing speak? Master, shall I strike?

Proteus. Who wouldst thou strike?   200

Launce. Nothing.

Proteus. Villain, forbear.

Launce. Why, sir, I'll strike nothing. I pray you—

Proteus. Sirrah, I say, forbear. Friend Valentine, a
    word.

Valentine. My ears are stopped, and cannot hear good
    news,   205
    So much of bad already hath possessed them.

Proteus. Then in dumb silence will I bury mine,
    For they are harsh, untunable, and bad.

Valentine. Is Silvia dead?

Proteus. No, Valentine.   210

Valentine. No Valentine, indeed, for sacred Silvia.
    Hath she forsworn me?

Proteus. No, Valentine.

Valentine. No Valentine, if Silvia have forsworn me.
    What is your news?   215

Launce. Sir, there is a proclamation that you are van-
    ished.

Proteus. That thou are banishèd—O, that's the
    news!—
    From hence, from Silvia, and from me thy friend.

Valentine. O, I have fed upon this woe already,   220
    And now excess of it will make me surfeit.
    Doth Silvia know that I am banishèd?

Proteus. Ay, ay, and she hath offered to the doom—
    Which, unreversed, stands in effectual force—
    A sea of melting pearl, which some call tears: 225
    Those at her father's churlish feet she tendered;

With them, upon her knees, her humble self;
Wringing her hands, whose whiteness so became
  them
As if but now they waxèd pale for woe.
230 But neither bended knees, pure hands held up,
Sad sighs, deep groans, nor silver-shedding tears,
Could penetrate her uncompassionate sire;
But Valentine, if he be ta'en, must die.
Besides, her intercession chafed him so,
235 When she for thy repeal was suppliant,
That to close prison he commanded her,
With many bitter threats of biding° there.

Valentine. No more; unless the next word that thou
  speak'st
Have some malignant power upon my life.
240 If so, I pray thee, breathe it in mine ear,
As ending anthem° of my endless dolor.

Proteus. Cease to lament for that thou canst not help,
And study help for that which thou lament'st.
Time is the nurse and breeder of all good.
245 Here if thou stay, thou canst not see thy love;
Besides, thy staying will abridge thy life.
Hope is a lover's staff; walk hence with that,
And manage it against despairing thoughts.
Thy letters may be here, though thou art hence;
250 Which, being writ to me, shall be delivered
Even in the milk-white bosom of thy love.
The time now serves not to expostulate.
Come, I'll convey thee through the city gate,
And, ere I part with thee, confer at large
255 Of all that may concern thy love affairs.
As thou lov'st Silvia, though not for thyself,
Regard thy danger, and along with me!

Valentine. I pray thee, Launce, and if° thou seest my
  boy,
Bid him make haste, and meet me at the Northgate.

237 **biding** i.e., permanent incarceration   241 **ending anthem** funeral
hymn   258 **and if** if

Proteus. Go, sirrah, find him out. Come, Valentine.   260

Valentine. O my dear Silvia! Hapless Valentine!
                    [*Exeunt Valentine and Proteus.*]

Launce. I am but a fool, look you, and yet I have the
   wit to think my master is a kind of a knave. But
   that's all one, if he be but one knave. He lives not
   now that knows me to be in love, yet I am in love;   265
   but a team of horse shall not pluck that from me,
   nor who 'tis I love, and yet 'tis a woman; but what
   woman, I will not tell myself, and yet 'tis a milk-
   maid; yet 'tis not a maid, for she hath had gossips;°
   yet 'tis a maid, for she is her master's maid, and   270
   serves for wages. She hath more qualities than a
   water spaniel—which is much in a bare Christian.
   [*Pulling out a paper*] Here is the cate-log of her
   condition. "Imprimis:° She can fetch and carry."
   Why, a horse can do no more: nay, a horse cannot   275
   fetch, but only carry; therefore is she better than a
   jade.° "Item: She can milk"; look you, a sweet virtue in a maid with clean hands.

                    [*Enter Speed.*]

Speed. How now, Signior Launce! What news with
   your mastership?   280

Launce. With my master's ship? Why, it is at sea.

Speed. Well, your old vice still; mistake the word.
   What news, then, in your paper?

Launce. The black'st news that ever thou heard'st.

Speed. Why, man, how black?   285

Launce. Why, as black as ink.

Speed. Let me read them.

Launce. Fie on thee, jolthead!° Thou canst not read.

---

269 **gossips** godparents (for her own child)   274 **Imprimis** in the first
place   277 **jade** nag   288 **jolthead** blockhead

Speed. Thou liest; I can.

290 *Launce.* I will try thee. Tell me this: who begot thee?

Speed. Marry, the son of my grandfather.

Launce. O illiterate loiterer! It was the son of thy grandmother. This proves that thou canst not read.

Speed. Come, fool, come; try me in thy paper.

295 *Launce.* There; and Saint Nicholas° be thy speed!°

Speed. [*Reads*] "Imprimis: She can milk."

Launce. Ay, that she can.

Speed. "Item: She brews good ale."

Launce. And thereof comes the proverb: "Blessing of
300 your heart, you brew good ale."

Speed. "Item: She can sew."

Launce. That's as much as to say, Can she so?

Speed. "Item: She can knit."

Launce. What need a man care for a stock° with a
305 wench when she can knit him a stock?

Speed. "Item: She can wash and scour."

Launce. A special virtue; for then she need not be washed and scoured.

Speed. "Item: She can spin."

310 *Launce.* Then may I set the world on wheels,° when she can spin for her living.

Speed. "Item: She hath many nameless virtues."

Launce. That's as much as to say, bastard virtues—
that, indeed, know not their fathers, and therefore
315 have no names.

---

295 **Saint Nicholas** patron saint of scholars (among others)   295 **speed** aid   304 **stock** dowry (pun follows)   310 **set the world on wheels** take life easy

Speed. "Here follow her vices."

Launce. Close at the heels of her virtues.

Speed. "Item: She is not to be kissed fasting, in respect of her breath."

Launce. Well, that fault may be mended with a break- 320
fast. Read on.

Speed. "Item: She hath a sweet mouth."°

Launce. That makes amends for her sour breath.

Speed. "Item: She doth talk in her sleep."

Launce. It's no matter for that, so she sleep not in her 325
talk.

Speed. "Item: She is slow in words."

Launce. O villain, that set this down among her vices!
To be slow in words is a woman's only virtue. I
pray thee, out with't, and place it for her chief 330
virtue.

Speed. "Item: She is proud."

Launce. Out with that too; it was Eve's legacy, and
cannot be ta'en from her.

Speed. "Item: She hath no teeth."   335

Launce. I care not for that neither, because I love
crusts.

Speed. "Item: She is curst."°

Launce. Well, the best is, she hath no teeth to bite.

Speed. "Item: She will often praise her liquor."   340

Launce. If her liquor be good, she shall; if she will
not, I will, for good things should be praised.

Speed. "Item: She is too liberal."

Launce. Of her tongue she cannot, for that's writ down

322 **hath a sweet mouth** i.e., likes sweets   338 **curst** shrewish

345 she is slow of; of her purse she shall not, for that I'll keep shut. Now, of another thing she may, and that cannot I help. Well, proceed.

Speed. "Item: She hath more hair than wit, and more faults than hairs, and more wealth than faults."

350 *Launce.* Stop there; I'll have her. She was mine, and not mine, twice or thrice in that last article. Rehearse that once more.

Speed. "Item: She hath more hair than wit"—

Launce. More hair than wit? It may be; I'll prove it.
355 The cover of the salt° hides the salt, and therefore it is more than the salt; the hair that covers the wit is more than the wit, for the greater hides the less. What's next?

Speed. "And more faults than hairs"—

360 *Launce.* That's monstrous. O, that that were out!

Speed. "And more wealth than faults."

Launce. Why, that word makes the faults gracious. Well, I'll have her; and if it be a match, as nothing is impossible—

365 *Speed.* What then?

Launce. Why, then will I tell thee—that thy master stays for thee at the Northgate?

Speed. For me?

Launce. For thee! Ay, who art thou? He hath stayed
370 for a better man than thee.

Speed. And must I go to him?

Launce. Thou must run to him, for thou hast stayed so long that going° will scarce serve the turn.

Speed. Why didst not tell me sooner? Pox of° your
375 love letters!　　　　　　　　　　　　　　[*Exit.*]

355 **salt** saltcellar　373 **going** i.e., merely walking　374 **Pox of** plague (literally, syphilis) on

Launce. Now will he be swinged for reading my letter
   —an unmannerly slave, that will thrust himself into
   secrets! I'll after, to rejoice in the boy's correction.
                                                        [*Exit.*]

Scene 2. [*Milan. The Duke's palace.*]

Enter Duke [and] Thurio.

Duke. Sir Thurio, fear not but that she will love you,
   Now Valentine is banished from her sight.

Thurio. Since his exile she hath despised me most,
   Forsworn my company, and railed at me,
   That I am desperate of obtaining her.   5

Duke. This weak impress° of love is as a figure
   Trenchèd in ice, which with an hour's heat
   Dissolves to water, and doth lose his form.
   A little time will melt her frozen thoughts,
   And worthless Valentine shall be forgot.   10

[Enter Proteus.]

   How now, Sir Proteus! Is your countryman,
   According to our proclamation, gone?

Proteus. Gone, my good lord.

Duke. My daughter takes his going grievously.

Proteus. A little time, my lord, will kill that grief.   15

Duke. So I believe, but Thurio thinks not so.
   Proteus, the good conceit° I hold of thee—
   For thou hast shown some sign of good desert—
   Makes me the better to confer with thee.

3.2.6 **impress** impression (dent, groove)   17 **conceit** opinion

20 *Proteus.* Longer than I prove loyal to your Grace,
Let me not live to look upon your Grace.

Duke. Thou know'st how willingly I would effect
The match between Sir Thurio and my daughter.

Proteus. I do, my lord.

25 *Duke.* And also, I think, thou art not ignorant
How she opposes her against my will.

Proteus. She did, my lord, when Valentine was here.

Duke. Ay, and perversely she persevers so.
What might we do to make the girl forget
30 The love of Valentine, and love Sir Thurio?

Proteus. The best way is to slander Valentine
With falsehood, cowardice, and poor descent,
Three things that women highly hold in hate.

Duke. Ay, but she'll think that it is spoke in hate.

35 *Proteus.* Ay, if his enemy deliver it;
Therefore it must with circumstance° be spoken
By one whom she esteemeth as his friend.

Duke. Then you must undertake to slander him.

Proteus. And that, my lord, I shall be loath to do.
40 'Tis an ill office for a gentleman,
Especially against his very friend.

Duke. Where your good word cannot advantage him,
Your slander never can endamage him;
Therefore the office is indifferent,°
45 Being entreated to it by your friend.

Proteus. You have prevailed, my lord. If I can do it
By aught that I can speak in his dispraise,
She shall not long continue love to him.
But say this weed her love from Valentine,
50 It follows not that she will love Sir Thurio.

Thurio. Therefore, as you unwind her love from him,

36 **circumstance** circumstantial detail 44 **indifferent** neutral in
effect

Lest it should ravel and be good to none,
You must provide to bottom° it on me;
Which must be done by praising me as much
As you in worth dispraise Sir Valentine. 55

Duke. And, Proteus, we dare trust you in this kind,°
Because we know, on Valentine's report,
You are already Love's firm votary
And cannot soon revolt and change your mind.
Upon this warrant shall you have access 60
Where you with Silvia may confer at large;
For she is lumpish, heavy, melancholy,
And, for your friend's sake, will be glad of you;
Where you may temper° her by your persuasion
To hate young Valentine and love my friend. 65

Proteus. As much as I can do, I will effect.
But you, Sir Thurio, are not sharp enough;
You must lay lime to tangle° her desires
By wailful sonnets, whose composèd rhymes
Should be full-fraught with serviceable vows.° 70

Duke. Ay,
Much is the force of heaven-bred poesy.

Proteus. Say that upon the altar of her beauty
You sacrifice your tears, your sighs, your heart.
Write till your ink be dry, and with your tears 75
Moist it again, and frame some feeling line
That may discover such integrity.°
For Orpheus' lute was strung with poets' sinews,
Whose golden touch could soften steel and stones,
Make tigers tame, and huge leviathans 80
Forsake unsounded deeps to dance on sands.°
After your dire-lamenting elegies,
Visit by night your lady's chamber window

53 **bottom** anchor, tie (as a weaver's thread)   56 **kind** i.e., an affair of this nature   64 **temper** make pliant, shape   68 **lime to tangle** birdlime to ensnare (birdlime is a sticky substance spread on branches to catch birds)   70 **full-fraught with serviceable vows** loaded with vows to serve faithfully   77 **discover such integrity** exhibit such devotion 78–81 **Orpheus' lute . . . sands** (cf. *Merchant of Venice*, 5.1, for a simpler tribute to the musician of Thrace)

With some sweet consort;° to their instruments
85 Tune a deploring dump.° The night's dead silence
Will well become such sweet-complaining grievance.
This, or else nothing, will inherit° her.

Duke. This discipline° shows thou hast been in love.

Thurio. And thy advice this night I'll put in practice.
90 Therefore, sweet Proteus, my direction-giver,
Let us into the city presently
To sort° some gentlemen well skilled in music.
I have a sonnet that will serve the turn
To give the onset° to thy good advice.

95 *Duke.* About it, gentlemen!

Proteus. We'll wait upon your Grace till after supper,
And afterward determine our proceedings.

Duke. Even now about it! I will pardon you.   *Exeunt.*

---

84 **sweet consort** i.e., company of musicians   85 **deploring dump**
doleful ditty   87 **inherit** obtain   88 **discipline** instruction   92 **sort** sort
out, select   94 **give the onset** make a beginning

ACT 4

Scene 1. [*A forest.*]

Enter certain Outlaws.

First Outlaw. Fellows, stand fast; I see a passenger.°

Second Outlaw. If there be ten, shrink not, but down
 with 'em.

[*Enter Valentine and Speed.*]

Third Outlaw. Stand, sir, and throw us that° you have
 about ye.
 If not, we'll make you sit, and rifle you.

Speed. Sir, we are undone; these are the villains 5
 That all the travelers do fear so much.

Valentine. My friends—

First Outlaw. That's not so, sir; we are your enemies.

Second Outlaw. Peace! We'll hear him.

Third Outlaw. Ay, by my beard, will we, for he's a
 proper° man. 10

Valentine. Then know that I have little wealth to lose.

4.1.1 **passenger** pedestrian   3 **that** that which   10 **proper** handsome

59

A man I am crossed with adversity.
My riches are these poor habiliments,
Of which if you should here disfurnish° me,
15   You take the sum and substance that I have.

Second Outlaw. Whither travel you?

Valentine. To Verona.

First Outlaw. Whence came you?

Valentine. From Milan.

20 *Third Outlaw.* Have you long sojourned there?

Valentine. Some sixteen months, and longer might
have stayed
If crooked fortune had not thwarted me.

First Outlaw. What, were you banished thence?

Valentine. I was.

25 *Second Outlaw.* For what offense?

Valentine. For that which now torments me to re-
hearse:
I killed a man, whose death I much repent;
But yet I slew him manfully in fight,
Without false vantage° or base treachery.

30 *First Outlaw.* Why, ne'er repent it, if it were done so.
But were you banished for so small a fault?

Valentine. I was, and held me glad of such a doom.°

Second Outlaw. Have you the tongues?°

Valentine. My youthful travel therein made me
happy,°
35   Or else I often had been miserable.

Third Outlaw. By the bare scalp of Robin Hood's fat
friar,
This fellow were a king for our wild faction!

14 **disfurnish** deprive   29 **false vantage** i.e., such advantage as is
gained by deceit   32 **doom** sentence   33 **Have you the tongues** do you
know foreign languages   34 **happy** fortunate

First Outlaw. We'll have him. Sirs, a word.

Speed. Master, be one of them; it's an honorable kind
of thievery.   *40*

Valentine. Peace, villain!

Second Outlaw. Tell us this: have you anything to
take to?°

Valentine. Nothing but my fortune.

Third Outlaw. Know, then, that some of us are gen-
tlemen,
Such as the fury of ungoverned youth   *45*
Thrust from the company of awful° men:
Myself was from Verona banishèd
For practicing° to steal away a lady,
An heir, and near allied unto the Duke.

Second Outlaw. And I from Mantua, for a gentleman   *50*
Who, in my mood, I stabbed unto the heart.

First Outlaw. And I for suchlike petty crimes as these.
But to the purpose—for we cite our faults,
That they may hold excused our lawless lives;
And partly, seeing you are beautified   *55*
With goodly shape, and by your own report
A linguist, and a man of such perfection
As we do in our quality much want°—

Second Outlaw. Indeed, because you are a banished
man,
Therefore, above the rest, we parley to you.   *60*
Are you content to be our general,
To make a virtue of necessity,
And live, as we do, in this wilderness?

Third Outlaw. What say'st thou? Wilt thou be of our
consort?
Say ay, and be the captain of us all.   *65*

---

42 **anything to take to** any trade to take up   46 **awful** deeply respectful
(but possibly a printer's slip for "lawful")   48 **practicing** plotting   58 **in
our quality much want** much lack in our profession

We'll do thee homage and be ruled by thee,
Love thee as our commander and our king.

First Outlaw. But if thou scorn our courtesy, thou
diest.

Second Outlaw. Thou shalt not live to brag what we
have offered.

70 *Valentine.* I take your offer, and will live with you,
Provided that you do no outrages
On silly° women or poor passengers.

Third Outlaw. No, we detest such vile base practices.
Come, go with us; we'll bring thee to our crews
75 And show thee all the treasure we have got,
Which, with ourselves, all rest at thy dispose.
Exeunt.

Scene 2. [*Milan. Beneath Silvia's window.*]

Enter Proteus.

Proteus. Already have I been false to Valentine,
And now I must be as unjust to Thurio.
Under the color° of commending him,
I have access my own love to prefer.°
5 But Silvia is too fair, too true, too holy
To be corrupted with my worthless gifts.
When I protest true loyalty to her,
She twits me with my falsehood to my friend;
When to her beauty I commend my vows,
10 She bids me think how I have been forsworn
In breaking faith with Julia whom I loved.
And notwithstanding all her sudden quips,
The least whereof would quell a lover's hope,
Yet, spaniel-like, the more she spurns my love,

72 **silly** defenseless   4.2,3 **color** pretense   4 **prefer** advance

The more it grows, and fawneth on her still.   15
But here comes Thurio; now must we to her window
And give some evening music to her ear.

[*Enter Thurio and Musicians.*]

Thurio. How now, Sir Proteus, are you crept before
   us?

Proteus. Ay, gentle Thurio, for you know that love
   Will creep in service where it cannot go.°   20

Thurio. Ay, but I hope, sir, that you love not here.

Proteus. Sir, but I do; or else I would be hence.

Thurio. Who? Silvia?

Proteus.   Ay, Silvia, for your sake.

Thurio. I thank you for your own. Now, gentlemen,
   Let's tune, and to it lustily awhile.   25

[*Enter, at a distance, Host, and Julia in boy's
   clothes.*]

Host. Now, my young guest, methinks you're allycholly.° I pray you, why is it?

Julia. Marry, mine host, because I cannot be merry.

Host. Come, we'll have you merry. I'll bring you where
   you shall hear music, and see the gentleman that   30
   you asked for.

Julia. But shall I hear him speak?

Host. Ay, that you shall.

Julia. That will be music.   [*Music plays.*]

Host. Hark, hark!   35

Julia. Is he among these?

Host. Ay, but, peace! Let's hear 'em.

20 **go** walk upright   26–27 **allycholly** i.e., melancholy

Song.

Who is Silvia, what is she,
    That all our swains commend her?
40 Holy, fair, and wise is she;
    The heaven such grace did lend her,
That she might admirèd be.

Is she kind as she is fair?
    For beauty lives with kindness.
45 Love doth to her eyes repair,
    To help him of his blindness,
And, being helped, inhabits there.

Then to Silvia let us sing,
    That Silvia is excelling;
50 She excels each mortal thing
    Upon the dull earth dwelling.
To her let us garlands bring.

Host. How now! Are you sadder than you were before?
    How do you, man? The music likes° you not.

55 *Julia.* You mistake; the musician likes me not.

Host. Why, my pretty youth?

Julia. He plays false, father.

Host. How? Out of tune on the strings?

Julia. Not so; but yet so false that he grieves my very
60 heartstrings.

Host. You have a quick ear.

Julia. Ay, I would I were deaf; it makes me have a
    slow° heart.

Host. I perceive you delight not in music.

65 *Julia.* Not a whit, when it jars so.

54 **likes** pleases   63 **slow** i.e., heavy

Host. Hark, what fine change° is in the music!

Julia. Ay, that change is the spite.

Host. You would have them always play but one thing?

Julia. I would always have one play but one thing.
    But, host, doth this Sir Proteus that we talk on   *70*
    Often resort unto this gentlewoman?

Host. I tell you what Launce, his man, told me—he
    loved her out of all nick.°

Julia. Where is Launce?

Host. Gone to seek his dog, which tomorrow, by his   *75*
    master's command, he must carry for a present to
    his lady.

Julia. Peace! Stand aside. The company parts.

Proteus. Sir Thurio, fear not you. I will so plead
    That you shall say my cunning drift excels.   *80*

Thurio. Where meet we?

Proteus.   At Saint Gregory's well.

Thurio.   Farewell.
    [*Exeunt Thurio and Musicians.*]

[*Enter Silvia above.*]

Proteus. Madam, good even to your ladyship.

Silvia. I thank you for your music, gentlemen.
    Who is that that spake?

Proteus. One, lady, if you knew his pure heart's truth,   *85*
    You would quickly learn to know him by his voice.

Silvia. Sir Proteus, as I take it.

Proteus. Sir Proteus, gentle lady, and your servant.

---

66 **change** modulation (in the next line Julia puns, alluding to the change in Proteus' affections)   73 **out of all nick** beyond measure

Silvia. What's your will?

Proteus.   That I may compass yours.

90 *Silvia.* You have your wish; my will is even this:
      That presently you hie you home to bed.
      Thou subtle, perjured, false, disloyal man!
      Think'st thou I am so shallow, so conceitless,°
      To be seducèd by thy flattery,
95   That hast deceived so many with thy vows?
      Return, return, and make thy love amends.
      For me, by this pale queen of night I swear,
      I am so far from granting thy request
      That I despise thee for thy wrongful suit,
100   And by and by intend to chide myself
      Even for this time I spend in talking to thee.

Proteus. I grant, sweet love, that I did love a lady;
      But she is dead.

Julia. [*Aside*] 'Twere false, if I should speak it,
105   For I am sure she is not burièd.

Silvia. Say that she be; yet Valentine thy friend
      Survives, to whom, thyself art witness,
      I am betrothed. And art thou not ashamed
      To wrong him with thy importunacy?

110 *Proteus.* I likewise hear that Valentine is dead.

Silvia. And so suppose am I, for in his grave
      Assure thyself my love is burièd.

Proteus. Sweet lady, let me rake it from the earth.

Silvia. Go to thy lady's grave, and call hers thence;
115   Or, at the least, in hers sepulcher thine.

Julia. [*Aside*] He heard not that.

Proteus. Madam, if your heart be so obdurate,
      Vouchsafe° me yet your picture for my love,
      The picture that is hanging in your chamber.
120   To that I'll speak, to that I'll sigh and weep;
      For since the substance of your perfect self

93 **conceitless** witless   118 **Vouchsafe** grant

Is else devoted,° I am but a shadow,
And to your shadow° will I make true love.

Julia. [*Aside*] If 'twere a substance, you would, sure,
    deceive it,
And make it but a shadow, as I am.   *125*

Silvia. I am very loath to be your idol, sir;
But since your falsehood shall become you well
To worship shadows and adore false shapes,
Send to me in the morning, and I'll send it.
And so, good rest.

Proteus.   As wretches have o'ernight   *130*
That wait for execution in the morn.
                    [*Exeunt Proteus and Silvia severally.*]

Julia. Host, will you go?

Host. By my halidom,° I was fast asleep.

Julia. Pray you, where lies° Sir Proteus?

Host. Marry, at my house. Trust me, I think 'tis almost *135*
day.

Julia. Not so; but it hath been the longest night
That e'er I watched, and the most heaviest.
                                        [*Exeunt.*]

Scene 3. [*Milan. Beneath Silvia's window.*]

Enter Eglamour.

Eglamour. This is the hour that Madam Silvia
Entreated me to call and know her mind.
There's some great matter she'd employ me in.
Madam, madam!

122 **else devoted** vowed to someone else   123 **shadow** portrait
133 **halidom** sacred relic (a mild oath)   134 **lies** lodges

[*Enter Silvia above.*]

Silvia. Who calls?

5   *Eglamour.*   Your servant and your friend,
    One that attends your ladyship's command.

Silvia. Sir Eglamour, a thousand times good morrow.

Eglamour. As many, worthy lady, to yourself.
    According to your ladyship's impose,°
10 I am thus early come to know what service
    It is your pleasure to command me in.

Silvia. O Eglamour, thou art a gentleman—
    Think not I flatter, for I swear I do not—
    Valiant, wise, remorseful,° well accomplished.
15 Thou art not ignorant what dear good will
    I bear unto the banished Valentine,
    Nor how my father would enforce me marry
    Vain Thurio, whom my very soul abhors.
    Thyself hast loved, and I have heard thee say
20 No grief did ever come so near thy heart
    As when thy lady and thy true love died,
    Upon whose grave thou vow'dst pure chastity.
    Sir Eglamour, I would to Valentine,
    To Mantua, where I hear he makes abode;
25 And, for the ways are dangerous to pass,
    I do desire thy worthy company,
    Upon whose faith and honor I repose.
    Urge not my father's anger, Eglamour,
    But think upon my grief, a lady's grief,
30 And on the justice of my flying hence
    To keep me from a most unholy match,
    Which heaven and fortune still rewards with plagues.
    I do desire thee, even from a heart
    As full of sorrows as the sea of sands,
35 To bear me company, and go with me:
    If not, to hide what I have said to thee,
    That I may venture to depart alone.

Eglamour. Madam, I pity much your grievances,

4.3.9 **impose** command   14 **remorseful** compassionate

Which since I know they virtuously are placed,
I give consent to go along with you, *40*
Recking as little what betideth me
As much I wish all good befortune you.
When will you go?

Silvia. This evening coming.

Eglamour. Where shall I meet you?

Silvia. At Friar Patrick's cell,
Where I intend holy confession. *45*

Eglamour. I will not fail your ladyship. Good morrow,
gentle lady.

Silvia. Good morrow, kind Sir Eglamour.
Exeunt [severally].

Scene 4. [*Milan. Beneath Silvia's window.*]

Enter Launce [, with his dog].

Launce. When a man's servant shall play the cur with
him, look you, it goes hard: one that I brought up
of° a puppy; one that I saved from drowning, when
three or four of his blind brothers and sisters went
to it! I have taught him, even as one would say pre- *5*
cisely, "thus I would teach a dog." I was sent to
deliver him as a present to Mistress Silvia from my
master, and I came no sooner into the dining chamber, but he steps me to her trencher° and steals her
capon's leg. O, 'tis a foul thing when a cur cannot *10*
keep° himself in all companies! I would have, as
one should say, one that takes upon him to be a
dog indeed, to be as it were, a dog at all things. If
I had not had more wit than he, to take a fault upon
me that he did, I think verily he had been hanged *15*

4.4.3 **of** from   9 **trencher** wooden plate   11 **keep** control for't; sure as I live, he had suffered for't. You shall judge. He thrusts me himself into the company of three or four gentlemanlike dogs under the Duke's table; he had not been there—bless the mark!—a pissing while, but all the chamber smelt him. "Out with the dog!" says one. "What cur is that?" says another. "Whip him out," says the third. "Hang him up," says the Duke. I, having been acquainted with the smell before, knew it was Crab, and goes me to the fellow that whips the dogs. "Friend," quoth I, "you mean to whip the dog?" "Ay, marry, do I," quoth he. "You do him the more wrong," quoth I; " 'twas I did the thing you wot° of." He makes me no more ado, but whips me out of the chamber. How many masters would do this for his servant? Nay, I'll be sworn, I have sat in the stocks for puddings° he hath stol'n; otherwise he had been executed. I have stood on the pillory for geese he hath killed; otherwise he had suffered for't. Thou think'st not of this now. Nay, I remember the trick you served me when I took my leave of Madam Silvia. Did not I bid thee still mark me, and do as I do? When didst thou see me heave up my leg, and make water against a gentlewoman's farthingale? Didst thou ever see me do such a trick?

[*Enter Proteus and Julia.*]

Proteus. Sebastian is thy name? I like thee well.
And will employ thee in some service presently.

Julia. In what you please. I'll do what I can.

Proteus. I hope thou wilt. [*To Launce*] How now, you
    whoreson peasant!
Where have you been these two days loitering?

Launce. Marry, sir, I carried Mistress Silvia the dog
    you bade me.

Proteus. And what says she to my little jewel?

28 **wot** know   31–32 **puddings** sausages

Launce. Marry, she says your dog was a cur, and tells
you currish thanks is good enough for such a present.   *50*

Proteus. But she received my dog?

Launce. No, indeed, did she not. Here have I brought
him back again.

Proteus. What, didst thou offer her this from me?

Launce. Ay, sir. The other squirrel° was stol'n from   *55*
me by the hangman's boys° in the market place, and
then I offered her mine own, who is a dog as big
as ten of yours, and therefore the gift the greater.

Proteus. Go get thee hence and find my dog again,
Or ne'er return again into my sight.   *60*
Away, I say! Stayest thou to vex me here?
                                          [*Exit Launce.*]
A slave, that still an end° turns me to shame!
Sebastian, I have entertainèd° thee
Partly that° I have need of such a youth
That can with some discretion do my business,   *65*
For 'tis no trusting to yond foolish lout;
But chiefly for thy face and thy behavior,
Which, if my augury deceive me not,
Witness good bringing up, fortune, and truth.
Therefore, know thou, for this I entertain thee.   *70*
Go presently, and take this ring with thee;
Deliver it to Madam Silvia.
She loved me well delivered it to me.

Julia. It seems you loved not her, to leave her token.
She is dead, belike?

Proteus.   Not so; I think she lives.   *75*

Julia. Alas!

Proteus. Why dost thou cry "Alas"?

---

55 **squirrel** i.e., little dog   56 **hangman's boys** i.e., boys who will
surely belong to the hangman (hang) at last   62 **still an end** forevermore
63 **entertainèd** retained   64 **Partly that** in part because

Julia.   I cannot choose
       But pity her.

Proteus.   Wherefore shouldst thou pity her?

Julia. Because methinks that she loved you as well
80   As you do love your lady Silvia.
       She dreams on him that has forgot her love;
       You dote on her that cares not for your love.
       'Tis pity love should be so contrary;
       And thinking on it makes me cry "Alas!"

85 *Proteus.* Well, give her that ring, and therewithal
       This letter. That's her chamber. Tell my lady
       I claim the promise for her heavenly picture.
       Your message done, hie home unto my chamber,
       Where thou shalt find me, sad and solitary.   [*Exit.*]

90 *Julia.* How many women would do such a message?
       Alas, poor Proteus! Thou hast entertained
       A fox to be the shepherd of thy lambs.
       Alas, poor fool! Why do I pity him
       That with his very heart despiseth me?
95   Because he loves her, he despiseth me;
       Because I love him, I must pity him.
       This ring I gave him when he parted from me,
       To bind him to remember my good will;
       And now am I, unhappy messenger,
100   To plead for that which I would not obtain,
       To carry that which I would have refused,
       To praise his faith which I would have dispraised.
       I am my master's true-confirmèd love,
       But cannot be true servant to my master
105   Unless I prove false traitor to myself.
       Yet will I woo for him, but yet so coldly
       As, heaven it knows, I would not have him speed.°

                 [*Enter Silvia, attended.*]

       Gentlewoman, good day! I pray you, be my mean
       To bring me where to speak with Madam Silvia.

107 **speed** prosper, succeed

Silvia. What would you with her, if that I be she?   *110*

Julia. If you be she, I do entreat your patience
  To hear me speak the message I am sent on.

Silvia. From whom?

Julia. From my master, Sir Proteus, madam.

Silvia. O, he sends you for a picture.   *115*

Julia. Ay, madam.

Silvia. Ursula, bring my picture there.
  Go give your master this. Tell him, from me,
  One Julia, that his changing thoughts forget,
  Would better fit his chamber than this shadow.   *120*

Julia. Madam, please you peruse this letter—
  Pardon me, madam; I have unadvised°
  Delivered you a paper that I should not.
  This is the letter to your ladyship.

Silvia. I pray thee, let me look on that again.   *125*

Julia. It may not be; good madam, pardon me.

Silvia. There, hold!
  I will not look upon your master's lines.
  I know they are stuffed with protestations,
  And full of new-found oaths which he will break   *130*
  As easily as I do tear his paper.

Julia. Madam, he sends your ladyship this ring.

Silvia. The more shame for him that he sends it me,
  For I have heard him say a thousand times
  His Julia gave it him at his departure.   *135*
  Though his false finger have profaned the ring,
  Mine shall not do his Julia so much wrong.

Julia. She thanks you.

Silvia. What say'st thou?

Julia. I thank you, madam, that you tender her.°   *140*

122 **unadvised** unintentionally   140 **tender her** i.e., have a care for her
interest

Poor gentlewoman! My master wrongs her much.

Silvia. Dost thou know her?

Julia. Almost as well as I do know myself.
To think upon her woes, I do protest
145   That I have wept a hundred several° times.

Silvia. Belike she thinks that Proteus hath forsook her.

Julia. I think she doth; and that's her cause of sorrow.

Silvia. Is she not passing° fair?

Julia. She hath been fairer, madam, than she is.
150   When she did think my master loved her well,
She, in my judgment, was as fair as you.
But since she did neglect her looking glass,
And threw her sun-expelling mask away,
The air hath starved the roses in her cheeks
155   And pinched the lily-tincture of her face,
That now she is become as black° as I.

Silvia. How tall was she?

Julia. About my stature: for, at Pentecost,°
When all our pageants of delight were played,
160   Our youth got me to play the woman's part,
And I was trimmed in Madam Julia's gown,
Which servèd me as fit, by all men's judgments,
As if the garment had been made for me.
Therefore I know she is about my height.
165   And at that time I made her weep agood,°
For I did play a lamentable part.
Madam, 'twas Ariadne° passioning
For Theseus' perjury and unjust flight,
Which I so lively acted with my tears
170   That my poor mistress, movèd therewithal,
Wept bitterly; and would I might be dead

145 **several** separate   148 **passing** surpassingly   156 **black** i.e., from
the sun   158 **Pentecost** (Whitsunday [seventh Sunday after Easter], an
occasion for morris dances, "pageants of delight," and such outdoor fes-
tivities)   165 **agood** aplenty   167 **Ariadne** (daughter of King Minos,
who aided Theseus' flight from the Cretan labyrinth, only to be abandoned on the isle of Naxos)

If I in thought felt not her very sorrow!

Silvia. She is beholding° to thee, gentle youth.
Alas, poor lady, desolate and left!
I weep myself to think upon thy words.   *175*
Here, youth, there is my purse. I give thee this
For thy sweet mistress' sake, because thou lov'st her.
Farewell.   [*Exit Silvia, with attendants.*]

Julia. And she shall thank you for't, if e'er you know
     her.
A virtuous gentlewoman, mild and beautiful!   *180*
I hope my master's suit will be but cold,
Since she respects my mistress' love so much.
Alas, how love can trifle with itself!
Here is her picture: let me see; I think,
If I had such a tire,° this face of mine   *185*
Were full as lovely as is this of hers.
And yet the painter flattered her a little,
Unless I flatter with myself too much.
Her hair is auburn, mine is perfect yellow:
If that be all the difference in his love,   *190*
I'll get me such a colored periwig.
Her eyes are gray as glass, and so are mine:
Ay, but her forehead's low, and mine's as high.
What should it be that he respects in her,
But I can make respective° in myself,   *195*
If this fond Love° were not a blinded god?
Come, shadow, come, and take this shadow up,°
For 'tis thy rival. O thou senseless form,
Thou shalt be worshiped, kissed, loved, and adored!
And, were there sense in his idolatry,   *200*
My substance should be statue in thy stead.
I'll use thee kindly for thy mistress' sake,
That used me so; or else, by Jove I vow,
I should have scratched out your unseeing eyes,
To make my master out of love with thee!   *Exit.* *205*

173 **beholding** indebted   185 **tire** headdress   195 **respective** worthy of
respect   196 **fond Love** i.e., foolish Cupid   197 **Come . . . shadow up**
come, shadow (of my former self), and "take on" this other shadow
(Silvia's portrait)

ACT 5

Scene 1. [*Milan. An abbey.*]

Enter Eglamour.

Eglamour. The sun begins to gild the western sky,
    And now it is about the very hour
    That Silvia, at Friar Patrick's cell, should meet me.
    She will not fail, for lovers break not hours,
5   Unless it be to come before their time,
    So much they spur their expedition.
    See where she comes.

[*Enter Silvia.*]

                    Lady, a happy evening!

Silvia. Amen, amen! Go on, good Eglamour,
    Out at the postern° by the abbey wall.
10 I fear I am attended° by some spies.

Eglamour. Fear not; the forest is not three leagues off.
    If we recover° that, we are sure enough.   *Exeunt.*

5.1.9 **postern** small door at side or rear   10 **attended** followed
12 **recover** reach

Scene 2. [*Milan. The Duke's palace.*]

Enter Thurio, Proteus, [and] Julia.

Thurio. Sir Proteus, what says Silvia to my suit?

Proteus. O, sir, I find her milder than she was;
And yet she takes exceptions at your person.

Thurio. What, that my leg is too long?

Proteus. No; that it is too little.   5

Thurio. I'll wear a boot, to make it somewhat rounder.

Julia. [*Aside*] But love will not be spurred° to what
it loathes.

Thurio. What says she to my face?

Proteus. She says it is a fair one.

Thurio. Nay then, the wanton lies; my face is black.   10

Proteus. But pearls are fair; and the old saying is,
Black men are pearls in beauteous ladies' eyes.

Julia. [*Aside*] 'Tis true, such pearls as put out ladies'
eyes;
For I had rather wink than look on them.

Thurio. How likes she my discourse?°   15

Proteus. Ill, when you talk of war.

Thurio. But well, when I discourse of love and peace?

Julia. [*Aside*] But better, indeed, when you hold your
peace.

5.2.7 **spurred** (with reference to preceding "boot")   15 **discourse** conversational ability

Thurio. What says she to my valor?

20   *Proteus.* O, sir, she makes no doubt of that.

Julia. [*Aside*] She needs not, when she knows it cowardice.

Thurio. What says she to my birth?

Proteus. That you are well derived.

Julia. [*Aside*] True, from a gentleman to a fool.

25   *Thurio.* Considers she my possessions?

Proteus. O, ay, and pities them.

Thurio. Wherefore?

Julia. [*Aside*] That such an ass should owe° them.

Proteus. That they are out by lease.°

30   *Julia.* Here comes the Duke.

[*Enter Duke.*]

Duke. How now, Sir Proteus! How now, Thurio!
Which of you saw Sir Eglamour of late?

Thurio. Not I.

Proteus.   Nor I.

Duke.   Saw you my daughter?

Proteus.   Neither.

Duke. Why then,
35   She's fled unto that peasant Valentine,
And Eglamour is in her company.
'Tis true; for Friar Laurence met them both
As he in penance wandered through the forest.
Him he knew well, and guessed that it was she,
40   But, being masked, he was not sure of it;
Besides, she did intend confession
At Patrick's cell this even, and there she was not.

28 **owe** own   29 **out by lease** i.e., because Thurio is such a fool, he will surely hold onto his possessions only temporarily

These likelihoods confirm her flight from hence.
Therefore, I pray you, stand not to discourse,
But mount you presently, and meet with me   45
Upon the rising of the mountain foot°
That leads toward Mantua, whither they are fled.
Dispatch, sweet gentlemen, and follow me.   [*Exit.*]

Thurio. Why, this it is to be a peevish girl
That flies her fortune when it follows her.   50
I'll after, more to be revenged on Eglamour
Than for the love of reckless Silvia.   [*Exit.*]

Proteus. And I will follow, more for Silvia's love
Than hate of Eglamour, that goes with her.   [*Exit.*]

Julia. And I will follow, more to cross that love   55
Than hate for Silvia, that is gone for love.   [*Exit.*]

Scene 3. [*A forest.*]

[*Enter*] *Silvia* [*and*] *Outlaws.*

First Outlaw. Come, come,
  Be patient; we must bring you to our captain.

Silvia. A thousand more mischances than this one
  Have learned me how to brook° this patiently.

Second Outlaw. Come, bring her away.   5

First Outlaw. Where is the gentleman that was with
  · her?

Third Outlaw. Being nimble footed, he hath outrun us,
  But Moyses and Valerius follow him.
  Go thou with her to the west end of the wood;
  There is our captain. We'll follow him that's fled;   10
  The thicket is beset;° he cannot 'scape.

46 **rising of the mountain foot** i.e., foothill   5.3.4 **learned me how to brook** taught me how to endure   11 **beset** surrounded

First Outlaw. Come, I must bring you to our captain's
    cave.
    Fear not; he bears an honorable mind,
    And will not use a woman lawlessly.

15 *Silvia.* O Valentine, this I endure for thee!   *Exeunt.*

Scene 4. [*Another part of the forest.*]

Enter Valentine.

Valentine. How use° doth breed a habit in a man!
    This shadowy desert,° unfrequented woods,
    I better brook than flourishing peopled towns.
    Here can I sit alone, unseen of any,
5   And to the nightingale's complaining notes
    Tune my distresses and record my woes.
    O thou that dost inhabit in my breast,
    Leave not the mansion so long tenantless,
    Lest, growing ruinous, the building fall,
10   And leave no memory of what it was!
    Repair me with thy presence, Silvia;
    Thou gentle nymph, cherish thy forlorn swain!
                                        [*Noise within.*]
    What halloing and what stir is this today?
    These are my mates, that make their wills their law,
15   Have° some unhappy passenger in chase.
    They love me well; yet I have much to do
    To keep them from uncivil outrages.
    Withdraw thee, Valentine. Who's this comes here?
                                        [*Retires.*]

[*Enter Proteus, Silvia, and Julia.*]

Proteus. Madam, this service I have done for you—
20   Though you respect not aught your servant doth—

5.4.1 **use** custom   2 **shadowy desert** wild place inhabited only with
shadows (of trees)   15 **Have** who have

To hazard life, and rescue you from him
That would have forced your honor and your love.
Vouchsafe me, for my meed, but one fair look;
A smaller boon than this I cannot beg,
And less than this, I am sure, you cannot give.   25

Valentine. [*Aside*] How like a dream is this I see and
    hear!
Love, lend me patience to forbear awhile.

Silvia. O miserable, unhappy that I am!

Proteus. Unhappy were you, madam, ere I came;
But by my coming I have made you happy.   30

Silvia. By thy approach thou mak'st me most unhappy.

Julia. [*Aside*] And me, when he approacheth to your
    presence.

Silvia. Had I been seizèd by a hungry lion,
I would have been a breakfast to the beast
Rather than have false Proteus rescue me.   35
O, Heaven be judge how I love Valentine
Whose life's as tender° to me as my soul!
And full as much, for more there cannot be,
I do detest false perjured Proteus.
Therefore be gone; solicit me no more.   40

Proteus. What dangerous action, stood it next to death,
Would I not undergo for one calm look!
O' tis the curse in love, and still approved,°
When women cannot love where they're beloved!

Silvia. When Proteus cannot love where he's beloved!   45
Read over Julia's heart, thy first, best love,
For whose dear sake thou didst then rend thy faith
Into a thousand oaths; and all those oaths
Descended into perjury, to love me.
Thou hast no faith left now, unless thou'dst two,   50
And that's far worse than none; better have none
Than plural faith, which is too much by one.
Thou counterfeit to thy true friend!

37 **tender** precious   43 **still approved** perennially proved true

Proteus.   In love,
   Who respects friend?

Silvia.   All men but Proteus.

55 *Proteus.* Nay, if the gentle spirit of moving words
      Can no way change you to a milder form,
      I'll woo you like a soldier, at arms' end,
      And love you 'gainst the nature of love—force ye.

Silvia. O heaven!

Proteus.   I'll force thee yield to my desire.

Valentine. [*Advancing*] Ruffian, let go that rude uncivil
60   touch,
      Thou friend of an ill fashion!°

Proteus.   Valentine!

Valentine. Thou common° friend, that's without faith
      or love—
      For such is a friend now; treacherous man!
      Thou hast beguiled my hopes; nought but mine eye
65   Could have persuaded me. Now I dare not say
      I have one friend alive; thou wouldst disprove me.
      Who should be trusted, when one's right hand
      Is perjured to the bosom? Proteus,
      I am sorry I must never trust thee more,
70   But count the world a stranger for thy sake.
      The private° wound is deepest. O time most accurst,
      'Mongst all foes that a friend should be the worst!

Proteus. My shame and guilt confounds° me.
      Forgive me, Valentine. If hearty sorrow
75   Be a sufficient ransom for offense,
      I tender't here; I do as truly suffer
      As e'er I did commit.°

Valentine.   Then I am paid;°

61 **friend of an ill fashion** i.e., false friend   62 **common** i.e., no better
than the ordinary   71 **private** intimate (here, given by a friend)
73 **confounds** destroys   76–77 **I do . . . did commit** i.e., I do indeed
suffer, as truly as I did commit the fault   77 **paid** satisfied

And once again I do receive thee honest.°
Who by repentance is not satisfied
Is nor of heaven nor earth, for these are pleased.   *80*
By penitence th' Eternal's wrath's appeased;
And, that my love may appear plain and free,
All that was mine in Silvia I give thee.

Julia. O me unhappy!   [*Swoons.*]

Proteus. Look to the boy.   *85*

Valentine. Why, boy! Why, wag! How now! What's
the matter? Look up; speak.

Julia. O good sir, my master charged me to deliver a
ring to Madam Silvia, which, out of my neglect, was
never done.   *90*

Proteus. Where is that ring, boy?

Julia.   Here 'tis; this is it.

Proteus. How! Let me see.
Why, this is the ring I gave to Julia.

Julia. O, cry you mercy,° sir, I have mistook.
This is the ring you sent to Silvia.   *95*

Proteus. But how cam'st thou by this ring? At my
depart I gave this unto Julia.

Julia. And Julia herself did give it me;
And Julia herself hath brought it hither.

Proteus. How! Julia!   *100*

Julia. Behold her that gave aim to° all thy oaths,
And entertained 'em deeply in her heart.
How oft hast thou with perjury cleft the root!
O Proteus, let this habit° make thee blush!
Be thou ashamed that I have took upon me   *105*
Such an immodest raiment, if shame live
In a disguise of love.°

78 **receive thee honest** accept you as being honorable   94 **cry you
mercy** I beg your pardon   101 **gave aim to** was the object (target) of
104 **habit** i.e., her boy's garb   106–07 **if shame . . . of love** if it can be
shameful to disguise oneself for the sake of love

It is the lesser blot, modesty finds,
Women to change their shapes than men their
minds.

Proteus. Than men their minds! 'Tis true. O heaven,
110   were man
But constant, he were perfect! That one error
Fills him with faults, makes him run through all th'
sins:
Inconstancy falls off ere it begins.°
What is in Silvia's face, but I may spy
115   More fresh in Julia's with a constant eye?

Valentine. Come, come, a hand from either.
Let me be blest to make this happy close;°
'Twere pity two such friends should be long foes.

Proteus. Bear witness, Heaven, I have my wish forever.

120 *Julia.* And I mine.

[*Enter Outlaws, with Duke and Thurio.*]

Outlaws. A prize, a prize, a prize!

Valentine. Forbear, forbear, I say! It is my lord the
Duke.
Your Grace is welcome to a man disgraced,
Banished Valentine.

Duke.   Sir Valentine!

125 *Thurio.* Yonder is Silvia, and Silvia's mine.

Valentine. Thurio, give back,° or else embrace thy
death.
Come not within the measure° of my wrath.
Do not name Silvia thine; if once again,
Verona° shall not hold thee. Here she stands.
130   Take but possession of her with a touch:
I dare thee but to breathe upon my love.

---

113 **Inconstancy . . . begins** i.e., the inconstant man proves false even
before he begins to love   117 **close** joining of hands   126 **give back**
back off   127 **measure** range, reach   129 **Verona** (i.e., Milan; see
3.1.81,n.)

Thurio. Sir Valentine, I care not for her, I.
  I hold him but a fool that will endanger
  His body for a girl that loves him not.
  I claim her not, and therefore she is thine.   135

Duke. The more degenerate and base art thou,
  To make such means for° her as thou hast done,
  And leave her on such slight conditions.
  Now, by the honor of my ancestry,
  I do applaud thy spirit, Valentine,   140
  And think thee worthy of an empress' love.
  Know, then, I here forget all former griefs,
  Cancel all grudge, repeal° thee home again,
  Plead a new state in thy unrivaled merit,°
  To which I thus subscribe: Sir Valentine,   145
  Thou art a gentleman, and well derived;
  Take thou thy Silvia, for thou hast deserved her.

Valentine. I thank your Grace; the gift hath made me
      happy.
  I now beseech you, for your daughter's sake,
  To grant one boon that I shall ask of you.   150

Duke. I grant it, for thine own, whate'er it be.

Valentine. These banished men that I have kept withal°
  Are men endued° with worthy qualities.
  Forgive them what they have committed here,
  And let them be recalled from their exile: 155
  They are reformèd, civil, full of good,
  And fit for great employment, worthy lord.

Duke. Thou hast prevailed; I pardon them and thee.
  Dispose of them as thou know'st their deserts.
  Come, let us go. We will include all jars°   160
  With triumphs, mirth, and rare solemnity.°

---

137 **means for** efforts to win   143 **repeal** recall (from banishment)
144 **Plead . . . merit** (the general sense appears to be one of the following: (1) plead to be restored to your good graces, having formerly
misjudged them (2) proclaim that you are elevated to a new place in my
favor, earned by your unrivaled merit) 152 **kept withal** lived with
153 **endued** endowed 160 **include all jars** conclude all discords
161 **triumphs . . . solemnity** celebrations . . . festivity

Valentine. And, as we walk along, I dare be bold
 With our discourse to make your Grace to smile.
 What think you of this page, my lord?

165 *Duke.* I think the boy hath grace in him; he blushes.

Valentine. I warrant you, my lord, more grace than
 boy.

Duke. What mean you by that saying?

Valentine. Please you, I'll tell you as we pass along,
 That you will wonder what hath fortunèd.°
170 Come, Proteus; 'tis your penance but° to hear
 The story of your loves discoverèd.°
 That done, our day of marriage shall be yours;
 One feast, one house, one mutual happiness.

            Exeunt.

FINIS

169 **fortunèd** chanced 170 **'tis your penance but** your only penance is
171 **discoverèd** revealed

Textual Note

The Two Gentlemen of Verona was first printed in the First Folio of 1623, which is the authority for the present text. In the Folio it is the second play, standing between *The Tempest* and *The Merry Wives of Windsor,* the title of the latter play mistakenly appearing at the top of the final two pages. Names of characters who participate in each scene are grouped at the head of the scene, without notice made of the point of their entrance. The present edition deletes these names, and provides them, in square brackets, at the appropriate places later in the scenes. The Folio gives "Protheus" for "Proteus" and places the dramatis personae at the end of the text. Certain irregularities occur in place names, as though Shakespeare had changed his mind or become confused about principal locations; thus in 2.5 Padua rather than Milan is identified as the place of action by Speed, and in 3.1 the Duke of Milan speaks of a lady "in Verona here." In the present edition, speech prefixes have been regularized, spelling and punctuation have been modernized, and obvious typographical errors have been corrected. Added material (stage directions, etc.) is set is brackets. Act and scene divisions are those of the Folio, translated from Latin into English. The relatively few emendations of the Folio text are indicated below: the present reading is given in italics, followed by the Folio reading in roman.

1.1.65 *leave* loue   77 *a sheep* Sheepe   144–45 *testerned* cestern'd

1.2.88 *your* you

1.3.91 *Exeunt* Exeunt. Finis

2.3.29 *wood* would

2.4.49 *father's in* father is in   107 *mistress* a Mistresse   165 *makes* make   195 *Is it mine eye* It is mine   213 *Exit* Exeunt

2.5.38 *that my* that that my

3.1.281 *master's ship* Mastership   318 *kissed fasting* fasting   378s.d. *Exit* Exeunt

4.1.10 *he's* he is   35 *miserable* often miserable   49 *An* And   49 *near* Neece

4.2.111 *his* her

4.3.18 *abhors* abhor'd

4.4.70 *thou* thee   74 *to leave* not leaue   205 *Exit* Exeunt

5.2.18 *your peace* you peace   32 *Sir Eglamour* Eglamoure   56 *Exit* Exeunt

The Source of
The Two Gentlemen of Verona

Both because its plot is filled with well-known romance elements and because its poetic style is laden with rhetorical devices fashionable at the time it was written, *The Two Gentlemen of Verona* appears inevitably to owe an unusual number of debts to a wide variety of materials. In its conventions as well as in its basic materials and their manner of use, it is as deeply embedded in the literary life of its time as any work of Shakespeare's.

The central theme of the play—conflict between the duties of friendship and love—had been used by Boccaccio in *La Teseide,* by Chaucer in *The Knight's Tale,* and by Lyly in *Euphues: The Anatomy of Wit* and *Endimion;* but, indeed, this theme is ancient and widespread, and Shakespeare would have encountered it in any event. Specific incidents and motifs in the play, such as Julia's disguise as a boy, may have been suggested by Sidney's pastoral romance of *Arcadia;* the abrupt election of Valentine as captain of the outlaws may derive from the same source. Many echoes of Brooke's *Romeus and Juliet,* the narrative poem which Shakespeare followed in *Romeo and Juliet,* occur in the play, perhaps the most notable being the device of the rope ladder, which figures prominently in both plays.

In poetic manner and attitude, the play shows the pervasive influence of Lyly, the fashionable stylist of courtly language and the master of dramatic artifice in dialogue, scene, and character. Long stretches of wit duels between servant and servant, servant and master, lady and attendant, filled with quips and quirks and turns of phrase, mark the play as Lylyan in its most basic conception. In *The Two Gentlemen of Verona* the artifices of Lyly are more than superficial ornamentation; they are organic.

For the core of the play, however, which is the love story of Julia and Proteus, Shakespeare went to a prose romance originally written in Spanish, the *Diana Enamorada,* by the Portuguese Jorge de Montemayor, published in 1542. How Shakespeare came to know this work is uncertain, for though it was translated into English by Bartholomew Yonge about 1582, the translation was not published until 1598—some four to six years after the play was written. It has been suggested that Shakespeare could have become acquainted with the *Diana* through a French translation made before 1590; that he may have seen Yonge's manuscript before it was published; or that the story was represented in a play now lost.

In any event, it is now generally accepted that Montemayor's romance somehow came to serve as Shakespeare's principal source, and, accordingly, an abridged version of the story follows. Inserted references to acts and scenes mark incidents of special interest.

Jorge de Montemayor
from *Diana Enamorada*

You shall therefore know, fair nymphs, that great Vandalia is my native country, a province not far hence, where I was born, in a city called Soldina, my mother called Delia, my father Andronius, for lineage and possessions the

Translated by Bartholomew Yonge, 1598

chiefest of all that province. It fell out that as my mother was married many years and had no children (by reason whereof she lived so sad and malcontent that she enjoyed not one merry day), with tears and sighs she daily importuned the heavens, and with a thousand vows and devout offerings besought God to grant her the sum of her desire: whose omnipotency it pleased, beholding from his imperial throne her continual orisons, to make her barren body (the greater part of her age being now spent and gone) to become fruitful. What infinite joy she conceived thereof, let her judge, that after a long desire of anything, fortune at last doth put it into her hands. Of which content my father Andronius being no less partaker, showed such tokens of inward joy as are impossible to be expressed. My mother Delia was so much given to reading of ancient histories that if, by reason of sickness or any important business, she had not been hindered, she would never (by her will) have passed the time away in any other delight; who (as I said) being now with child and finding herself on a night ill at ease, entreated my father to read something unto her, that her mind being occupied in contemplation thereof, she might the better pass her grief away. My father, who studied for nothing else but to please her in all he might, began to read unto her the history of Paris, when the three ladies referred their proud contention for the golden apple to his conclusion and judgment. But as my mother held it for an infallible opinion that Paris had partially given that sentence (persuaded thereunto by a blind passion of beauty), so she said, that without all doubt he did not with due reason and wisdom consider the goddess of battles; for, as martial and heroical feats (said she) excelled all other qualities, so with equity and justice the apple should have been given to her. My father answered that since the apple was to be given to the fairest, and that Venus was fairer than any of the rest, Paris had rightly given his judgment, if that harm had not ensued thereof, which afterwards did. To this my mother replied that, though it was written in the apple that it should be given to the fairest, it was not to be understood of corporal beauty, but of the intellectual beauty of the mind. And therefore since fortitude was a thing that made one most beautiful, and the exercise of arms an exterior act of this virtue, she affirmed that to the goddess of battles this apple should be given, if Paris had judged like a prudent and unappassionate judge. So that, fair nymphs, they spent a great part of the night in this controversy, both of them alleging the most reasons they could to confirm their own purpose. They persisting in this point, sleep began to overcome her whom the reasons and arguments of her husband could not once move; so that being very deep in her disputations, she fell into as deep a sleep, to whom (my father being now gone to his chamber) appeared the goddess Venus, with as frowning a countenance as fair, and said, "I marvel, Delia, who hath moved thee to be so contrary to her that was never opposite to thee? If thou hadst but called to mind the time when thou wert so overcome in love for Andronius, thou wouldest not have paid me the debt thou owest me with so ill coin. But thou shalt not escape free from my due anger; for thou shalt bring forth a son and a daughter, whose birth shall cost thee no less than thy life, and them their contentment, for uttering so much in disgrace of my honor and beauty: both which shall be as unfortunate in their love as any were ever in all their lives, or to the age wherein, with remediless sighs, they shall breathe forth the sum of their ceaseless sorrows." And having said thus, she vanished away: when, likewise, it seemed to my mother that the goddess Pallas came to her in a vision, and with a merry countenance said thus unto her: "With what sufficient rewards may I be able to requite the due regard, most happy and discreet Delia, which thou hast alleged in my favor against thy husband's obstinate opinion, except it be by making thee understand that thou shalt bring forth a son and a daughter, the most fortunate in arms that have been to their times." Having thus said, she vanished out of her sight, and my mother, through exceeding fear, awaked immediately. Who, within a month after, at one birth was delivered of me and of a brother of mine, and died in childbed, leaving my father the most sorrowful man in the world for her sudden death; for grief whereof, within a little while after, he also died. And because you may know, fair nymphs, in what great extremities love hath put me, you must understand that (being a woman of that quality and disposition as you have heard) I have been forced by my cruel destiny to leave my natural habit and liberty, and the due respect of mine honor, to follow him who thinks (perhaps) that I do but lose it by loving him so extremely. Behold how bootless and unseemly it is for a woman to be so dextrous in arms, as if it were her proper nature and kind, wherewith, fair nymphs, I had never been indued, but that, by means thereof, I should come to do you this little service against these villainies; which I account no less than if fortune had begun to satisfy in part some of those infinite wrongs that she hath continually done me. The nymphs were so amazed at her words that they could neither ask nor answer anything to that the fair shepherdess told them, who, prosecuting her history, said:

My brother and I were brought up in a nunnery, where an aunt of ours was abbess, until we had accomplished twelve years of age, at what time we were taken from thence again, and my brother was carried to the mighty and invincible King of Portugal his court (whose noble fame and princely liberality was bruited over all the world) where, being grown to years able to manage arms, he achieved as valiant and almost incredible enterprises by them as he suffered unfortunate disgraces and foils by love. And with all this he was so highly favored of that magnificent king that he would never suffer him to depart from his court. Unfortunate I, reserved by my sinister destinies to greater mishaps, was carried to a grandmother of mine, which place I would I had never seen, since it was an occasion of such a sorrowful life as never any woman suffered the like. And because there is not anything, fair nymphs, which I am not forced to tell you, as well for the great virtue and deserts which your excellent beauties do testify, as also for that for my mind doth give me, that you shall be no small part and means of my comfort, know that as I was in my grandmother's house, and almost seventeen years old, a certain young gentleman fell in love with me, who dwelt no further from our house than the length of a garden terrace, so that he might see me every summer's night when I walked in the garden. Whenas therefore ingrateful Felix had beheld in that place the unfortunate Felismena (for this is the name of the woeful woman that tells you her mishaps) he was extremely enamored of me, or else did cunningly dissemble it, I not knowing then whether of these two I might believe, but am now assured that whosoever believes least, or nothing at all in these affairs, shall be most at ease. Many days Don Felix spent in endeavoring to make me know the pains which he suffered for me, and many more did I spend in making the matter strange, and that he did not suffer them for my sake. And I know not why love delayed the time so long by forcing me to love him, but only that (when he came indeed) he might enter into my heart at once, and with greater force and violence. [1.1] When he had, therefore, by sundry signs, as by tilt and tourneys, and by prancing up and down upon his proud jennet before my windows, made it manifest that he was in love with me (for at the first I did not so well perceive it) he determined in the end to write a letter unto me; and having practiced divers times before with a maid of mine, and at length, with many gifts and fair promises, gotten her good will and furtherance, he gave her the letter to deliver to me. [1.2] But to see the means that Rosina made unto me (for so was she called), the dutiful services and unwonted circumstances, before she did deliver it, the oaths that she sware unto me, and the subtle words and serious protestations she used, it was a pleasant thing, and worthy the noting. To whom (nevertheless) with an angry countenance I turned again, saying, "If I had not regard of mine own estate, and what hereafter might be said, I would make this shameless face of thine be known ever after for a mark of an impudent and bold minion: but because it is the first time, let this suffice that I have said and give thee warning to take heed of the second."

Methinks I see now the crafty wench, how she held her peace, dissembling very cunningly the sorrow that she conceived by my angry answer; for she feigned a counterfeit smiling, saying, "Jesus, Mistress! I gave it you, because you might laugh at it, and not to move your patience with it in this sort; for if I had any thought that it would have provoked you to anger, I pray God He may show His wrath as great towards me as ever He did to the daughter of any mother." And with this she added many words more (as she could do well enough) to pacify the feigned anger and ill opinion that I had conceived of her, and taking her letter with her, she departed from me. This having passed thus, I began to imagine what might ensue thereof, and love (methought) did put a certain desire into my mind to see the letter, though modesty and shame forbade me to ask it of my maid, especially for the words that had passed between us, as you have heard. And so I continued all that day until night, in variety of many thoughts; but when Rosina came to help me to bed, God knows how desirous I was to have her entreat me again to take the letter, but she would never speak unto me about it, nor (as it seemed) did so much as once think thereof. Yet to try, if by giving her some occasion I might prevail, I said unto her: "And is it so, Rosina, that Don Felix, without any regard to mine honor, dares write unto me?" "These are things, mistress," said she demurely to me again, "that are commonly incident to love, wherefore I beseech you pardon me, for if I had thought to have angered you with it, I would have first pulled out the balls of mine eyes." How cold my heart was at that blow, God knows, yet did I dissemble the matter and suffer myself to remain that night only with my desire, and with occasion of little sleep. And so it was, indeed, for that (methought) was the longest and most painful night that ever I passed. But when, with a slower pace (than I desired) the wished day was come, the discreet and subtle Rosina came into my chamber to help me to make me ready, in doing whereof, of purpose she let the letter closely fall, which when I perceived, "What is that that fell down?" said I. "Let me see it." "It is nothing, mistress," said she. "Come, come, let me see it," said I. "What! Move me not, or else tell me what it is." "Good Lord, mistress," said she, "why will you see it: it is the letter I would have given you yesterday." "Nay, that it is not," said I. "Wherefore show it me, that I may see if you lie or no." I had no sooner said so but she put it into my hands, saying, "God never give me good if it be any other thing"; and although I knew it well indeed, yet I said, "What, this is not the same, for I know that well enough, but it is one of thy lover's letters: I will read it, to see in what need he standeth of thy favor." And opening it, I found it contained this that followeth.

I ever imagined, dear mistress, that your discretion and wisdom would have taken away the fear I had to write unto you, the same knowing well enough (without any letter at all) how much I love you, but the very same hath so cunningly dissembled that wherein I hoped the only remedy of my griefs had been, therein consisted my greatest harm. If according to your wisdom you censure my boldness, I shall not then (I know) enjoy one hour of life; but if you do consider of it according to love's accustomed effects, then will I not exchange my hope for it. Be not offended, I beseech you, good lady, with my letter, and blame me not for writing unto you, until you see by experience whether I can leave off to write: and take me besides into the possession of that which is yours, since all is mine doth wholly consist in your hands, the which, with all reverence and dutiful affection, a thousand times I kiss.

When I had now seen my Don Felix his letter, whether it was for reading it at such a time, when by the same he showed that he loved me more than himself, or whether he had disposition and regiment over part of this wearied soul to imprint that love in it whereof he wrote unto me, I began to love him too well (and, alas, for my harm!), since he was the cause of so much sorrow as I have passed for his sake. Whereupon, asking Rosina forgiveness of what was past (as a thing needful for that which was to come) and committing the secrecy of my love to her fidelity, I read the letter once again, pausing a little at every word (and a very little indeed it was), because I concluded so soon with myself to do that I did, although in very truth it lay not otherwise in my power to do. Wherefore, calling for paper and ink, I answered his letter thus.

Esteem not so slightly of mine honor, Don Felix, as with feigned words to think to inveigle it, or with thy vain pretenses to offend it any ways. I know well enough what manner of man thou art, and how great thy desert and presumption is; from whence thy boldness doth arise (I guess), and not from the force (which thing thou wouldst fain persuade me) of thy fervent love. And if it be so (as my suspicion suggesteth) thy labor is as vain as thy imagination presumptuous, by thinking to make me do anything contrary to that which I owe unto mine honor. Consider (I beseech thee) how seldom things commenced under subtlety and dissimulation have good success; and that it is not the part of a gentleman to mean them one way and speak them another. Thou prayest me (amongst other things) to admit thee into possession of that that is mine: but I am of so ill an humor in matters of this quality, that I trust not things experienced, how much less then thy bare words; yet, nevertheless, I make no small account of that which thou hast manifested to me in thy letter; for it is enough that I am incredulous, though not unthankful.

This letter did I send, contrary to that I should have done, because it was the occasion of all my harms and griefs; for after this, he began to wax more bold by unfolding his thoughts and seeking out the means to have a parley with me. In the end, fair nymphs, a few days being spent in his demands and my answers, false love did work in me after his wonted fashions, every hour seizing more strongly upon my unfortunate soul. The tourneys were now renewed, the music by night did never cease; amorous letters and verses were recontinued on both sides; and thus passed I away almost a whole year, at the end whereof I felt myself so far in his love that I had no power to retire nor stay myself from disclosing my thoughts unto him, the thing which he desired more than his own life. [1.3] But my adverse fortune afterwards would, that of these our mutual loves (when as now they were most assured) his father had some intelligence, and whosoever revealed them first persuaded him so cunningly that his father (fearing lest he would have married me out of hand) sent him to the great Princess Augusta Caesarina's court, telling him it was not meet that a young gentleman, and of so noble a house as he was, should spend his youth idly at home, where nothing could be learned but examples of vice, whereof the very same idleness (he said) was the only mistress. He went away so pensive that his great grief would not suffer him to acquaint me with his departure; which when I knew, how sorrowful I remained, she may imagine that hath been at any time tormented with like passion. To tell you now the life that I led in his absence, my sadness, sighs, and tears, which every day I poured out of these wearied eyes, my tongue is far unable: if then my pains were such that I cannot now express them, how could I then suffer them? [2.7] But being in the midst of my mishaps, and in the depth of those woes which the absence of Don Felix caused me to feel, and it seeming to me that my grief was without remedy, if he were once seen or known of the ladies in that court (more beautiful and gracious than myself), by occasion whereof, as also by absence (a capital enemy to love) I might easily be forgotten, I determined to adventure that which I think never any woman imagined; which was to apparel myself in the habit of a man and to hie me to the court to see him in whose sight all my hope and content remained. Which determination I no sooner thought of than I put in practice, love blinding my eyes and mind with an inconsiderate regard of mine own estate and condition. To the execution of which attempt I wanted no industry; for, being furnished with the help of one of my approved friends and treasuress of my secrets, who bought me such apparel as I willed her, and a good horse for my journey, I went not only out of my country but out of my dear reputation, which (I think) I shall never recover again; and so trotted directly to the court, passing by the way many accidents, which (if time would give me leave to tell them) would not make you laugh a little to hear them. Twenty days I was in going thither, at the end of which, being come to the desired place, I took up mine inn in a street less frequented with concourse of people: and the great desire I had to see the destroyer of my joy did not suffer me to think of any other thing but how or where I might see him. To inquire of him of mine host I durst not, lest my coming might (perhaps) have been discovered; and to seek him forth I thought it not best, lest some inopinate mishap might have fallen out, whereby I might have been known. Wherefore I passed all that day in these perplexities while night came on, each hour whereof (methought) was a whole year unto me. [4.1] But midnight being a little past, mine host called at my chamber door and told me if I was desirous to hear some brave music I should arise quickly and open a window towards the street. The which I did by and by, and making no noise at all, I heard how Don Felix his page, called Fabius (whom I knew by his voice), said to others that came with him, "Now it is time, my masters, because the lady is in the gallery over her garden, taking the fresh air of the cool night." He had no sooner said so but they began to wind three cornets and a sackbut, with such skill and sweetness that it seemed celestial music; and then began a voice to sing, the sweetest (in my opinion) that ever I heard. And though I was in suspense by hearing Fabius speak, whereby a thousand doubts and imaginations (repugnant to my rest) occurred in my mind, yet I neglected not to hear what was sung, because their operations were not of such force that they were able to hinder the desire nor distemper the delight that I conceived by hearing it. That therefore which was sung were these verses:

> Sweet mistress, harken unto me,
>   (If it grieves thee to see me die)
> And hearing though it grieveth thee,
>   To hear me yet, do not deny.

> O grant me then this short content,
>   For forced I am to thee to fly:
> My sighs do not make thee relent,
>   Nor tears thy heart do mollify.

> Nothing of mine doth give thee pain,
>   Nor thou think'st of no remedy:
> Mistress, how long shall I sustain
>   Such ill as still thou dost apply?

> In death there is no help, be sure,
>   But in thy will, where it doth lie:
> For all those ills which death doth cure,
>   Alas, they are but light to try.

> My troubles do not trouble thee,
>   Nor hope to touch thy soul so nigh:
> O! From a will that is so free,
>   What should I hope when I do cry?

How can I mollify that brave
    And stony heart, of pity dry?
Yet mistress, turn those eyes (that have
    No peers) shining like stars in sky;

But turn them not in angry sort,
    If thou wilt not kill me thereby:
Though yet in anger, or in sport,
    Thou killest only with thine eye.

After they had first, with a concert of music, sung this song, two played, the one upon a lute, the other upon a silver-sounding harp, being accompanied with the sweet voice of my Don Felix. The great joy that I felt in hearing him cannot be imagined, for (methought) I heard him now as in that happy and passed time of our loves. But after the deceit of this imagination was discovered, seeing with mine eyes and hearing with mine ears that this music was bestowed upon another and not on me, God knows what a bitter death it was unto my soul: and with a grievous sigh that carried almost my life away with it, I asked mine host if he knew what the lady was for whose sake the music was made? He answered me that he could not imagine on whom it was bestowed, because in that street dwelled many noble and fair ladies. And when I saw he could not satisfy my request, I bent mine ears again to hear my Don Felix, who now, to the tune of a delicate harp, whereon he sweetly played, began to sing this sonnet following:

A SONNET

My painful years impartial Love was spending
    In vain and bootless hopes my life appaying,
    And cruel Fortune to the world bewraying
Strange samples of my tears that have no ending.

Time everything to truth at last commending,
    Leaves of my steps such marks, that now betraying,
    And all deceitful trusts shall be decaying,
And none have cause to 'plain of his offending.
She, whom I loved to my obliged power,
    That in her sweetest love to me discovers
Which never yet I knew (those heavenly pleasures),
And I do say, exclaiming every hour,
    Do not you see what makes you wise, O lovers?
Love, Fortune, Time, and my fair mistress' treasures.

The sonnet being ended, they paused a while, playing on four lutes together, and on a pair of virginals, with such heavenly melody that the whole world (I think) could not afford sweeter music to the ear nor delight to any mind not subject to the pangs of such predominant grief and sorrow as mine was. But then four voices, passing well tuned and set together, began to sing this song following:

A SONG

That sweetest harm I do not blame,
First caused by thy fairest eyes,
But grieve, because too late I came
To know my fault, and to be wise.

I never knew a worser kind of life,
To live in fear, from boldness still to cease:
Nor worse than this, to live in such a strife,
Whether of both, to speak or hold my peace?

And so the harm I do not blame,
Caused by thee or thy fair eyes;
But that to see how late I came
To know my fault, and to be wise.

I ever more did fear that I should know
Some secret things and doubtful in their kind,
Because the surest things do ever go
Most contrary unto my wish and mind.

And yet by knowing of the same
There is no hurt; but it denies
My remedy, since late I came
To know my fault, and to be wise.

When this song was ended, they began to sound divers sort of instruments and voices most excellently agreeing together and with such sweetness that they could not choose but delight any very much who were so far from it as I. About dawning of the day the music ended, and I did what I could to espy out my Don Felix, but the darkness of the night was mine enemy therein. And seeing now that they were gone, I went to bed again, where I bewailed my great mishap, knowing that he whom most of all I loved had so unworthily forgotten me, whereof his music was too manifest a witness. And when it was time I arose and, without any other consideration, went straight to the princess her palace, where (I thought) I might see that which I so greatly desired, determining to call myself Valerius, if any (perhaps) did ask my name. Coming therefore to a fair broad court before the palace gate, I viewed the windows and galleries, where I saw such store of blazing beauties and gallant ladies that I am not able now to recount nor then to do any more but wonder at their graces, their gorgeous attire, their jewels, their brave fashions of apparel and ornaments wherewith they were so richly set out. Up and down this place, before the windows, rode many lords and brave gentlemen in rich and sumptuous habits and mounted upon proud jennets, every one casting his eye to that part where his thoughts were secretly placed. God knows how greatly I desired to see Don Felix there, and that his injurious love had been in that famous palace;

because I might then have been assured that he should never have got any other guerdon of his suits and services, but only to see and to be seen, and sometimes to speak to his mistress, whom he must serve before a thousand eyes, because the privilege of that place doth not give him any further leave. But it was my ill fortune that he had settled his love in that place where I might not be assured of this poor help. Thus, as I was standing near to the palace gate, I espied Fabius, Don Felix his page, coming in great haste to the palace, where, speaking a word or two with a porter that kept the second entry, he returned the same way he came. I guessed his errand was to know whether it were fit time for Don Felix to come to dispatch certain business that his father had in the court, and that he could not choose but come thither out of hand. And being in this supposed joy which his sight did promise me, I saw him coming along with a great train of followers attending on his person, all of them being bravely appareled in a livery of watchet silk, guarded with yellow velvet and stitched on either side with threads of twisted silver, wearing likewise blue, yellow, and white feathers in their hats. But my lord Don Felix had on a pair of ash-color hose, embroidered and drawn forth with watchet tissue; his doublet was of white satin, embroidered with knots of gold, and likewise an embroidered jerkin of the same colored velvet; and his short cape cloak was of black velvet, edged with gold lace, and hung full of buttons of pearl and gold and lined with a razed watchet satin: by his side he wore, at a pair of embroidered hangers, a rapier and dagger, with engraven hilts and pommel of beaten gold. On his head, a hat beset full of golden stars, in the midst of every which a rich orient pearl was enchased, and his feather was likewise blue, yellow, and white. Mounted he came upon a fair dapple gray jennet, with a rich furniture of blue, embroidered with gold and seed pearl. When I saw him in this rich equipage, I was so amazed at his sight that how extremely my senses were ravished with sudden joy I am not able, fair nymphs, to tell you. Truth it is that I could not but shed some tears for joy and grief, which his sight did make me feel, but, fearing to be noted by the standers-by, for that time I dried them up. But as Don Felix (being now come to the palace gate) was dismounted, and gone up a pair of stairs into the chamber of presence, I went to his men, where they were attending his return; and seeing Fabius, whom I had seen before amongst them, I took him aside and said unto him, "My friend, I pray you tell me what lord this is, which did but even now alight from his jennet, for (methinks) he is very like one whom I have seen before in another far country." Fabius then answered me thus: "Art thou such a novice in the court that thou knowest not Don Felix? I tell thee there is not any lord, knight, or gentleman better known in it than he." "No doubt of that," said I, "but I will tell thee what a novice I am and how small a time I have been in the court, for yesterday was the first that ever I came to it." "Nay then, I cannot blame thee," said Fabius, "if thou knowest him not. Know, then, that this gentleman is called Don Felix, born in Vandalia, and hath his chiefest house in the ancient city of Soldina, and is remaining in this court about certain affairs of his father's and his own." "But I pray you tell me," said I, "why he gives his liveries of these colors?" "If the cause were not so manifest, I would conceal it," said Fabius, "but since there is not any that knows it not and canst not come to any in this court who cannot tell thee the reason why, I think by telling thee it I do no more than in courtesy I am bound to do. Thou must therefore understand that he loves and serves a lady here in this city named Celia and therefore wears and gives for his livery an azure blue which is the color of the sky, and white and yellow, which are the colors of his lady and mistress." When I heard these words, imagine, fair nymphs, in what a plight I was; but dissembling my mishap and grief, I answered him: "This lady certes is greatly beholding to him, because he thinks not enough, by wearing her colors, to show how willing he is to serve her, unless also he bear her name in his livery; whereupon I guess she cannot but be very fair and amiable." "She is no less, indeed," said Fabius, "although the other whom he loved and served in our own country in beauty far excelled this and loved and favored him more than ever this did. But this mischievous absence doth violate and dissolve those things which men think to be most strong and firm." At these words, fair nymphs, was I fain to come to some composition with my tears, which, if I had not stopped from issuing forth, Fabius could not have chosen but suspected, by the alteration of my countenance, that all was not well with me. And then the page did ask me what countryman I was, my name and of what calling and condition I was: whom I answered that my country where I was born was Vandalia, my name Valerius, and till that time served no master. "Then by this reckoning," said he, "we are both countrymen and may be both fellows in one house if thou wilt; for Don Felix my master commanded me long since to seek him out a page. Therefore if thou wilt serve him, say so. As for meat, drink, and apparel, and a couple of shillings to play away, thou shalt never want; besides pretty wenches, which are not dainty in our street, as fair and amorous as queens, of which there is not any that will not die for the love of so proper a youth as thou art. And to tell thee in secret (because, perhaps, we may be fellows), I know where an old canon's maid is, a gallant fine girl, whom if thou canst but find in thy heart to love and serve as I do, thou shalt never want at her hands fine handkerchers, pieces of bacon, and now and then wine of St. Martin." When I heard this, I could not choose but laugh to see how naturally the unhappy page played his part by depainting forth their properties in their lively colors. And because I thought nothing more commodious for my rest, and for the enjoying of my desire, than to follow Fabius his counsel, I answered him thus: "In truth, I determined to serve none; but now, since fortune hath offered me so good a service and at such a time, when I am constrained to take this course of life, I shall not do amiss if I frame myself to the service of some lord or gentleman in this court, but especially of your master, because he seems to be a worthy gentleman, and such an one that makes more reckoning of his servants than another." "Ha, thou knowest him not so well as I," said Fabius, "for I promise thee, by the faith of a gentleman (for I am one indeed, for my father comes of the Cachopines of Laredo), that my master Don Felix is the best-natured gentleman that ever thou knewest in thy life, and one who useth his pages better than any other. And were it not for those troublesome loves, which makes us run up and down more and sleep less than we would, there were not such a master in the whole world again." [4.4] In the end, fair nymphs, Fabius spake to his master Don Felix as soon as he was come forth, in my behalf, who commanded me the same night to come to him at his lodging. Thither I went, and he entertained me for his page, making the most of me in the world; where, being but a few days with him, I saw the messages, letters, and gifts that were brought and carried on both sides, grievous wounds (alas! and corr'sives to my dying heart), which made my soul to fly sometimes out of my body, and every hour in hazard to lose my forced patience before every one. But after one month was past, Don Felix began to like so well of me that he disclosed his whole love unto me from the beginning unto the present estate and forwardness that it was then in, committing the charge thereof to my secrecy and help; telling me that he was favored of her at the beginning and that afterwards she waxed weary of her loving and accustomed entertainment, the cause whereof was a secret report (whosoever it was that buzzed it into her ears) of the love that he did bear to a lady in his own country, and that his present love unto her was but to entertain the time while his business in the court were dispatched. "And there is no doubt," said Don Felix unto me, "but that, indeed, I did once commence that love that she lays to my charge; but God knows if now there be anything in the world that I love and esteem more dear and precious than her." When I heard him say so, you may imagine, fair nymphs, what a mortal dagger pierced my wounded heart. But with dissembling the matter the best I could, I answered him thus: "It were better, sir (methinks), that the gentlewoman should complain with cause, and that it were so indeed; for if the other lady, whom you served before, did not deserve to be forgotten of you, you do her (under correction, my lord) the greatest wrong in the world." "The love," said Don Felix again, "which I bear to my Celia will not let me understand it so; but I have done her (methinks) the greater injury, having placed my love first in another and not in her." "Of these wrongs," said I to myself, "I know who bears the worst away." And (disloyal) he, pulling a letter out of his bosom, which he had received the same hour from his mistress, read it into me, thinking he did me a great favor thereby, the contents whereof were these:

CELIA'S LETTER TO DON FELIX

Never anything that I suspected, touching thy love, hath been so far from the truth that hath not given me occasion to believe more often mine own imagination than thy innocence; wherein, if I do thee any wrong, refer it but to the censure of thine own folly. For well thou mightest have denied or not declared thy passed love, without giving me occasion to condemn thee by thine own confession. Thou sayest I was the cause that made thee forget thy former love. Comfort thyself, for there shall not want another to make thee forget thy second. And assure thyself of this, Lord Don Felix, that there is not anything more unbeseeming a gentleman than to find an occasion in a gentlewoman to lose himself for her love. I will say no more, but that in an ill, where there is no remedy, the best is not to seek out any.

After he had made an end of reading the letter, he said unto me, "What thinkest thou, Valerius, of these words?" "With pardon be it spoken, my lord, that your deeds are showed by them." "Go to," said Don Felix, "and speak no more of that." "Sir," said I, "they must like me well if they like you, because none can judge better of their words that love well than they themselves. But that which I think of the letter is that this gentlewoman would have been the first, and that Fortune had entreated her in such sort that all others might have envied her estate." "But what wouldest thou counsel me?" said Don Felix. "If thy grief doth suffer any counsel," said I, "that thy thoughts be divided into this second passion, since there is so much due to the first." Don Felix answered me again, sighing and knocking me gently on the shoulder, saying, "How wise art thou, Valerius, and what good counsel dost thou give me if I could follow it. Let us now go in to dinner, for when I have dined I will have thee carry me a letter to my lady Celia, and then thou shalt see if any other love is not worthy to be forgotten in lieu of thinking only of her." These were words that grieved Felismena to the heart, but because she had him before her eyes, whom she loved more than herself, the content that she had by only seeing him was a sufficient remedy of the pain that the greatest of these stings did make her feel. After Don Felix had dined, he called me unto him, and giving me a special charge what I should do (because he had imparted his grief unto me, and put his hope and remedy in my hands), he willed me to carry a letter to Celia, which he had already written, and reading it first unto me, it said thus:

DON FELIX HIS LETTER TO CELIA

The thought that seeks an occasion to forget the thing which it doth love and desire, suffers itself so easily to be known that (without troubling the mind much) it may be quickly discerned. And think not, fair lady, that I seek a remedy to excuse you of that wherewith it pleased you to use me, since I never came to be so much in credit with you that in lesser things I would do it. I have confessed unto you that indeed I once loved well, because that true love, without dissimulation, doth not suffer anything to be hid, and you, dear lady, make that an occasion to forget me, which should be rather a motive to love me better. I cannot persuade me that you make so small an account of yourself to think that I can forget you for anything that is, or hath ever been, but rather imagine that you write clean contrary to that which you have tried by my zealous love and faith towards you. Touching all those things that, in prejudice of my good will towards you, it pleaseth you to imagine, my innocent thoughts assure me to the contrary, which shall suffice to be ill recompensed besides being so ill thought of as they are.

After Don Felix had read this letter unto me, he asked me if the answer was correspondent to those words that his lady Celia had sent him in hers, and if there was anything therein that might be amended; whereunto I answered thus: "I think, sir, it is needless to amend this letter, or to make the gentlewoman amends to whom it is sent, but her whom you do injury so much with it. Which under your lordship's pardon I speak, because I am so much affected to the first love in all my life that there is not anything that can make me alter my mind." "Thou hast the greatest reason in the world," said Don Felix, "if I could persuade myself to leave off that which I have begun. But what wilt thou have me do, since absence hath frozen the former love, and the continual presence of a peerless beauty rekindled another more hot and fervent in me?" "Thus may she think herself," said I again, "unjustly deceived, whom first you loved, because that love which is subject to the power of absence cannot be termed love, and none can persuade me that it hath been love." These words did I dissemble the best I could, because I felt so sensible grief to see myself forgotten of him who had so great reason to love me, and whom I did love so much that I did more than any would have thought to make myself still unknown. But taking the letter and mine errand with me, I went to Celia's house, imagining by the way the woeful estate whereunto my hapless love had brought me; since I was forced to make war against mine own self, and to be the intercessor of a thing so contrary to mine own content. But coming to Celia's house, and finding a page standing at the door, I asked him if I might speak with his lady: who being informed of me from whence I came, told Celia how I would speak with her, commending therewithal my beauty and person unto her, and telling her besides that Don Felix had but lately entertained me into his service; which made Celia say unto him, "What, Don Felix so soon disclose his secret loves to a page, but newly entertained? He hath (belike) some great occasion that moves him to do it. Bid him come in, and let us know what he would have." In I came, and to the place where the enemy of my life was, and with great reverence kissing her hands, I delivered Don Felix his letter unto her. Celia took it and, casting her eyes upon me, I might perceive how my sight had made a sudden alteration in her countenance, for she was so far besides herself that for a good while she was not able to speak a word, but remembering herself at last, she said unto me, "What good fortune hath been so favorable to Don Felix to bring thee to this court, to make thee his page?" "Even that, fair lady," said I, "which is better than ever I imagined, because it hath been an occasion to make me behold such singular beauty and perfections as now I see clearly before mine eyes. And if the pains, the tears, the sighs, and the continual disquiets that my lord Don Felix hath suffered have grieved me heretofore, now that I have seen the source from whence they flow and the cause of all his ill, the pity that I had on him is now wholly converted into a certain kind of envy. But if it be true, fair lady, that my coming is welcome unto you, I beseech you by that which you owe to the great love which he bears you, that your answer may import no less unto him." "There is not anything," said Celia, "that I would not do for thee, though I were determined not to love him at all, who for my sake hath forsaken another. For it is no small point of wisdom for me to learn by other women's harms to be more wise and wary in mine own." "Believe not, good lady," said I, "that there is anything in the world that can make Don Felix forget you. And if he hath cast off another for your sake, wonder not thereat, when your beauty and wisdom is so great and the other's so small that there is no reason to think that he will (though he hath worthily forsaken her for your sake) or ever can forget you for any woman else in the world." "Dost thou then know Felismena," said Celia, "the lady whom thy master did once love and serve in his own country?" "I know her," said I, "although not so well as it was needful for me to have prevented so many mishaps" (and this I spake softly to myself). "For my father's house was near to hers; but seeing your great beauty adorned with such perfections and wisdom, Don Felix cannot be blamed if he hath forgotten his first love only to embrace and honor yours." To this did Celia answer, merrily and smiling, "Thou hast learned quickly of thy master to soothe." "Not so, fair lady," said I, "but to serve you would I fain learn: for flattery cannot be where (in the judgment of all) there are so manifest signs and proofs of this due commendation." Celia began in good earnest to ask me what manner of woman Felismena was, whom I answered that, touching her beauty, some thought her to be very fair; but I was never of that opinion, because she hath many days since wanted the chiefest thing that is requisite for it. "What is that?" said Celia. "Content of mind," said I, "because perfect beauty can never be, where the same is not adjoined to it." "Thou hast the greatest reason in the world," said she, "but I have seen some ladies whose lively hue sadness hath not one whit abated, and others whose beauty anger hath increased, which is a strange thing methinks." "Hapless is that beauty," said I, "that hath sorrow and anger the preservers and mistresses of it, but I cannot skill of these impertinent things. And yet that woman that must needs be molested with continual pain and trouble, with grief and care of mind and with other passions to make her look well, cannot be reckoned among the number of fair women, and for mine own part I do not account her so." "Wherein thou hast great reason," said she, "as in all things else that thou hast said, thou hast showed thyself wise and discreet." "Which I have dearly bought," said I again. "But I beseech you, gracious lady, to answer this letter, because my lord Don Felix may also have some contentment, by receiving this first well-employed service at my hands." "I am content," said Celia, "but first thou must tell me if Felismena in matters of discretion be wise and well advised?" "There was never any woman," said I again, "more wise than she, because she hath been long since beaten to it by her great mishaps; but she did never advise herself well, for if she had (as she was accounted wise) she had never come to have been so contrary to herself." "Thou speakest so wisely in all thy answers," said Celia, "that there is not any that would not take great delight to hear them." "Which are not viands," said I, "for such a dainty taste, nor reasons for so ingenious and fine a conceit, fair lady, as you have, but boldly affirming that by the same I mean no harm at all." "There is not anything," said Celia, "whereunto thy wit cannot attain, but because thou shalt not spend thy time so ill in praising me, as thy master doth in praying me, I will read thy letter and tell thee what thou shalt say unto him from me." Whereupon unfolding it, she began to read it to herself, to whose countenance and gestures in reading of the same, which are oftentimes outward signs of the inward disposition and meaning of the heart, I gave a watchful eye. And when she had read it, she said unto me, "Tell thy master that he that can so well by words express what he means, cannot choose but mean as well as he saith," and coming nearer to me, she said softly in mine ear, "and this for the love of thee, Valerius, and not so much for Don Felix thy master his sake, for I see how much thou lovest and tenderest his estate." "And from thence, alas," said I to myself, "did all my woes arise." Whereupon kissing her hands for the great courtesy and favor she showed me, I hied me to Don Felix with this answer, which was no small joy to him to hear it, and another death to me to report it, saying many times to myself (when I did either bring him home some joyful tidings or carry letters or tokens to her), "O thrice unfortunate Felismena, that with thine own weapons art constrained to wound thy ever-dying heart, and to heap up favors for him who made so small account of thine." And so did I pass away my life with so many torments of mind that if by the sight of my Don Felix they had not been tempered, it could not have otherwise been but that I must needs have lost it. More than two months together did Celia hide from me the fervent love she bare me, although not in such sort but that by certain apparent signs I came to the knowledge thereof, which was no small lighting and ease of that grief which incessantly haunted my wearied spirits; for as I thought it a strong occasion, and the only mean to make her utterly forget Don Felix, so likewise I imagined that, perhaps, it might befall to him as it hath done to many that the force of ingratitude and contempt of his love might have utterly abolished such thoughts out of his heart. But, alas, it happened not so to my Don Felix; for the more he perceived that his lady forgot him, the more was his mind troubled with greater cares and grief, which made him lead the most sorrowful life that might be, whereof the least part did not fall to my lot. For remedy of whose sighs and piteous lamentations, poor Felismena (even by main force) did get favors from Celia, scoring them up (whensoever she sent them by me) in the catalogue of my infinite mishaps. For if by chance he sent her anything by any of his other servants, it was so slenderly accepted that he thought it best to send none unto her but myself, perceiving what inconvenience did ensue thereof. But God knows how many tears my messages cost me, and so many they were that in Celia's presence I ceased not to pour them forth, earnestly beseeching her with prayers and petitions not to entreat him so ill who loved her so much, because I would bind Don Felix to me by the greatest bond as never man in like was bound to any woman. My tears grieved Celia to the heart, as well for that I shed them in her presence, as also for that she saw if I meant to love her, I would not (for requital of hers to me) have solicited her with such diligence nor pleaded with such pity to get favors for another. And thus I lived in the greatest confusion that might be, amidst a thousand anxieties of mind, for I imagined with myself that if I made not a show that I loved her, as she did me, I did put it in hazard lest Celia, for despite of my simplicity or contempt, would have loved Don Felix more than before, and by loving him that mine could not have any good success; and if I feigned myself, on the other side, to be in love with her, it might have been an occasion to have made her reject my lord Don Felix, so that with the thought of his love neglected and with the force of her contempt, he might have lost his content, and after that, his life, the least of which two mischiefs to prevent I would have given a thousand lives, if I had them. Many days passed away in this sort, wherein I served him as a third between both, to the great cost of my contentment, at the end whereof the success of his love went on worse and worse, because the love that Celia did bear me was so great that the extreme force of her passion made her lose some part of that compassion she should have had of herself. And on a day after that I had carried and recarried many messages and tokens between them, sometimes feigning some myself from her unto him, because I could not see him (whom I loved so dearly) so sad and pensive, with many supplications and earnest prayers I besought Lady Celia with pity to regard the painful life that Don Felix passed for her sake, and to consider that by not favoring him she was repugnant to that which she owed to herself: which thing I entreated, because I saw him in such a case that there was no other thing to be expected of him but death, by reason of the continual and great pain which his grievous thoughts made him feel. But she with swelling tears in her eyes, and with many sighs, answered me thus: "Unfortunate and accursed Celia, that now in the end dost know how thou livest deceived with a false opinion of thy great simplicity (ungrateful Valerius) and of thy small discretion. I did not believe till now that thou didst crave favors of me for thy master, but only for thyself, and to enjoy my sight all that time that thou didst spend in suing to me for them. But now I see thou dost ask them in earnest, and that thou art so content to see me use him well, that thou canst not (without doubt) love me at all. O how ill dost thou acquit the love I bear thee, and that which, for thy sake, I do now forsake? O that time might revenge me of thy proud and foolish mind, since love hath not been the means to do it. For I cannot think that Fortune will be so contrary unto me, but that she will punish thee for contemning that great good which she meant to bestow on thee. And tell thy lord Don Felix that if he will see me alive, that he see me not at all: and thou, vile traitor, cruel enemy to my rest, come no more (I charge thee) before these wearied eyes, since their tears were never of force to make thee know how much thou art bound unto them." And with this she suddenly flang out of my sight with so many tears that mine were not of force to stay her. For in the greatest haste in the world she got her into her chamber where, locking the door after her, it availed me not to call and cry unto her, requesting with amorous and sweet words to open me the door and to take such satisfaction on me as it pleased her: nor to tell her many other things, whereby I declared unto her the small reason she had to be so angry with me and to shut me out. But with a strange kind of fury she said unto me, "Come no more, ungrateful and proud Valerius, in my sight, and speak no more unto me, for thou art not able to make satisfaction for such great disdain, and I will have no other remedy for the harm which thou hast done me, but death itself, the which with mine own hands I will take in satisfaction of that which thou deservest." Which words when I heard, I stayed no longer, but with a heavy cheer came to my Don Felix his lodging, and, with more sadness than I was able to dissemble, told him that I could not speak with Celia, because she was visited of certain gentlewomen her kinswomen. But the next day in the morning it was bruited over all the city that a certain trance had taken her that night, wherein she gave up the ghost, which struck all the court with no small wonder. But that which Don Felix felt by her sudden death, and how near it grieved his very soul, as I am not able to tell, so cannot human intendment conceive it, for the complaints he made, the tears, the burning sighs, and heartbreak sobs, were without all measure and number. But I say nothing of myself, when on the one side the unlucky death of Celia touched my soul very near, the tears of Don Felix on the other did cut my heart in two with grief: and yet this was nothing to that intolerable pain which afterwards I felt. For Don Felix heard no sooner of her death, but the same night he was missing in his house, that none of his servants nor anybody else could tell any news of him.

Whereupon you may perceive, fair nymphs, what cruel torments I did then feel: then did I wish a thousand times for death to prevent all these woes and miseries which afterwards befell unto me: for Fortune (it seemed) was but weary of those which she had but till then given me. But as all the care and diligence which I employed in seeking out my Don Felix was but in vain, so I resolved with myself to take this habit upon me as you see, wherein it is more than two years since I have wandered up and down, seeking him in many countries: but my Fortune hath denied me to find him out, although I am not a little now bound unto her by conducting me hither at this time, wherein I did you this small piece of service. Which, fair nymphs, believe me, I account (next after his life in whom I have put all my hope) the greatest content that might have fallen unto me. . . .

[There follows a discussion of the relationship of love to reason.]

The shepherdess having made an end of her sharp answer and Felismena beginning to arbitrate the matter between them, they heard a great noise in the other side of the meadow, like to the sound of blows and smiting of swords upon harness, as if some armed men had fought together, so that all of them with great haste ran to the place where they heard the noise, to see what the matter was. And being come somewhat near, they saw in a little island (which the river with a round turning had made) three knights fighting against one. And although he defended himself valiantly, by showing his approved strength and courage, yet the three knights gave him so much to do that he was fain to help himself by all the force and policy he could. They fought on foot, for their horses were tied to little trees that grew thereabout. And now by this time, the knight that fought all alone and defended himself had laid one of them at his feet with a blow of his good sword, which ended his life. But the other two that were very strong and valiant redoubled their force and blows so thick on him that he looked for no other thing than death. The shepherdess Felismena seeing the knight in so great danger, and if she did not speedily help him, that he could not escape with life, was not afraid to put hers in jeopardy by doing that which in such a case she thought she was bound to perform: wherefore putting a sharp-headed arrow into her bow, she said unto them: "Keep out, knights, for it is not beseeming men that make account of this name and honor, to take advantage of their enemies with so great odds." And aiming at the sight of one of their helmets, she burst it with such force that the arrow running into his eyes came out of the other side of his head so that he fell down dead to the ground. When the distressed knight saw two of his enemies dead, he ran upon the third with such force as if he had but then begun the combat; but Felismena helped him out of more trouble by putting another arrow into her bow, the which transpiercing his armor, she left under his left pap, and so justly smote his heart that this knight also followed his two companions. When the shepherds and the knight beheld what Felismena had done, and how at two shoots she had killed two such valiant knights, they were all in great wonder. The knight therefore, taking off his helmet and coming unto her, said: "How am I able, fair shepherdess, to requite so great a benefit and good turn as I have received at thy hands this day, but by acknowledging this debt forever in my grateful mind?" When Felismena beheld the knight's face and knew him, her senses were so troubled that being in such a trance she could scarce speak, but coming to herself again, she answered him: "Ah, my Don Felix, this is not the first debt wherein thou art bound unto me. And I cannot believe that thou wilt acknowledge this (as thou sayest) no more than thou hast done greater than this before. Behold to what a time and end my fortune and thy forgetness hath brought me, that she what was wont to be served of thee in the city with tilt and tourneys, and honored with many other things, whereby thou didst deceive me (or I suffered myself to be deceived), doth now wander up and down, exiled from her native country and liberty, for using thus thine own. If this brings thee not into the knowledge of that which thou owest me, remember how one whole year I served thee as thy page in the Princess Caesarina's court: and how I was a solicitor against myself, without discovering myself or my thoughts unto thee; but only to procure thy remedy and to help the grief which thine made thee feel. How many times did I get thee favors from thy mistress Celia to the great cost of my tears and griefs: all which account but small, Don Felix, in respect of those dangers (had they been unsufficient) wherein I would have spent my life for redress of thy pains, which thy injurious love afforded thee. And unless thou art weary of the great love that I have borne thee, consider and weigh with thyself the strange effects which the force of love hath caused me to pass. I went out of my native country and came to serve thee, to lament the ill that thou didst suffer, to take upon me the injuries and disgraces that I received therein; and to give thee any content, I cared not to lead the most bitter and painful life that ever woman lived. In the habit of a tender and dainty lady I loved thee more than thou canst imagine, and in the habit of a base page I served thee (a thing more contrary to my rest and reputation than I mean now to rehearse) and yet now in the habit of a poor and simple shepherdess I came to do thee this small service. What remains then more for me to do, but to sacrifice my life to thy loveless soul, if with the same yet I could give thee more content—and if in lieu thereof thou wouldest but remember how much I have loved and do yet love thee! Here hast thou thy sword in thy hand; let none therefore but thy self revenge the offense that I have done thee." When the knight heard Felismena's words and knew them all to be as true as he was disloyal, his heart by this strange and sudden accident recovered some force again to see what great injury he had done her, so that thought thereof and the plenteous effusion of blood that issued out of his wounds made him like a dead man fall down in a swoon at fair Felismena's feet; who with great care and no less fear, laying his head in her lap, with showers of tears that rained from her eyes upon the knight's pale visage, began thus to lament: "What means this cruel Fortune? Is the period of my life come just with the last end of my Don Felix his days? Ah, my Don Felix (the cause of all my pain), if the plenteous tears, which for thy sake I have now shed, are not sufficient; and these which I now distill upon thy lovely cheeks, too few to make thee come to thyself again, what remedy shall this miserable soul have to prevent that this bitter joy by seeing thee turn not to occasion of utter despair. Ah, my Don Felix, awake my love, if thou dost but sleep or be'st in a trance, although I would not wonder if thou dost not, since never anything that I could do prevailed with thee to frame my least content." And in these and other lamentations was fair Felismena plunged, whom the Portugal shepherdesses with their tears and poor supplies endeavored to encourage, when on the sudden they saw a fair nymph coming over the stony causey that led the way into the island, with a golden bottle in one hand and a silver one in the other, whom Felismena knowing by and by, said unto her: "Ah, Doria, could any come at this time to succor me but thou, fair nymph? Come hither then, and thou shalt see the cause of all my troubles, the substance of my sighs, and the object of my thoughts, lying in the greatest danger of death that may be." "In like occurrents," said Doria, "virtue and a good heart most take place. Recall it then, fair Felismena, and revive thy daunted spirits, trouble not thyself any more, for now is the end of thy sorrows and the beginning of thy contentment come." And speaking these words, she besprinkled his face with a certain odoriferous water which she brought in the silver bottle, whereby he came to his memory again, and then said unto him: "If thou wilt recover thy life, sir knight, and give it her that hath passed such an ill one for thy sake, drink of the water in this bottle." The which Don Felix, taking in his hand, drunk a good draught and, resting upon it a little, found himself so whole of his wounds, which the three knights had given him, and of that which the love of Celia had made in his breast, that now he felt the pain no more which either of them had caused him than if he had never had them. And in this sort he began to rekindle the old love that he bore to Felismena, the which (he thought) was never more zealous than now. Whereupon sitting down upon the green grass, he took his lady and shepherdess by the hands and, kissing them many times, said thus unto her: "How small account would I make of my life, my dearest Felismena, for canceling that great bond wherein (with more than life) I am forever bound unto thee: for since I enjoy it, by thy means, I think it no more than right to restore thee that which is thine own. . . . What words are sufficient to excuse the faults that I have committed against thy faith and firmest love and loyalty? . . . Truth is that I loved Celia well and forgot thee, but in such sort that thy wisdom and beauty did ever slide out of my mind. And the best is that I know not wherein to put this fault that may be so justly attributed to me; for if I will impute it to the young age that I was then in, since I had it to love thee, I should not have wanted it to have been firm in the faith that I owed thee. If to Celia's beauty it is clear that thine did far excel hers and all the world's besides. If to the change of time, this should have been the touchstone which should have showed the force and virtue of my firmness. If to injurious and traitorous absence, it serves as little for my excuse, since the desire of seeing thee should not have been absent from supporting thy image in my memory. Behold then, Felismena, what assured trust I put in thy goodness that (without any other means) I dare put before thee the small reason thou hast to pardon me. But what shall I do to purchase pardon at thy gracious hands, or after thou hast pardoned me, to believe that thou art satisfied: for one thing grieves me more than anything else in the world, and this it is. That, though the love which thou hast borne me, and wherewith thou dost yet bless me, is an occasion (perhaps) to make thee forgive me and forget so many faults: yet I shall never lift up mine eyes to behold thee, but that every injury which I have done thee will be worse than a mortal incision in my guilty heart." The shepherdess Felismena, who saw Don Felix so penitent for his past misdeeds and so affectionately returned to his first thoughts, with many tears told him that she did pardon him, because the love that she had ever borne him would suffer her to do no less: which if she had not thought to do, she would never have taken so great pains and so many weary journeys to seek him out, and many other things, wherewith Don Felix was confirmed in his former love. . . . And Don Felix wondered not a little to understand how his lady Felismena had served him so many days as his page, and that he was so far gone out of his wits and memory that he knew her not for all that while. And his joy on the other side to see that his lady loved him so well, was so great that by no means he could hide it. Thus therefore, riding on their way, they came to Diana's temple, where the sage Felicia was looking for their coming: and likewise the shepherd Arsileus, and Belisa, Sylvanus, and Selvagia, who were now come thither not many days before. They were welcomed on every side and with great joy entertained; but fair Felismena especially, who for her rare virtues and singular beauty was greatly honored of them all. There they were all married with great joy, feasts, and triumphs, which were made by all the goodly nymphs and by the sage and noble lady Felicia. . . .

Commentaries

GEORGE BERNARD SHAW

From Our Theatres in the Nineties

THE TWO GENTLEMEN OF VERONA. Daly's Theatre, 2 July 1895. [6 *July* 1895]

The piece founded by Augustin Daly on Shakespear's *Two Gentlemen of Verona,* to which I looked forward last week, is not exactly a comic opera, though there is plenty of music in it, and not exactly a serpentine dance, though it proceeds under a play of changing colored lights. It is something more old-fashioned than either: to wit, a vaudeville. And let me hasten to admit that it makes a very pleasant entertainment for those who know no better. Even I, who know a great deal better, as I shall presently demonstrate rather severely, enjoyed myself tolerably. I cannot feel harshly towards a gentleman who works so hard as Mr. Daly does to make Shakespear presentable: one feels that he loves the bard, and lets him have his way as far as he thinks it good for him. His rearrangement of the scenes of the first two acts

From *Our Theatres in the Nineties* by George Bernard Shaw. 3 vols. London: Constable & Co., Ltd., 1932. Reprinted by permission of the Public Trustee and the Society of Authors.

is just like him. Shakespear shews lucidly how Proteus lives with his father (Antonio) in Verona, and loves a lady of that city named Julia. Mr. Daly, by taking the scene in Julia's house between Julia and her maid, and the scene in Antonio's house between Antonio and Proteus, and making them into one scene, convinces the unlettered audience that Proteus and Julia live in the same house with their father Antonio. Further, Shakespear shews us how Valentine, the other gentleman of Verona, travels from Verona to Milan, the journey being driven into our heads by a comic scene in Verona, in which Valentine's servant is overwhelmed with grief at leaving his parents, and with indignation at the insensibility of his dog to his sorrow, followed presently by another comic scene in Milan in which the same servant is welcomed to the strange city by a fellow servant. Mr. Daly, however, is ready for Shakespear on this point too. He just represents the two scenes as occurring in the same place; and immediately the puzzle as to who is who is complicated by a puzzle as to where is where. Thus is the immortal William adapted to the requirements of a nineteenth-century audience.

In preparing the text of his version Mr. Daly has proceeded on the usual principles, altering, transposing, omitting, improving, correcting, and transferring speeches from one character to another. Many of Shakespear's lines are mere poetry, not to the point, not getting the play along, evidently stuck in because the poet liked to spread himself in verse. On all such unbusinesslike superfluities Mr. Daly is down with his blue pencil. For instance, he relieves us of such stuff as the following, which merely conveys that Valentine loves Silvia, a fact already sufficiently established by the previous dialogue:

> My thoughts do harbor with my Silvia nightly;
>> And slaves they are to me, that send them flying:
> Oh, could their master come and go as lightly,

> Himself would lodge where senseless they are lying.
> My herald thoughts in thy pure bosom rest them,
>> While I, their king, that thither them importune,
> Do curse the grace that with such grace hath blessed them,
>> Because myself do want my servant's fortune.
> I curse myself, for they are sent by me,
>> That they should harbor where their lord would be.

Slaves indeed are these lines and their like to Mr. Daly, who "sends them flying" without remorse. But when he comes to passages that a stage manager can understand, his reverence for the bard knows no bounds. The following awkward lines, unnecessary as they are under modern stage conditions, are at any rate not poetic, and are in the nature of police news. Therefore they are piously retained:

> What halloing, and what stir, is this today?
> These are my mates, that make their wills their law,
> Have some unhappy passenger in chase.
> They love me well; yet I have much to do,
> To keep them from uncivil outrages.
> Withdraw thee, Valentine: who's this comes here?

The perfunctory metrical character of such lines only makes them more ridiculous than they would be in prose. I would cut them out without remorse to make room for all the lines that have nothing to justify their existence except their poetry, their humor, their touches of character—in short, the lines for whose sake the play survives, just as it was for their sake it originally came into existence. Mr. Daly, who prefers the lines which only exist for the sake of the play, will doubtless think me as great a fool as Shakespear; but I submit to him, without disputing his judgment, that he is, after all, only a man with a theory of dramatic composition, going with a blue pencil over the work of a great dramatist, and striking out everything that does not fit his theory. Now, as it happens, nobody cares about Mr. Daly's theory; whilst everybody who pays to see what is, after all, advertised as a performance of Shakespear's play entitled *The Two Gentlemen of Verona,* and not as a demonstration of Mr. Daly's theory, does care more or less about the art of Shakespear. Why not give them what they ask for, instead of going to great trouble and expense to give them something else?

In those matters in which Mr. Daly has given the rein to his own taste and fancy: that is to say, in scenery, costumes, and music, he is for the most part disabled by a want of real knowledge of the arts concerned. I say for the most part, because his pretty fifteenth-century dresses, though probably inspired rather by Sir Frederic Leighton than by Benozzo Gozzoli, may pass. But the scenery is insufferable. First, for "a street in Verona" we get a Bath bun colored operatic front cloth with about as much light in it as there is in a studio in Fitzjohn's Avenue in the middle of October. I respectfully invite Mr. Daly to spend his next holiday looking at a real street in Verona, asking his conscience meanwhile whether a manager with eyes in his head and the electric light at his disposal could not advance a step on the Telbin (senior) style. Telbin was an admirable scene painter; but he was limited by the mechanical conditions of gas illumination; and he learnt his technique before the great advance made during the Impressionist movement in the painting of open-air effects, especially of brilliant sunlight. Of that advance Mr. Daly has apparently no conception. The days of Macready and Clarkson Stanfield still exist for him; he would probably prefer a water-color drawing of a foreign street by Samuel Prout to one of Mr. T. M. Rooke; and I daresay every relic of the original tallow candlelight that still clings to the art of scene painting is as dear to him as it is to most old playgoers, including, unhappily, many of the critics.

As to the elaborate set in which Julia makes her first entrance, a glance at it shews how far Mr. Daly prefers the

Marble Arch to the loggia of Orcagna. All over the scene we have Renaissance work, in its genteelest stages of decay, held up as the perfection of romantic elegance and beauty. The school that produced the classicism of the First Empire, designed the terraces of Regent's Park and the façades of Fitzroy Square, and conceived the Boboli Gardens and Versailles as places for human beings to be happy in, ramps all over the scenery, and offers as much of its pet colonnades and statues as can be crammed into a single scene, by way of a compendium of everything that is lovely in the city of San Zeno and the tombs of the Scaligers. As to the natural objects depicted, I ask whether any man living has ever seen a pale green cypress in Verona or anywhere else out of a toy Noah's Ark. A man who, having once seen cypresses and felt their presence in a north Italian landscape, paints them lettuce color, must be suffering either from madness, malice, or a theory of how nature should have colored trees, cognate with Mr. Daly's theory of how Shakespear should have written plays.

Of the music let me speak compassionately. After all, it is only very lately that Mr. Arnold Dolmetsch, by playing fifteenth-century music on fifteenth-century instruments, has shewn us that the age of beauty was true to itself in music as in pictures and armor and costumes. But what should Mr. Daly know of this, educated as he no doubt was to believe that the court of Denmark should always enter in the first act of *Hamlet* to the march from *Judas Maccabaeus*? Schubert's setting of "Who Is Silvia?" he knew, but had rashly used up in *Twelfth Night* as "Who's Olivia." He has therefore had to fall back on another modern setting, almost supernaturally devoid of any particular merit. Besides this, all through the drama the most horribly common music repeatedly breaks out on the slightest pretext or on no pretext at all. One dance, set to a crude old English popular tune, sundry eighteenth- and nineteenth-century musical banalities, and a titivated plantation melody in the first act which produces an indescribably atrocious effect by coming in behind the scenes as a sort of coda to Julia's curtain speech, all turn the play, as I have said, into a vaudeville. Needless to add, the accompaniments are not played on lutes and viols, but by the orchestra and a guitar or two. In the forest scene, the outlaws begin the act by a chorus. After their encounter with Valentine they go off the stage singing the refrain exactly in the style of *La Fille de Madame Angot.* The wanton absurdity of introducing this comic opera convention is presently eclipsed by a thunderstorm, immediately after which Valentine enters and delivers his speech sitting down on a bank of moss, as an outlaw in tights naturally would after a terrific shower. Such is the effect of many years of theatrical management on the human brain.

Perhaps the oddest remark I have to make about the performance is that, with all its glaring defects and blunders, it is rather a handsome and elaborate one as such things go. It is many years now since Mr. Ruskin first took the Academicians of his day aback by the obvious remark that Carpaccio and Giovanni Bellini were better painters than Domenichino and Salvator Rosa. Nobody dreams now of assuming that Pope was a greater poet than Chaucer, that Mozart's Twelfth Mass is superior to the masterpieces of Orlandus Lassus and Palestrina, or that our "ecclesiastical Gothic" architecture is more enlightened than Norman axe work. But the theatre is still wallowing in such follies; and until Mr. Comyns Carr and Sir Edward Burne-Jones, Baronet, put King Arthur on the stage more or less in the manner natural to men who know these things, Mr. Daly might have pleaded the unbroken conservatism of the playhouse against me. But after the Lyceum scenery and architecture I decline to accept a relapse without protest. There is no reason why cheap photographs of Italian architecture (sixpence apiece in infinite variety at the bookstall in the South Kensington Museum) should not rescue us from Regent's Park Renaissance colonnades on the stage just as the electric light can rescue us from Telbin's dun-colored sunlight. The opera is the last place in the world where any wise man would look for adequate stage illusion; but the fact is that Mr. Daly, with all his colored lights, has not produced a single Italian scene comparable in illusion to that provided by Sir Augustus Harris at Covent Garden for *Cavalleria Rusticana.*

Of the acting I have not much to say. Miss Rehan provided a strong argument in favor of rational dress by looking much better in her page's costume than in that of her own sex; and in the serenade scene, and that of the wooing of Silvia for Proteus, she stirred some feeling into the part, and reminded us of what she was in *Twelfth Night,* where the same situations are fully worked out. For the rest, she moved and spoke with imposing rhythmic grace. That is as much notice as so cheap a part as Julia is worth from an artist who, being absolute mistress of the situation at Daly's Theatre, might and should have played Imogen for us instead. The two gentlemen were impersonated by Mr. Worthing and Mr. Craig. Mr. Worthing charged himself with feeling without any particular reference to his lines; and Mr. Craig struck a balance by attending to the meaning of his speeches without taking them at all to heart. Mr. Clarke, as the Duke, was emphatic, and worked up every long speech to a climax in the useful old style; but his tone is harsh, his touch on his consonants coarse, and his accent ugly, all fatal disqualifications for the delivery of Shakespearean verse. The scenes between Launce and his dog brought out the latent silliness and childishness of the audience as Shakespear's clowning scenes always do: I laugh at them like a yokel myself. Mr. Lewis hardly made the most of them. His style has been formed in modern comedies, where the locutions are so familiar that their meaning is in no danger of being lost by the rapidity of his quaint utterance; but Launce's phraseology is another matter: a few of the funniest lines missed fire because the audience did not catch them. And with all possible allowance for Mr. Daly's blue pencil, I cannot help suspecting that Mr. Lewis's memory was responsible for one or two of his omissions. Still, Mr. Lewis has always his comic force, whether he makes the most or the least of it; so that he cannot fail in such a part as Launce. Miss Maxine Elliot's Silvia was the most considerable performance after Miss Rehan's Julia. The whole company will gain by the substitution on Tuesday next of a much better play, *A Midsummer Night's Dream,* as a basis for Mr. Daly's operations. No doubt he is at this moment, like Mrs. Todgers, "a dodgin' among the tender bits with a fork, and an eatin' of 'em"; but there is sure to be enough of the original left here and there to repay a visit.

H. B. CHARLTON

From Shakespearian Comedy

In its first intention, Elizabethan romantic comedy was an attempt to adapt the world of romance and all its implications to the service of comedy. *The Two Gentlemen of Verona* shows that intention at its crudest. In the story of it, there are all the main marks of the medieval tradition as that tradition had been modified, elaborated, and extended by the idealism of Petrarch and by the speculations of the Platonists. It is yet the same tradition in its essence, corroborated rather than altered by the modifying factors; as, for instance, at the hands of Ficino, Platonism brought a medico-metaphysical theory to explain the love-laden gleam of a beautiful eye. Shakespeare's play embodies a literary manner and a moral code; its actions are conducted according to a conventional etiquette and are determined by a particular creed; and every feature of it, in matter and in sentiment, is traceable to the romantic attitude of man to woman. It presents as its setting a world constituted in such fashion that the obligations and the sanctions of its doctrines could best be realized. The course of the whole play is determined by the values such doctrine attaches to the love of man and woman.

A note struck early in the play recalls one of the few passionate love stories of classical legend—"how young

From *Shakespearian Comedy* by H. B. Charlton. London: Methuen and Co., Ltd.; New York: The Macmillan Company, 1938. Reprinted by permission of Methuen and Co., Ltd.

Leander crossed the Hellespont"—and at another moment, Ariadne is remembered "passioning for Theseus' perjury." But the real color of the tale is given unmistakably by the presence amongst its characters of Sir Eglamour. By his name is he known and whence he springs. He points straight back to the source of the religious cult of love: "servant and friend" of Silvia, he is ready at call to rush to any service to which she may command him. His own lady and his true love died, and on her grave he vowed pure chastity, dedicating himself to the assistance of lovers in affliction, recking nothing what danger should betide him in the venture. His home is in the land of medieval romance; and his brethren are those consecrated warriors who will undertake all danger, though it stands next to death, for one calm look of Love's approval. He comes to life again in a play where knightly vows are spoken, where errantry is the normal mode of service, where the exercise of tilt and tournament is the traditional recreation, where lovers name themselves habitually the servants of their ladies, where such service may impose as a duty the helping of one's lady to a rival, and where the terms of infamy to which the utmost slander can give voice are "perjured, false, disloyal." And that is the world in which Shakespeare makes his Two Gentlemen live.

Throughout the play, "Love's a mighty lord,"

> There is no woe to his correction
> Nor to his service no such joy on earth.

This is the state of the lover as the old *Romaunt of the Rose* had depicted it:

> The sore of love is merveilous,
> For now is the lover joyous,
> Now can he pleyne, now can he grone,
> Now can he syngen, now maken mone;
> To day he pleyneth for hevynesse,

> To morowe he pleyeth for jolynesse.
> The lyf of love is full contrarie,
> Which stounde-mele can ofte varie.

Heavy penance is visited on unbelievers

> for contemning Love,
> Whose high imperious thoughts will punish him
> With bitter fasts, with penitential groans,
> With nightly tears and daily heartsore sighs.

Sleep is chased from such a rebel's now enthralled eyes, to make them watchers of his own heart's sorrow. From true votaries, nothing less than absolute devotion is required. They must hold no discourse except it be of love. Absent from their lady, they must let no single hour o'erslip without its ceremonial sigh for her sake. The more such languishing fidelity appears to be spurned, the more must it grow and fawn upon its recalcitrant object. Apart from love, nothing in life has the least significance:

> banished from her,
> Is self from self, a deadly banishment.
> What light is light, if Silvia be not seen?
> What joy is joy, if Silvia be not by?
> Except I be by Silvia in the night,
> There is no music in the nightingale.
> Unless I look on Silvia in the day,
> There is no day for me to look upon.
> She is my essence, and I leave to be,
> If I am not by her fair influence
> Fostered, illumined, cherished, kept alive.

Such is the consecrated desolation of the romantic lover: the medieval sense of a world emptied of its content persists through romantic poetry and is the undertone of the Renaissance sonneteers' woe. Bembo puts it not unlike Valentine in the play:

> Tu m'hai lasciato senza sole i giorni,
> Le notte senza stelle, e grave e egro
> Tutto questo, ond'io parlo, ond'io respiro:
> La terra scossa, e'l ciel turbato e negro;
> Et pien di mille oltraggi e mille scorni
> Me sembra ogni parte, quant'io miro.
> Valor e cortesia si dipartiro
> Nel tuo partire; e'l mondo infermo giacque;
> Et virtu spense i suoi chiari lumi;
> Et le fontane e i fiumi
> Nega la vena antica e l'usate acque:
> Et gli augelletti abandonaro il canto,
> Et l'herbe e i fior lasciar nude le piaggie,
> Ne piu di fronde il bosco si consperse.

But the lover has ample recompense for his sorrow. Setting the world at nought, he gains a heaven in its stead:

> she is mine own,
> And I as rich in having such a jewel
> As twenty seas if all their sand were pearl,
> The water nectar, and the rocks pure gold.

Inevitably, a creed of such ardent devotion has its appropriate liturgy. Stuffed with protestation, and full of new-found oaths, the lover utters his fears in wailful sonnets, whose composed rhymes are fully fraught with serviceable vows:

> . . . and on the altar of her beauty
> You sacrifice your tears, your sighs, your heart:
> Write till your ink be dry, and with your tears

Moist it again, and frame some feeling line
That may discover such integrity:
For Orpheus' lute was strung with poets' sinews,
Whose golden touch could soften steel and stones,
Make tigers tame, and huge leviathans
Forsake unsounded deeps to dance on sands.
After your dire-lamenting elegies,
Visit by night your lady's chamber window
With some sweet concert; to their instruments
Tune a deploring dump: the night's dead silence
Will well become such sweet-complaining grievance.
This, or else nothing, will inherit her.

With oceans of tears, and twenty thousand soul-confirming oaths, the lover excites himself to a fervid bacchanalian orgy, and in his braggardism proclaims his lady "sovereign to all the creatures on the earth," threatening destruction to all who will not at once subscribe, and extermination to any who but dare to breathe upon her. In the intervals of these ecstatic outbursts, the lover stands before the picture of his love, sighing and weeping, wreathing his arms like a malcontent, until at length he walks off alone like one that hath the pestilence.

When cruel circumstance separates him from his lady, etiquette prescribes the proper behavior and the right demeanor. He resorts to the congenial solitude of woods or wilderness. In the earlier days of the cult, his manner on these occasions was more violent than ceremonious. Tristan, as Malory tells us, exiled and separated from his love, goes mad for grief; he would unlace his armor and go into the wilderness, where he "brast down the trees and bowes, and otherwhyle, when he found the harp that the lady sent him, then wold he harpe and playe therupon and wepe togethre." But in the course of time the manners of solitaries became more polite. Chaucer (or the author of the *Romaunt of the Rose*) advises the lover to cultivate a proper solitude:

> For ofte, whan thou bithenkist thee
> Of thy lovyng, where so thou be,
> Fro folk thou must departe in hie,
> That noon perceyve thi maladie.
> But hyde thyne harme thou must alone,
> And go forthe sole, and make thy mone.

It is only one more stage to the final artistic decorum of the habit. The lover in the French romance *Flamenca* "in the dark of night goes of custom to listen to the nightingale in the wood." Just, in fact, as does Valentine: in the intervals between inspecting the arms or allocating the booty of his bandit band, he takes his laments for Silvia into the woods for orchestral effects from the nightingales:

> These shadowy, desert, unfrequented woods
> I better brook than flourishing peopled towns:
> Here can I sit alone, unseen of any,
> And to the nightingale's complaining notes
> Tune my distresses and record my woes.

Such is the way of lovers in romances, and in *The Two Gentlemen of Verona*. Their state of spiritual ecstasy is revealed by the progressive etherialization of their sustenance. A collection of the menus of romantic feasts is more than a gastronomic document. In the beginnings of romance, eating and drinking was a major occupation. Owein ate and drank "whilst it was late in the time of the nones"; and once he was bidden to a feast which took three months to consume and had taken three years to prepare. But later, the initiate have so far purged their mortal grossness that eating and loving begin to appear incompatible. Again the *Romaunt of the Rose* brings the evidence:

> Such comyng and such goyng
> Such hevynesse and such wakyng

> Makith lovers, withouten wene,
> Under her clothes pale and lene.
> For love leveth colour ne cleernesse,
> Who loveth trewe hath no fatnesse;
> Thou shalt wel by thy-silf ysee
> That thou must nedis assaied be;
> For men that shape hem other weye
> Falsly her ladyes to bitraye,
> It is no wonder though they be fatt,
> With false othes her loves they gatt.
> For oft I see suche losengours
> Fatter than abbatis or priours.

On occasion, the true lover, like Jehan in *Jehan and Blonde,* is like to fade away, and can only eat when his lady serves the dishes to him with her own delicate hands. Our Valentine had been a good trencherman before he became a romantic lover; in those days, when he fasted, it was presently after dinner. But once he becomes a votary, not even ambrosia nor nectar is good enough for his ethereal table: "now can I break my fast, dine, sup, and sleep upon the very naked name of love." How he thrives on this diet will become a primary article of the literary and dramatic criticism of *The Two Gentlemen of Verona.*

So much for the spirit of romance in the play. Now for the world in which it is set—since, taking its religion thence, it must also take the romantic world in which such religion may reveal itself. Not men living dully sluggardized at home, but those bred and tutored in the wider world, seeking preferment out, trying their fortunes in war or discovering islands far away—these are they who have scope to put such religion to the proof. So in *The Two Gentlemen of Verona,* the scene is laid in Italy, the country which to Shakespeare's fellows was the hallowed land of romance. But it is an Italy of romance, not of physiographic authenticity. It has inland waterways unknown to geographers; the journey from

Verona to Milan is a sea voyage; it is indeed a scenario in which all the material trappings of romance may be assembled. Mountain and forest are indispensable, mountains which are brigand-haunted, and forests in the gloom of which are abbeys from whose postern gates friars creep into the encircling woods, so wrapt in penitential mood that lurking lions, prowling hungrily for food, are utterly forgotten. In such a locality, the tale of true love may run its uneven course. The poetically gifted lover meets such obstacles as a rival, at whom he hurls his cartel, and a perverse father whose plans for his daughter are based on such irrelevant considerations as the rivals' bank balances. The father's castle has its upper tower far from the ground, and built so shelving that to climb it is at apparent hazard of one's life. And here is the angelic daughter's chamber wherein she is nightly lodged, within doors securely locked, so that rescue can only be by a corded ladder to her chamber window. Then unexpected difficulties will be expected to intrude: the best-laid plot to carry her away is foiled by the machinations of a villain out of the least suspected quarter. Banishment naturally follows, and at length, with the flight of the heroine and the pursuit of her by the entire court, all will work out well by a series of surprising coincidences, to which rivals, brigands, friars, and lions are all somehow contributory. In this way, romantic love makes its romantic universe; and this in fact is the setting and the story of *The Two Gentlemen of Verona.*

This, both in matter and in spirit, is the tradition which the Elizabethan dramatists desired to lift bodily onto their comic stage. But something somehow went wrong. The spirit of medieval romance seemed to shrivel in the presence of comedy. Something similar had in fact happened in the real world outside the theater. The last hero of romance had lived gloriously and had died quite out of his part. Jacques de Lalaing, le bon chevalier, the mirror of knighthood who adorned the Burgundian court in the middle of the fifteenth century, had become the pattern of chivalry for all Europe. To his contemporaries, "fair was he as Paris, pious as Aeneas, wise as Ulysses, and passionate as Hector": and his exploits in tournament and in knight-errantry had carried his fame through many lands. He died an early death in 1453. But he did not die of a lover's broken heart; nor was he slain in tourney by a foeman worthy of his steel and of his thirty-two emblazoned pennants. He was shot down by a cannon ball in an expedition against the merchants and shop-keepers of Ghent. The gross ponderable facts of a very material world swept the symbol of an outworn ideal from off the face of the earth. So in *The Two Gentlemen,* a sheer clod of earth, Launce by name, will, quite unwittingly, expose the unsubstantiality of the romantic hero with whom the play throws him into contact. But we are anticipating. The consequences of Shakespeare's attempt to dramatize romance must be watched in closer detail.

There is little wonder that the Elizabethan dramatists saw the dramatic possibilities of such material, and did not at first perceive its dramatic disadvantages. They felt the dramatic thrill of following these lovers and setting the world at nought. Nor is it very difficult to set the geographical world at nought, at least to the extent of making inland seas in Italy or liberating living lions in its woods. Yet sometimes the distortions of the physical universe necessarily ventured by the romanticist entail violent wrenches of our common consciousness. The dukes of Shakespeare's Italy, for instance, apparently have magic power over the flight of time; for whilst a banished man is speaking but ten lines, the proclamation of his banishment is ratified, promulgated, and has become publicly known throughout the duchy, and sentinels have already been posted along the frontiers to prevent a surreptitious return of the exile to the land which he has not yet had time to pack his suitcase for leaving. It is a land too where optical illusions, or perhaps optical delusions, are the normal way of vision. A man seeking a page boy interviews an applicant for the post; he is just enough of a businessman to know that some sort of reason must be advanced for taking on a servant who can show neither character nor reference from previous employers, and so Proteus, engaging the disguised Julia, says that the engagement is specifically on the recommendation of the applicant's face; but he does not recognize, as he gazes into this face, that it was the one he was smothering with kisses a few weeks before when its owner, in her proper dress, was his betrothed. Yet these are really only minor impediments, requiring but a little and a by no means reluctant suspension of our disbelief. They are altogether insignificant compared with the reservations involved when romance displays its peculiar propensity for setting the world of man at nought. To satisfy its own obligations, it perforce demanded supermen; at all events, the heroes it puts forward as its votaries in the play are something either more or less than men.

Romantically speaking, Valentine is the hero, and not alone in the technical sense. In classical comedy the hero is simply the protagonist, the central figure who is the biggest butt of the comic satire. But here the protagonist is the upholder of the faith on which the play is built, the man with whom the audience is called upon to rejoice admiringly, and not the fellow at whom it is derisively to laugh. He is to play the hero in every sense of the word. Yet in the event, the prevailing spirit of romance endows him with sentiments and provides him with occupations which inevitably frustrate the heroic intention. The story renders him a fool. Convention may sanctify his sudden conversion from the mocker to the votary of love, and may even excuse or palliate his fractious braggardism when he insults Proteus with ill-mannered comparisons between Silvia and Julia. But his helplessness and his impenetrable stupidity amount to more than the traditional blindness of a lover. Even the clown Speed can see through Silvia's trick, when she makes Valentine write a letter to himself. But Valentine plays out the excellent motion as an exceeding puppet, unenlightened by the faintest gleam of common insight. And despite his vaunt that he knows Proteus as well as he knows himself, he is blind to villainies so palpable that Launce, the other clown of the piece, though he be but a fool, has the wits to recognize them for what they plainly are. The incidents are dramatically very significant, for both Launce and Speed come into the play for no reason whatever but to be unmistakable dolts. One begins to feel that it will be extremely difficult to make a hero of a man who is proved to be duller of wit than the patent idiots of the piece. Even when Valentine might have shone by resource in action, he relapses into conventional laments, and throws himself helplessly into the arms of Proteus for advice and consolation. Heroic opportunity stands begging round him when he encounters the brigands. But besides demonstrating that he can tell a lie—witness his tale of cock and bull about having killed a man—the situation only serves to discredit him still more: for the words of his lie, his crocodile tears for the fictitious man he claims to have slain, and his groundless boast that he slew him manfully in fight without false vantage or base treachery, are in fact nothing but an attempt to make moral capital by means of forgery and perjury. They have not even the recommendation of the Major General's tears for the orphan boy. When at length Valentine is duly installed as captain of the brigands, his chief occupation is to vary highway robbery with sentimental descants on the beauty of nature in her "shadowy, desert, unfrequented woods":

> Here can I sit alone, unseen of any—

and we already know his favorite hobby on these saunterings—

> And to the nightingale's complaining notes
> Tune my distresses and record my woes.

He is own brother to Gilbert's coster, who, when he isn't jumping on his mother, loves to lie abasking in the sun, and to the cutthroat, who, when not occupied in crimes, loves to hear the little brook agurgling and listen to the merry village chimes. But Valentine's utmost reach of ineptitude comes with what, again romantically speaking, is meant to be the heroic climax of the play. When he has just learnt the full tale of the villainy of Proteus, the code permits him neither resentment nor passion. Like a cashier addressing a char-woman who has pilfered a penny stamp, he sums up his rebuke—"I am sorry I must never trust thee more." And worse follows immediately. With but five lines of formal apology from the villain, Valentine professes himself so completely satisfied that he enthusiastically resigns his dar-ling Silvia to the traitor. Even Valentine must have seen that the gesture was a little odd, because he quotes the legal sanc-tion. It is the code, a primary article in the romantic faith— "that my love may appear plain and free." But it makes a man a nincompoop. Nor does it help much that after this pre-posterous episode Valentine is allowed to spit a little fire in an encounter with another rival, Thurio. He has already proved himself so true a son of romance that he can never again be mistaken for a creature of human nature.

Proteus is less hampered by romantic obligations; because the plot requires him to have just sufficient of salutary vil-lainy to make him throw over their commandments for his own ends. Yet the villain of romance suffers almost as much from the pressure of romanticism as does the hero. The noble fellows whom he, as villain, is called upon to deceive are such gullible mortals that little positive skill is necessary. Proteus can fool Thurio and Valentine and the Duke without exerting himself. But on the one occasion when he might have shown his wits, he only reveals his lack of them. Making love to Silvia, he meets her protest against his dis-loyalty to Julia by inventing the easy excuse that Julia is dead. Silvia replies that, even so, he should be ashamed to wrong Valentine. It is, of course, a tight corner: but the best Proteus can do is to say "I likewise hear that Valentine is dead." He might at least have displayed a little more ingenuity in invention; he fails in precisely such a situation as would have permitted the clown of classical comedy to triumph. Moreover, the main plot requires Proteus to be guilty of incredible duplicity, and of the most facile rapidity in changing morals and mistresses. But he need scarcely have made the change explicit in words so ineptly casual and banal as his remark: *"Methinks* my zeal to Valentine is cold." The phrase is accidentally in keeping with the unintended complacence he displays when, wooing the lady who will have none of him, he begins by informing her that "he has made her happy" by his coming. The trait becomes intolerably ludicrous when, all his sins forgiven him, and Julia restored to his arms, all he can utter in confession is his own fatuous self-conceit:

> O heaven, were man
> But constant, he were perfect.

It is, of course, a fine sentiment; but the audience, having seen Valentine, simply will not believe it.

Even the brigands of romance will scarcely stand the test of the stage. They enter with metaphorical daggers in mouths bristling with black mustachios and with desperate oaths. Callous and bloodthirsty ruffians, spoiling for a fight, their chief regret is that fate is sending only one defenseless traveler to be rifled instead of ten. But when the destined victim turns out to be two, courage perhaps abates a little: at all events, the travelers are warned to keep their distance, and throw over the booty or otherwise to assume a sitting posture, whilst the rifling is safely done by the desperadoes themselves. Perhaps this, and not his customary ineptitude in speech, is what makes Valentine address the villains as "My friends." But, of course, his assumption is, for the trade of brigandage, economically unsound. And so, with apologies for correcting him, Valentine is informed that he is not playing the game—"that's not so, sir; we are your enemies." But the outlaws are connoisseurs of masculine beauty, and Valentine's fine figure secures him an opportunity for a hearing: one cannot but note that this is the first time that any of his romantic attributes has made for his advantage, and that he misuses it scandalously for his lying brag. Hearing the fiction, however, the bandits feel at once that here is a fellow spirit, given, like themselves, to "so small a fault" as homicide. Straightway they implore him to show them his diploma in the modern languages, promising him the kingship of the band if it is of good honors' standard. Becoming convivial, they reveal their amiable dispositions in snatches of their life history. One has amused himself with attempts at abduction. Another, when the whim takes him, "in his mood," has the merry trick of stabbing gentlemen unto the heart; and his gaiety makes us forget that a mood in Shakespeare's English was not quite the casual fancy it now is. Another acclaims these and other "such like petty crimes" as congenial peccadilloes in his own repertory. By this time, the brigands have become so hilarious with their reminiscences, that they are no longer minded to scrutinize Valentine's academic credentials. They will take him for a linguist merely "on his own report," and, mainly because he "is beautified with goodly shape," they offer him the leadership, pathetically promising to love him as their commander and their king. Clearly such a thoroughly unbrigandlike procedure as this election has almost put them out of their parts. They must be allowed to recover in a traditional tableau. Daggers are whipped out, threats become fierce, and Valentine, with steel points at his throat, is given the choice of being a king or a corpse. Perhaps his fear is responsible for the odd proviso that "silly women" shall be exempt from the depredations of the gang over which he is to rule; but it is of course too much to expect of better men than Valentine to require them to anticipate a variation in the meaning of a word. Neither before nor after *The Two Gentlemen of Verona* has dramatic literature known a band of outlaws like to these—except once: there are the Pirates of Penzance: but then Gilbert meant his to be funny.

One begins to suspect that everything which is hallowed by the tradition of romance is made thereby of no avail for the purposes of drama. But there are Julia and Launce to reckon with; and these are figures universally accounted the most substantial beings in the play. So indeed they are. But they owe it entirely to the fact that they are under no obligation whatever to the code of romance. The behavior of Valentine is entirely conditioned by the doctrine of romantic love. But the code allowed to woman no duty but to excite by her beauty the devoted worship of her knight. If England instead of France had performed the final codification of chivalry, its women might have had other and less ladylike propensities, such, for instance, as King Horn's Rimenhild displayed. But when a French romance elaborates its portrait of womanhood, it gives her patience rather than character: women with the forcefulness of a distinct personality might have turned the energies of their knights away from consecrated paths of knighthood, as Chretien's Enide turned her Erec:

> Mes tant l'ama Erec d'amors
> Que d'armes mes ne li chaloit,
> Ne a tornoiemant n'aloit
> N'avoit mes soing de tornoiier.

Wherefore Chretien's romance tells of Erec's regeneration through the discipline by which he reduces his Enide to absolute submission. At the end, she has attained complete self-suppression—

Ne je tant hardie ne sui
Que je os regarder vers lui—

and, to the modern eye, has become the perfect pattern of an exquisitely charming nonentity.

When Shakespeare takes over a tradition whose women are like these, so long as he preserves the beauty of their faces, he can endow them with whatever character he may please. His Julia is a creation, not a convention. As she is a woman, acting on a woman's instinct—"I have no other but a woman's reason, I think him so because I think him so"— she is depicted in moods, whimsies, and vagaries which are in fact the stuff of dramatic characterization. Like the heroine of romance, she will cover her first love letter with kisses and press the precious manuscript to her heart. But like the spirited independent young lady of the world, she will not expose herself to the chuckles of her maid by exhibiting the common symptoms of her affections. Hence the pretended contempt, and the struggle to keep up appearances, even at considerable risk to the sacred document. But for what seriously concerns her love, Julia is too levelheaded to overreach herself. As far as may be, she will avoid the disapproval of opinion: but where there is no remedy, she will defy a scandalized world and undertake her pilgrimage of love. She knows the hazards of the road and the many weary steps it will involve. But she also knows her own capacities, and has duly taken note of all material things she will stand in need of. And although Proteus is a poor thing on whom to lavish so much love, Julia knows that love is indeed a blinded god; and in her capable hands even a Proteus may be molded to something worth the having.

Launce is another who insists on remaining in the memory. He has no real right within the play, except that gentlemen must have servants and Elizabethan audiences must have clowns. But coming in thus by a back door, he earns an unexpected importance in the play. Seen side by side with Speed, his origin is clear. Whilst Speed belongs to the purely theatrical family of the Dromios, with their punning and logic-chopping asininities, Launce harks back to the native Costard. And as Costard shows his relationship to Bottom by his skill in village theatricals, so Launce reveals by his wooing his family connection with Touchstone, and Touchstone's Audrey, who was a poor thing, but his own. All the kind of the Launces are thus palpably a mighty stock. Their worth, compared with that of the Speeds and the Dromios, is admirably indicated by Launce's consummate use of Speed's curiosity and of his better schooling. Launce gets his letter deciphered; he gets also an opportunity to display his own superior breeding and to secure condign punishment for the ill-mannered Speed: "now will he be swinged for reading my letter; an unmannerly slave, that will thrust himself into secrets! I'll after, to rejoice in the boy's correction."

Launce is happiest with his dog. Clownage can go no farther than the pantomimic representation, with staff and shoe and dog, of the parting from his home folks. Laughter is hilarious at Launce's bitter grief that his ungrateful cur declined to shed a tear. That Launce should expect it is, of course, the element of preposterous incongruity which makes him a clown. But when he puts his complaint squarely, that his "dog has no more pity in him than a dog," the thrust pierces more than it was meant to. Romance itself has expected no less largely of Valentine, of Proteus, and of the rest. It has demanded that man shall be more than man, and has laid upon him requisitions passing the ability of man to fulfill. At the bidding of romance, Valentine and Proteus have become what they are in the play, and the one thing they are not is men like other men. A further incident in which Launce is concerned takes on a similarly unexpected significance. He has made as great a sacrifice as did Valentine himself: he has given up his own cur in place of the one which Proteus entrusted to him to take to Silvia. But the effect hardly suggests that self-sacrifice is worldly-wise. And so once more it seems to bring into question the worldly worth of the code which sanctifies such deeds. Unintentionally, Launce has become the means by which the incompatibilities and the unrealities of romantic postulates are laid bare. And Launce is palpably the stuff of comedy: awakening our comedy sense, he inevitably sharpens our appreciation of the particular range of incongruities which are the province of comedy—the incongruity between what a thing really is and what it is taken to be.

Romance, and not comedy, has called the tune of *The Two Gentlemen of Verona* and governed the direction of the action of the play. That is why its creatures bear so little resemblance to men of flesh and blood. Lacking this, they are scarcely dramatic figures at all; for every form of drama would appear to seek at least so much of human nature in its characters. But perhaps the characters of the Two Gentlemen are comic in a sense which at first had never entered the mind of their maker. Valentine bids for the sympathy, but not for the laughter of the audience: the ideals by which he lives are assumed to have the world's approbation. But in execution they involve him in most ridiculous plight. He turns the world from its compassionate approval to a mood of skeptical questioning. The hero of romantic comedy appears no better than its clowns. And so topsy-turvy is the world of romance that apparently the one obvious way to be reputed in it for a fool is to show at least a faint sign of discretion and of common sense. Thurio, for instance, was cast for the dotard of the play, and of course he is not without egregious folly. But what was meant in the end to annihilate him with contempt turns out quite otherwise. Threatened by Valentine's sword, he resigns all claim to Silvia, on the ground that he holds him but a fool that will endanger his body for a girl that loves him not. The audience is invited to call Thurio a fool for thus showing himself to be the one person in the play with a modicum of worldly wisdom, a respect for the limitations of human nature, and a recognition of the conditions under which it may survive. Clearly, Shakespeare's first attempt to make romantic comedy had only succeeded so far that it had unexpectedly and inadvertently made romance comic. The real problem was still to be faced.

MARK VAN DOREN

From Shakespeare

In its kind *The Two Gentlemen of Verona* is not nearly as good as *The Taming of the Shrew* is in the kind called farce. But Shakespeare will soon do better in the kind he now discovers, and with one exception, *The Merry Wives of Windsor,* he is never to follow any other. *The Two Gentlemen of Verona* is a slight comedy and it minces uncertainly to an implausible conclusion, but it is Shakespeare's own and it sets his course. His problem henceforth is not to keep his fun outside the range of feeling but to keep his feeling within the range of fun; or rather it is to mingle them so that wit and emotion are wedded in an atmosphere which is as grave as it is smiling, as golden as it is bright. This atmosphere, so natural to man's life, so easy to breathe, and so mellow in its hue, is uniquely Shakespeare's, and it will be sufficient for his purposes in comedy; in its amber light he can go anywhere and consider everything, and his people can speak with the richest variety. Its elements are scarcely compounded in *The Two Gentlemen of Verona,* which is only a copy of what is to come; but for that very reason they are separately recognizable, they can be witnessed in the process of creation.

Valentine's opening speech announces the tone as he dis-

From *Shakespeare* by Mark Van Doren. New York: Henry Holt and Co., 1939; London: George Allen & Unwin, Ltd., 1941. Copyright 1939 by Mark Van Doren. Reprinted by permission of Holt, Rinehart and Winston, Inc.

courses to his fellow gentleman concerning the advantages of travel. "Such wind as scatters young men through the world" will soon blow both the heroes—rather stiff and humorless figures, newborn in Shakespeare's comic universe—from Verona to Milan, where one of them will forget his beloved Julia and plot to steal the other's Silvia. So far they are at peace, and their voices move lightly through the cadences of a graceful, breeze-haunted music. Valentine's speech is indeed a poem:

> Cease to persuade, my loving Proteus.
> Home-keeping youth have ever homely wits.
> Were 't not affection chains thy tender days
> To the sweet glances of thy honor'd love,
> I rather would entreat thy company
> To see the wonders of the world abroad
> Than, living dully sluggardiz'd at home,
> Wear out thy youth with shapeless idleness.
> But since thou lov'st, love still and thrive therein,
> Even as I would when I to love begin.

$$(1.1.1-10)$$

The rhyme at the end is amateur, but Valentine has caught the tone which will be heard henceforth in the golden world of gentlemen where Shakespeare's comedy will occur. It is a world whose free and graceful movement finds a symbol for itself in the travel of young men:

> Some to the wars, to try their fortune there;
> Some to discover islands far away;
> Some to the studious universities.

$$(1.3.8-10)$$

They are awaited somewhere by ladies of fine and disciplined feeling; or they will be followed, as Proteus in the present case is followed by Julia, in brave disguise and be served as pages by the very sweethearts they have lost. The ladies will be accustomed to compliment:

Valentine.   Sweet lady, entertain him
   To be my fellow servant to your ladyship. . . .

Silvia.   Servant, you are welcome to a worthless mistress.

Proteus.   I'll die on him that says so but yourself.

Silvia.   That you are welcome?

Proteus.   That you are worthless.
                                   (2.4.103–04, 112–14)

In their grace they understand the arts both of bestowing and of receiving praise. And their ideal might be such a man as Eglamour, whom Silvia invites to be her escort as she follows Valentine:

> Thyself hast lov'd; and I have heard thee say
> No grief did ever come so near thy heart
> As when thy lady and thy true love died. . . .
> I do desire thee, even from a heart
> As full of sorrows as the sea of sands,
> To bear me company.
>   (4.3.19–21, 33–35)

They are not wailing women; their grief is delicate, well-taught, tender, and half-concealed. They are at home in romance: Valentine must climb to Silvia by a corded ladder, Julia must knit up her hair in silken strings with twenty odd-conceited truelove knots (2.7.45–46), and there will be outlaws in the dangerous forest—hardly dangerous themselves, once a sweet lady adventures among them. And they live for that love which is both "a mighty lord" (2.4.135) and as tenderly capricious as

The uncertain glory of an April day   (1.3.85)

So do their gentlemen live for love of each other. Friendship is one of the gods here, and he has given laws which Proteus will find it going against the grain to break, so that soliloquies will be necessary before he can comprehend the depth of his default. He has not heard Valentine describe him to the Duke of Milan, but the language would have been familiar:

> I knew him as myself, for from our infancy
> We have convers'd and spent our hours together;
> And though myself have been an idle truant,
> Omitting the sweet benefit of time
> To clothe mine age with angel-like perfection,
> Yet hath Sir Proteus, for that's his name,
> Made use and fair advantage of his days. . . .
> He is complete in feature and in mind
> With all good grace to grace a gentleman.
>
> (2.4.61–67, 72–73)

It is such a friend that Proteus betrays, and his exclamation at the close, after the reconciliation which no one believes,

> O heaven! Were man
> But constant, he were perfect. That one error
> Fills him with faults,
>
> (5.4.110–12)

covers his untruth to Valentine no less than his abandonment of Julia.

"Heaven-bred poesy," as the Duke puts it, is natural to the mood of this world. And music is so much so that we cannot be surprised to find an excellent sweet song, Who is Silvia, built into the key scene of the play—laced firmly into it with more than simple irony, for Julia, who hears it sung to her rival, does not know that Proteus is pretending to sing it for

Thurio. Nor can we fail to note the balances set up here and there—between Julia's coyness (1.2) and Silvia's (2.1), between Proteus's concealment of a letter (1.3) and Valentine's concealment of a ladder (3.1)—as phrases are balanced in music. And the favorite subjects for quibble are note, burden, sharp, flat, bass, string, and change.

Of quibbles there are many in the play; too many, since they are the only device yet known by Shakespeare for securing the effect of wit and he must overwork them. Valentine and Proteus turn directly in the first scene from talk of travel to an exchange of puns; and the servants, Speed and Launce, are soon at it in their own different fashions. Wit belongs of course in such a world, but this early sample of it is dry and curiously spiritless. It is almost purely verbal. "Your old vice still," says Speed to Launce (3.1.282); "mistake the word." Both masters and men, not to speak of Julia with her maid Lucetta, have caught it like the plague. It does not give them the gaiety which their successors in Shakespearean comedy will have, and which will never depend on puns for its expression, though puns will by no means disappear. There is in fact no gaiety in *The Two Gentlemen of Verona* outside of a few scenes dealing with the sensible Launce and his unwanted dog. Launce looks forward not merely to the Launcelot Gobbo whose name he suggests but to a whole line of clowns whose humor is in their hearts and stomachs rather than on their tongues. Speed looks backward to barrenness and will not thrive.

One of the interesting things about *The Two Gentlemen of Verona* is the studies it contains of things to come in Shakespeare. Julia is something like Portia when she discusses suitors with her maid (1.2), and something like Viola when she discusses herself in disguise (4.4). Proteus tells almost as many lies as Bertram does in *All's Well That Ends Well*. The Friar Patrick at whose cell Silvia can arrange to meet Eglamour is soon, in *Romeo and Juliet*, to change his name to Laurence; and indeed there is already a Friar Laurence here (5.2.37). And the forest near Mantua which Valentine finds so much more agreeable than "flourishing peopled towns" is a promise of Arden. But *The Two Gentlemen of Verona* is at best half-grown. Its seriousness is not mingled with its mirth. It has done a great deal in that it has set a scene and conceived an atmosphere. It has done no more.

PAULA S. BERGGREN

"More Grace Than Boy":
Male Disguise in *The Two Gentlemen of Verona*

Very few readers come to *The Two Gentlemen of Verona* before having read at least one of Shakespeare's later comedies; thus Julia's conventional decision to put on boy's clothes is likely to be judged by the measure of *As You Like It* or *Twelfth Night*, surely the two plays that exploit the convention most fully. Yet to understand how male disguise works in *The Two Gentlemen of Verona*, one must adjust assumptions drawn from the later comedies. For this play, as its title suggests, takes a male-centered view of the world and consequently, as we shall see, asks for special qualities in its disguised heroine.

In some ways Julia's experience seems typical: like most of the later comic heroines, she announces that she puts on boy's clothes for self-protection, to "prevent / The loose encounters of lascivious men" (2.7.40–41). In *As You Like It* and *Twelfth Night*, the heroine's initial caution proves unnecessary, with the happy and unexpected result that wearing men's clothing primarily promotes the heroine's fortunes in love. Julia's disguise, by contrast, achieves its original purpose: in a play where "lascivious men" do attack women, she proceeds unmolested.

Julia's disguise fails, on the other hand, to further her

This essay was written for the Signet Classics Shakespeare.

relationship with Proteus. Rosalind has only just met Orlando at the beginning of *As You Like It,* and Viola only heard of Orsino when *Twelfth Night* begins. Their transformed states allow them to know the men they love, who, in turn find themselves drawn to unusually attractive boys. Conversely, Julia and Proteus are in love when *The Two Gentlemen of Verona* begins. Her disguise makes her invisible rather than desirable; unseen by Proteus, she must stand by and hear him blithely declare her dead. When she does present herself to him as a page boy, she may awaken subconscious memories of her female self that lead Proteus to hand her the ring she had herself given him. Yet her "face" and "behavior" (4.4.67) recommend her only to serve as a go-between, to deliver her ring to "Madam Silvia." To the page boy Sebastian, Proteus acknowledges that the ring's owner lives, but no sensitivity to the owner's proximity shakes his determination to sue for Silvia's favors.

Not only does Julia's disguise fail to move the man she loves, its original purpose is undercut by the strong presence of Silvia in *The Two Gentlemen of Verona.* All the comic heroines in male disguise share the romantic spotlight with another major heroine, but none is so much in the other's shadow as Julia. For while dressed as a woman, Silvia undertakes to do precisely what Julia felt she needed to disguise herself to manage. Silvia too decides to follow her love, and exceeds Julia in devotion by following him into banishment after contriving to escape from her father's control. She enlists protection, certainly, as did Julia, and in choosing a male escort in place of self-concealment seems at first less courageous than a girl who goes a further distance disguised and on her own. But Silvia from the start is prepared to do without Sir Eglamour if necessary (4.3.37), and, of course, Sir Eglamour abandons her at the first sign of danger. Twice outraged by "lascivious men," Silvia nevertheless emerges unharmed and successfully reunited with

Valentine, who saves her, while Julia contents herself with Proteus, who betrayed her.

The feckless Sir Eglamour, it may be recalled, is spoken of early in the play as one of Julia's suitors in Verona. His unexplained removal to the court of Milan, often taken as evidence of an unfortunate lack of concentration on Shakespeare's part, may more profitably be interpreted as a sign of an unusual symbiotic relationship between the two heroines of *The Two Gentlemen of Verona.** At first, Silvia threatens to subsume much of the interest originated by Julia. Although we hear Julia pondering the merits of three suitors (among them Sir Eglamour) who "every day with parle encounter" her (1.2.5), the lady we actually see surrounded by three suitors is Silvia. In the opening scene of the play, Proteus fears and Speed confirms Julia's disdain of his letter: "she's as hard as steel," the messenger reports (1.1.140–41). The men in Verona, it seems, stereotype Julia as the traditional hard-hearted mistress of Petrarchan love poetry. The audience knows better, however, for in the next scene we learn that Speed has mistakenly delivered the letter to Lucetta. As her lady's surrogate, she makes a more convincing Petrarchan mistress than does Julia herself, whom we soon see scrambling on the floor to pick up the pieces of her letter. We must wait for Act 2 to discover in Silvia a more authentic embodiment of the masculine fantasy of feminine power that Proteus attributes to Julia but relocates the instant he sees the real thing.

By its stage deployment of the two heroines, *The Two Gentlemen of Verona* frequently gives theatrical force to the relative subordination of Julia. Praising Silvia, Valentine deems Julia fit merely to be his lady's handmaid,

*In "Identity and Representation in Shakespeare," *ELH* 49 (1982): 339–62, Barry Weller says that Proteus and Valentine "provide patterns for each other's actions and emotions, so that their progress through the play is not so much mirrored as filled with echoes and syncopated repetition" (p. 350). A similar syncopation, it seems to me, may be observed in the relationship of Silvia to Julia.

　　　　　　　　　dignified with this high honor—
To bear my lady's train, lest the base earth
Should from her vesture chance to steal a kiss.

　　　　　　　　　　　　　　　　　(2.4.157–59)

Girls in doublet and hose forfeit such sartorial compliments; and the implied posture envisaged for Julia here, stooping down to lift up Silvia's garment, is one we have already seen her in as she retrieves Proteus's letter. When the two heroines actually appear on stage together for the first time, Julia in her page boy's outfit lurks in shadow below while Silvia shines down from her tower, above, like the "pale queen of night" (4.2.97) by whom she swears.*

　　Even when Julia is the social superior, as in her scenes at home with Lucetta, she plays an oddly subordinate role. Bertrand Evans points out that in *The Merchant of Venice,* where mistress and maid review the lady's suitors in a scene very like Act 1, Scene 2 of *The Two Gentlemen of Verona,* "Shakespeare knew to give the witty descriptive lines to Portia, not Nerissa."† Let us consider, however, that Julia's reticence fits better a young woman who (quite unlike the preening Portia) dwells on her "modesty" (1.2.41,55), both here and in the momentous scene where, having boldly proposed to follow Proteus in male disguise, she leaves it to Lucetta to work out the details of her physical imposture. Still, she sets careful limits on Lucetta's ingenuity: she must be a "well-reputed page" (2.7.43), she will not cut her hair (which would be a drastic step, akin to self-mutilation, for a

---

*Silvia's name, of course, links her to the woods, and the goddess of the moon is also the goddess of the hunt. See the discussion of Silvia as "the moon goddess" in W. Thomas MacCary, *Friends and Lovers: The Phenomenology of Desire in Shakespearean Comedy* (New York: Columbia University Press, 1985), pp. 99–108. For a different view of the significance of Silvia's name, cf. Jonathan Goldberg, "Shakespearean characters: the generation of Silvia," in *Voice Terminal Echo: Postmodernism and English Renaissance Texts* (New York: Methuen, 1986), pp. 68–100.

†Introduction, *The Two Gentlemen of Verona,* ed. Bertrand Evans (New York: New American Library, Signet Classics, 1964), p. lxv.

Renaissance woman), and she shrinks even from discussing the sexual indelicacy of an ornamental codpiece. She asks Lucetta to think what will be "meet" and "mannerly" (58) and then drops the issue. By the time we see her as a page boy, she has journeyed to Milan and located Proteus. Whatever charm her disguise may initially have held for her has long since passed and goes unremarked.

The pun on "mannerly" and Lucetta's saucy consideration of codpieces should remind us that in the sixteenth and seventeenth centuries, these scenes of boy actors playing girls who dress up as boys had an extra-dramatic dimension difficult for modern audiences to appreciate. Twentieth-century Americans assign one set of meanings to a woman wearing pants, having to do with taking control of, perhaps even displacing, men. We believe the woman in pants empowered, in other words, a belief that (especially) Rosalind's dominant role in *As You Like It* seems to affirm existed even in Shakespeare's day. Having boys successfully play the roles of Rosalind and Portia, female characters who then successfully play boys, must have added a concrete piquancy to the abstract notion of a strong-willed woman's "manliness." Yet since the same boys were equally successful playing shy or unobtrusive women (and since not all men are strong), there is nothing intrinsically assertive about wearing male disguise. In *The Two Gentlemen of Verona,* a play where Proteus's proclivity for change endangers friendship, love, and social harmony, a boy-heroine exulting in deft and tantalizing self-metamorphosis would exacerbate rather than resolve the dramatic crisis.

As You Like It and *Twelfth Night* go on to investigate the process by which the thrice-disguised boys acquire a fluid sexual identity, recognizing that, as potential partners, they seem capable of satisfying any sexual taste. Once conscious of the universal appeal inherent in their multiple selves, the disguised heroines of the later comedies take on almost superhuman powers. Julia does not. But a Rosalind, a Portia, or even a Viola would be an impediment in *The Two Gentlemen of Verona,* where male disguise provides little occasion for erotic dazzle. Although sexually titillating considerations have a place in the critique of male fashion conducted by Lucetta and Julia in 2.7, the early play fails to dramatize them, and with good reason: ultimately it is not the sexual but the social ingredient of Julia's disguise that counts. Julia becomes so faithful a servant to Proteus that, as Sebastian, she perseveres in an errand whose success would be fatal to her deepest desires. In a play focused more on selfishness than on sex, her selflessness restores order.

The Two Gentlemen of Verona explores the virtues of service in a variety of characters. Two of them serve for reward: Valentine, a courtly lover whom Silvia briskly calls "servant" (2.1.97; 2.4.1), wants love; Speed, a witty messenger, wants money. Launce and Julia, as several critics have astutely noted, are set against them and each other.* Launce enters the play directly after Julia's silent farewell to Proteus and leaves it, demoted to a "slave" (4.4.62), just as Sebastian prepares to follow him into Proteus's service. In his last speech, Launce shows us that Proteus is like a dog and Julia like Launce, for both clown and page boy pay for the willful indiscretions perpetrated by creatures whom they love better than themselves.

The special quality of male disguise in *The Two Gentlemen of Verona* is most evident in the scene where the messenger Julia approaches Silvia as her rival and discovers instead her staunchest supporter. The symbiotic blending of the two heroines reaches its apex when Silvia projects herself empathetically into the plight of a woman she thinks she has never seen, while speaking directly to this woman. To

---

*Most notable is Harold F. Brooks, "Two Clowns in a Comedy (to say nothing of the Dog): Speed, Launce (and Crab) in 'The Two Gentlemen of Verona,' " *Essays and Studies 1963,* ed. S. Gorley Putt (London: John Murray, 1963), pp. 91–100. See too the introduction to the play in the Arden series by the editor, Clifford Leech (London: Methuen, 1969), pp. lv–lvi, lxi.

cover "his" inadvertent expression of gratitude on Julia's behalf, "Sebastian" must remember that he speaks *for* rather than *as* Julia. Julia in male disguise then demonstrates that one best reaches others by suppressing the self. Although we hear a remote, fictional Julia described as having wept at the sight of Sebastian playing Ariadne, the Julia we see does not weep at the raw truth of her own loss (and in Sebastian's invention we have no way of knowing whether the weeping Julia is to be thought of as already abandoned by the Theseus-like Proteus or not). These are tears of empathy,* shed by the fictive Julia and the "real" Silvia in response to the acting boy in boy's clothes who projects himself as fully into the woman's part as he fits perfectly into the heroine's dress.

This invented scene is supposed to have taken place at Pentecost, the Christian festival that comes fifty days after Easter and celebrates the descent of the Holy Ghost, a descent that reenacts the willingness of divinity to take on an inferior form in order to achieve the salvation of others. In *The Two Gentlemen of Verona,* taking on male disguise is to assume inferior status, for it is a world of "lascivious men," not to be trusted. By becoming a man, Julia does nothing for herself. She is moved by grace to give up her own claims in order to move and serve others.

The Petrarchan male fantasy that animates gentlemen in Verona is dangerous because it falsely imputes power to women and then appeals to that power as a justification for unmannerly, unmanly behavior. If Proteus is the worse offender, neither is Valentine, who would violate the Duke's hospitality, free of blame. Julia and Silvia must work symbiotically, in tandem rather than in opposition, to expose the self-regarding masculine view of the feminine that their

---

*Cf. Lisa Jardine, *Still Harping on Daughters* (Brighton: Harvester, 1983), pp. 30–33: Jardine, arguing against the presence of any real emotion on the part of two boys pretending to be women, compares weeping for Ariadne to weeping for Hecuba in *Hamlet.*

lovers' mindless rehearsal of Petrarchan metaphors endorses. Silvia's job is to counter directly the fatuous praise of the false Proteus: "I am very loath to be your idol, sir" (4.2.126). But used to flattery, the Duke's daughter does give out her picture, even though she insists that it is an insubstantial "shadow" (4.4.120).

Julia's task in the play is to eradicate idolatry completely and to excavate the truth beneath the falsehood; she begins herself in falsehood, refusing a letter that matters more to her than anything except an unconsidered image of propriety. Yet moments later, she falls to the floor to retrieve the essential meaning if not the form of that letter.* She closes the play on the same note: again an emotion she would repress but cannot overtakes her and again she falls to the ground, now in a swoon, which reveals her to be the girl Julia and not the boy Sebastian. First and last, Julia reaches down to truth, like Ariadne, prostrate in her grief, and perhaps more tellingly, like the Holy Ghost descending on Pentecost.

The religious note heard in the reference to Pentecost reverberates in the name that the disguised Julia takes—Sebastian. To the extent that her choice evokes the image of a saint whose near-nude posture in martyrdom was a favorite artistic subject combining religious and erotic elements,† we recognize a link to Rosalind's taking the name of Ganymede, the Trojan boy loved by Zeus. Rosalind, loved by Phebe and Orlando, and ultimately seconded by the god of marriage in arranging for the ensuing confusion to be put right, revels in her androgynous charms. Sebastian's beauty may be as celebrated as Ganymede's, but Ganymede was not a Christian martyr. No one falls in love with Julia in male disguise; her costume offers her no gratification but the

---

*See Inga-Stina Ewbank, " 'Were man but constant, he were perfect': Constancy and Consistency in *The Two Gentlemen of Verona,*" in *Shakespearian Comedy,* ed. Malcolm Bradbury and David Palmer (New York: Crane, Russak, 1972), p. 41. This essay offers a brilliant account of the Petrarchan motifs in the play.

†Jardine calls Sebastian a "homosexual prototype," p. 19.

opportunity to serve others. In an age accustomed to see religious content in apparently secular images, Julia in male disguise lightly bodies forth a solemn sacrifice.

Even as it falsifies, then, male disguise is a device that reveals truth. As Sebastian explains to Silvia, the abandoned Julia has given up her Petrarchan affectations in the wake of Proteus's deceit:

> . . . since she did neglect her looking glass,
> And threw her sun-expelling mask away,
> The air hath starved the roses in her cheeks
> And pinched the lily-tincture of her face,
> That now she is become as black as I.

> (4.4.152–56)

The boy actor presumably has scrubbed off his makeup to become a girl in male disguise, and in this very act calling attention to his adolescent male self, he proclaims the generosity of the girl Julia, "more grace than boy" (5.4.166). If the page boy Julia misses both the pleasure and the power that male disguise affords the later disguised heroines, paradoxically in the moment when the boy actor shows himself as a boy, Julia proclaims the essence if not the form of Petrarchan spiritual beauty. To demean oneself for love, to throw away the mirror, to give up self-regarding—these central truths give substance to the disguised heroine of *The Two Gentlemen of Verona*.

PETER HOLLAND

The Two Gentlemen of Verona at Stratford-upon-Avon, 1991

In David Lodge's novel *Small World* (1984), Persse McGarrigle proposes to write a book on the influence of T. S. Eliot on Shakespeare; Thacker's production was surely about the influence of Dennis Potter on Shakespeare. But where in Potter's work the thirties songs mark the gap between the sordid and painful action of *Pennies from Heaven* and the language of sentimental song, in Thacker's *Two Gentlemen* the songs were a reassurance, translating the action to a thirties context in which the characters' obsession with love was validated. The audience needed to have no anxiety, for the songs guaranteed that the characters' sharp pains could and would be resolved within the terms of this romance world. Gershwin and Cole Porter inhabited the same world as the play, sharing the same perceptions of love as an uncontrollable anthropomorphized force which the characters so often voice; Valentine could have said with Gershwin "Love walked in." The play matched our yearning, that yearning that Potter's salesman so unavailingly voiced, that the songs should turn out to be true. As the opening and closing song reminded us, "Love is the sweetest thing."

The songs were also there as part of the play's visual—as well as aural—design. The band and chanteuse, placed

From *English Shakespeares* by Peter Holland. Cambridge: Cambridge University Press, 1997, pp. 87–91. Used by permission of the author and Cambridge University.

upstage, made sure the audience could enjoy the scene changes, making an entertainment of the fairly laborious process of moving rather too much furniture. But they also belonged with the spring blossom that decorated the stage, sharing with it the visual language of romantic springtime, the belief in the painful seriousness as well as the joyful immaturity of the play's view of love. One might want to say, with the wisdom supposedly born of age, that there is a great deal in the world that is more important than the concerns of this play but the production, with unflagging charm, denied the space for such cynicism. One had to be feeling really curmudgeonly to dislike this production.

Only at one point did Thacker misjudge the play: in the final company song that sentimentalized an ending that, up to that point, he had carefully and successfully refused to see as sentimental at all. Elsewhere the production proved capable of harsh pain and hard thinking. It was, in particular, remarkably successful at showing a character reconsidering himself or herself. Proteus's shift of tenses after first seeing Silvia was part of this: "She is fair; and so is Julia that I love— / That I did love" (2.4.198–99), Barry Lynch's pause after "that I love" creating the space for the character's oleaginous awareness of the need to redefine the time of that emotion.

When the Duke banished Valentine in 3.1, Richard Bonneville found in Valentine's soliloquy (170–87) a newly serious and wondering comprehension of the depth of Valentine's love for Silvia, showing Valentine puzzling out the ramifications of a love that was proving to be far more profound than he had yet considered it to be. From being a string of romantic clichés the speech moved the character into a new realm of feeling. I am not entirely convinced that the speech will quite do all that; the language still seems to be caught up in the narrowness of feeling possible in the range of romantic simile: "Except I be by Silvia in the night, /

There is no music in the nightingale" (178–79). But I respected the actor's attempt here, the ability to discard the Woosterish silly-ass style of Valentine earlier in the play, a style made possible both by his gullibility and by the way the thirties setting allowed for a tinge of P. G. Wodehouse.

Certainly the Duke's tricking of Valentine into a revelation of his elopement plot was beautifully handled, as the Duke prepared a picnic with malign intent; I had never before taken the instruction in recipes to remove the seeds from a melon as an encouragement to mimic disemboweling. The audience was way ahead of Valentine here and could be heard registering with a certain glee how innocently he strode into the trap. This was the Valentine that had become familiar in the production: young, handsome, good and very stupid. But the new access of the pain of love immediately afterward, in the soliloquy, refused the audience the right to patronize Valentine and forced them to reevaluate their view of the rather naive emotions and very naive confidence that had driven the character thus far.

Something similar happened in the fine playing of the scene between Silvia (Saskia Reeves) and Julia (Clare Holman) over Proteus's ring (4.4.108ff.). Again there was the transition between the audience's superiority to the action and its being surprised by the movement of the play. The audience's pain and sympathy for Julia when Proteus handed over the ring earlier in the scene was transformed into Silvia's pain and sympathy, a pain which was a precise expression of the women's similar positions, both vulnerable to the duplicity of Proteus. This scene, above all, managed to question and nearly to shatter the limits of romance, making of the women's vulnerability and the oppressive power of the man something that cut through the limited terms in which we are usually prepared to consider action in such a play. The transition was marked by the difference between Julia's comic tearing of Proteus's letter at

1.2.99s.d. and the harsh truths that lay behind Silvia's pained tearing of another letter from him here (4.4.131).

All problems in the play pale into insignificance beside Valentine's handing over of the nearly raped Silvia to the rapist: "All that was mine in Silvia I give thee" (5.4.83). Thacker's production, while not making the line unproblematic, offered it as a problem squarely confronted and tentatively solved. The production had, slowly and thoughtfully, allowed the significance of the women to grow as the play progressed, accepting their rights to decide what happens to them, their ability to initiate action and to actualize a form of friendship that the men talk of but cannot carry through into action. It seemed only logical and fully justifiable therefore to see Silvia resolving the play's crux. Anne Barton has argued that the moment is "Shakespeare's blunder . . . when without warning he gives ideal friendship precedence over love," seeing the "gift of Silvia to his friend" as "an intolerable clumsiness" which "has the effect here of negating the whole previous development of the comedy." Thacker's modest and highly intelligent solution reintegrated the moment into the development of the comedy as this production had explored it. After Proteus's "My shame and guilt confounds me" (73) Barry Lynch left a colossal pause, showing Proteus considering the possibility of conning Valentine again, before finally resolving on genuine repentance. If the audience hesitated slightly as to the genuineness of the repentance—and Lynch's smirk was so beguiling that one had to have a moment's pause—it was Silvia's silent intercession, a calm gesture of moving toward Proteus, that reassured them. Her judgment that this man was worth forgiveness justified Valentine's generosity, a symbolic act of love and respect for Silvia as much as of friendship for Proteus. Such work, accepting the play's difficulty, was as honest and intelligent as one could wish for.

Robert Smallwood, while applauding the subtlety of this revisionist treatment, had a moment's hesitation:

It was a daring and in many ways brilliant solution to what has so often been regarded, on the page, as an intractable problem: from seeming to many readers merely a property, a chattel, in the scene, the silent Silvia was made its motor, and comic form was thus preserved. One could argue, of course, that from the character being the chattel of the dramatist's chauvinist vision the actress had become the chattel of the director's sentimental inversion.

At such intractable moments of text, directors are confronted by three choices: to abandon the production completely, to attempt to recreate a Renaissance context for understanding the event or to redefine the moment in a way that, while the text may inadequately support it, at least allows the moment to be transformingly and intriguingly playable. Unwilling to take the first option, some directors attempt the second, as academic critics often now demand that such authenticity of referential meaning should be achieved or at least attempted.

It would be possible to play this climactic moment of *The Two Gentlemen of Verona* in terms of Renaissance concepts of friendship, though audiences probably would not be able to follow it; it is certainly possible to play it as a moment of male oppression that denies Silvia any of the space and power she has slowly started to achieve in the course of the play, but that would be to make the ending's mechanisms a bleak vision of the inevitable reassertion of patriarchal control. Thacker's version, a fellow-traveling male vision of female strength and generosity, allowed the play to reach its ending through an exploration of silence, the text's "failure" to mark Silvia's reaction allowing an open space for her approval, rejection or, as here, intervention, in the reconciliation of Valentine and Proteus.

FREDERICK KIEFER

The Two Gentlemen of Verona on Stage and Screen

Anyone who has seen *Two Gentlemen* in performance knows that although the play contains comic speech and stage business, it contains serious matter too: the betrayal of a friend, the betrayer's attempted rape of the woman he desires, and the wronged man's curious offer of his beloved to his rival. The mixture of elements has proved a challenge to directors and actors, who have achieved a balance only with difficulty. Earlier productions accentuated the lighter side of the play by cutting troubling speeches and adding music and spectacle. Some recent productions have had a dark tone, emphasizing the disturbing nature of sexual rivalry and the psychology responsible for it. Whatever the approach, this play has tested the ingenuity of directors and the patience of audiences.

Although no documentary evidence exists, *Two Gentlemen* was apparently first staged ca. 1593. We know virtually nothing of the original production. The staging requirements, however, are quite simple: a stage and a space "above" for Silvia's window. Like many other comedies of the time, the play requires no trapdoor, curtains, or descent machinery. Moreover, there would have been no scenery, no stage properties, and only a few hand properties: a ring, a portrait, a rope ladder, and several letters. The actors would have worn costumes, of course, but most of these would probably have been supplied from the company's wardrobe.

The earliest recorded performance of *Two Gentlemen* was David Garrick's production at the Theatre Royal, Drury Lane, on December 22, 1762. This proved a harbinger of future productions, for instead of using the earliest surviving script—that in the First Folio of 1623—Garrick used an adaptation with "alterations and additions" by Benjamin Victor. The "improvements" included the rearrangement of various scenes so that those situated in Verona were clustered together in the first act, while all of acts 2 and 3 were situated in Milan. Although this now seems eccentric, Victor recast the original chiefly because theatrical producers were using painted scenery, and it therefore made sense to minimize changes in the scenes. (We know about the scenery because a report survives from January 25, 1763, saying that one of the actors saved it from destruction during a riot at the theater.) Other of Victor's changes were motivated by a more profound discomfiture with the play. For instance, Victor omitted the offer of Silvia to Proteus in the last act, doubtless owing to the puzzling nature of Valentine's generosity. And in order to enhance the play's comedy, Victor brought Launce and Speed back onstage in the last act. Despite this extensive reworking of the play, Victor seems not to have found the right combination of adaptations to win and hold an audience; this production had only six performances.

When John Philip Kemble became manager of Drury Lane, he decided to stage *Two Gentlemen,* which he rightly saw as neglected. The playbills for his 1790 production announced that the play had not been acted in twenty years, and if this was not strictly accurate (there had been a single performance at Covent Garden in 1784), *Two Gentlemen* was certainly among the least performed of Shakespeare's plays in the eighteenth century. Although he restored the original script, this production failed. Kemble called the play "ineffectual," confessing, "I am sorry I ever took the trouble to revive it." Nevertheless, he tried again, producing the play at Covent Garden in 1808 and playing the role of Valentine himself. This time he used Benjamin Victor's version though he corrected some errors introduced by Victor (such as Julia's answering Proteus' letter before she receives it!). And Kemble, who had a penchant for naming Shakespeare's unnamed characters, made some changes his own: he christened the outlaws Ubaldo, Luigi, Carlos, Stephano, Giacomo, and Valerio. None of this tinkering saved the production, which had only three performances.

Instead of presenting *Two Gentlemen* in either of its extant forms, Frederick Reynolds in 1821 decided to recast the play completely, converting it into a music extravaganza at Covent Garden, where Charles Kemble was manager. Henry Rowley Bishop supplied the music; Shakespeare's other plays and sonnets were ransacked for lyrics. Responding to a growing taste for spectacle, Reynolds sought to delight the eye as well as the ear. The audience saw a ducal palace and the great square of Milan; a procession of actors exotically costumed as the Seasons and the Four Elements; Cleopatra's galley floating down a river; and a carnival featuring masquers, dancing girls, and mountebanks. Reynolds also capitalized on the new sophistication of spectacle that allowed spectators to see, in the Duke's garden, "an artificial mountain reaching to the clouds, the explosion of which discovered a gorgeous temple of Apollo." Although this entertainment departed even further from Shakespeare than Victor's version had, Reynolds at least found an enthusiastic reception: his production ran for twenty-nine performances.

Lavish spectacle alone, however, could not guarantee the success of *Two Gentlemen* in the form that Shakespeare wrote it. William Charles Macready had become manager of Drury Lane when he decided to restore Shakespeare's script in 1841. He prepared playbills that meticulously explained the significance of each set. The opening scene, for example, consisted of "the tombs of the Scaligeri, the former princes of Verona"; and the Duke's palace was adorned with escutcheons of the Sforza and Visconti families. Reviewers acknowledged the "beautiful scenery" but felt that the (apparently drab) costumes were deficient: "The characters were, in truth, rather underdressed (for the comedy in its spirit seems to demand a gay costume)." It was a sign of current taste that one reviewer carefully described the theater's new curtain: "crimson velvet with a broad gold fringe, and ornamented with large gold wreaths of laurel." Once again a respected theatrical manager found only frustration in staging *Two Gentlemen*.

Five years later Charles Kean tried his hand, cutting some scenes and altering the language. He presented *Two Gentlemen* at New York's Park Theater in 1846, playing the role of Valentine himself; his wife, Ellen Tree, played Julia. Neither this nor Benjamin Webster's production in London (with Kean) was a commercial triumph. Nor was the production by Samuel Phelps at Sadler's Wells during the 1856–57 season; although this staging received some critical acclaim, the record of three performances suggests a financial disappointment. Not surprisingly, the play went into eclipse for the next four decades.

Near the end of the nineteenth century, *Two Gentlemen* attracted new interest. The American manager and playwright Augustin Daly presented the comedy, with Ada Rehan as Julia, at his theater in New York during 1895 and, later, at his theater in London. He succeeded in finding some of the play's humor, for George Bernard Shaw wrote: "The scenes between Launce and his dog brought out the latent silliness and childishness of the audience as Shakespeare's clowning scenes always do: I laugh at them like a yokel myself." Shaw, however, found little else to praise. Although Daly was following long-established custom by employing musical embellishment, painted scenery, and special effects (including a thunderstorm in the last act), Shaw objected to Daly's practice of "altering, transposing, omitting, improving, correcting, and transferring speeches from one character to another." At last a thoughtful playgoer was beginning to wonder whether theatrical directors had gone too far in adapting Shakespeare.

Although developments in stagecraft and the new mode of lighting the show by gas and then by electricity drew huge audiences to Victorian theaters, the technical advances moved productions even further from Elizabethan practice. So did the widespread use of proscenium arch and front curtain, which created a sharp demarcation between audience and stage, inhibiting rapport between actor and spectator. Fortunately, scholarly directors began an effort to recover the theatrical conditions of Shakespeare's time. Prominent among the pioneers was William Poel, who became instructor for the Shakespeare Reading Society in 1887. This group sponsored recital performances: Shakespeare's plays were read aloud without distinct act and scene divisions, thus emulating the continuous action of the Elizabethan public playhouse; the plays were also recited without the cuts that had become commonplace in Victorian England. In 1892 the Society gave a recital of *Two Gentlemen* at St. James's Hall. And in 1896 Poel's Elizabethan Stage Society used the Merchant Taylors' Hall for a production (repeated at the Great Hall of the Charterhouse in 1897). Here Poel sought to break down the invisible barrier separating actors from audience; when Valentine, on his way into exile, left the stage, he moved through the midst of the audience, and the outlaws entered through the same space. Poel tried an even bolder experiment when Herbert Beerbohm Tree invited the Elizabethan Stage Society to present *Two Gentlemen* at a Shakespeare Festival in 1910 (the production was later repeated at the Gaiety Theatre, Manchester). Poel departed from contemporary practice in two important ways: he built an apron stage out over the orchestra pit of His Majesty's Theatre, and he eliminated the footlights that had become a theatrical fixture (the lights were instead hung from the balconies). By bringing actors closer to spectators, Poel demonstrated that such Elizabethan conventions as the soliloquy and the aside could be more effective than anyone had realized, and Shakespeare's verse had a new immediacy. A reviewer wrote of this *Two Gentlemen*: ". . . the lyric beauty of many of its passages came out with unusual freshness."

The first half of the twentieth century witnessed a number of productions, many influenced by Poel's example. These included the work of Harley Granville-Barker at the Court Theatre in 1904, Ben Greet at Stratford-upon-Avon in 1916, W. Bridges-Adams at Stratford in 1925, Robert Atkins in the same year at the Apollo Theatre (with John Gielgud as Valentine), and B. Iden Payne at Stratford in 1938. It was not until after the Second World War, however, that *Two Gentlemen* proved an unqualified hit. Denis Carey achieved this at the Bristol Old Vic in 1952. His production was innovative in its spirit: the play was animated by lyric grace and charm. The comedy of Launce and Speed (played by Michael Aldridge and Newton Blick) delighted audiences by making the wordplay, which can seem labored when the play is read in the study, come alive onstage. This production, which surprised people by its very success, was subsequently brought to London to redeem a lackluster season there.

Five years later, in 1957, Michael Langham's production opened at the Old Vic, London. Instead of seeing the play's contrivance and artificiality as impediments, Langham accentuated them. The actors wore costumes of the Regency: frilled shirts, tall hats, swirling cloaks. The unit set, representing Verona, Milan, and the forest by way of changing a backcloth, looked like a Romantic painting: a central fountain flanked by an ivy-covered tower and a ruined building. And the actors in their manner appeared to be imbued with the spirit of Gilbert and Sullivan. The costumes, set, and acting style worked collectively to produce an atmosphere, festive and frivolous, in which the play's potentially troubling action seemed less disturbing. Instead of coming across as a cad, Proteus, played by Keith Michell, emerged as a Byronic hero, overwhelmed by his own youthful passion.

At the same time that *Two Gentlemen* was finding receptive audiences in England, the play was having success in America, too. The challenge was daunting, for relatively few American actors were trained in speaking blank verse, and they had a tendency to emulate the features of British speech. In 1957, however, the Oregon Shakespeare Festival in Ashland presented the play without the affectation that sometimes marred American treatments of Shakespeare; a "relaxed naturalness" marked this production. The actors, directed by James Sandoe, seemed at home in their roles. That same year saw an even more celebrated production at the New York Shakespeare Festival in Central Park. This outdoor performance, directed by Stuart Vaughan, was characterized by vigor, ebullience, and physical action: the actors were literally kept in motion, using stairs on either side of the stage that led to an upper playing area. Jerry Stiller as Launce was singled out for praise, as was Anne Meara as Julia. Harold Clurman wrote: "Here was a consummate ensemble—down to the best cast dog I have ever seen on the stage." The joy of the actors and the directors was reflected in the stage business and sight gags they invented: the Duke was a horticulturist, with pruning shears and watering can at the ready; Eglamour was equipped with a huge sword that he kept tripping over; Silvia inspected purchases from a shopping spree. No longer was there any doubt that Shakespeare's play could, in the right hands, be a huge popular success. What Vaughan discovered, like Carey and Langham before him, was that the key to unlocking the play's humor was a deft touch, a buoyant spirit, and confidence that the potential for brilliant comedy was present in the script.

Curiously, no sooner had *Two Gentlemen* finally proved itself onstage than it suffered a relapse. Peter Hall's Stratford production of 1960 represented a giant step backward.

Reviewers complained of awkward pauses and inappropriate emphases in the speeches. Even worse, Hall used a revolving stage to accommodate changes in the scenery; this had the effect of making the action seem choppy and fragmented. Not even good performances by Eric Porter as the Duke and Derek Godfrey as Proteus could save this treatment. Paradoxically, it may have been the very success of productions in the 1950s that led to Hall's debacle, for as Shakespeare festivals proliferated around the globe and as even the most neglected of his plays began to receive their share of attention, directors felt increasing pressure to justify their own particular efforts. In practice this often meant finding an approach different from all those that had already been (successfully) tried. Sometimes the willingness to take risks has breathed life into a production, preventing it from becoming a stale duplication of earlier triumphs. But at times the effort has fallen flat.

Directorial ingenuity has worked best when it has made a Shakespearean play more accessible to an audience, as Robin Phillips demonstrated with his Royal Shakespeare Company production at Stratford-upon-Avon in 1970. He presented the play in modern dress; and Daphne Dare's set evoked the Riviera, with diving board and pool, monogrammed beachwear, and sunglasses. Phillips' purpose was apparent in the opening scenes where an athletic Valentine, in swimming attire, exercised with a beach ball. By contrast, Proteus was puny and watched his friend enviously. When Valentine exited, Proteus tested his muscles and found them wanting. By this means the director supplied a psychological explanation for the character's later behavior. Ian Richardson's playboy Proteus suffered from a sense of his own inadequacy, which led to the betrayal of his friend and to the wooing of Silvia. In 1975 Phillips again directed *Two Gentlemen,* this time at the Stratford Shakespeare Festival in Ontario, Canada. This production, codirected by David Toguri, had much in common with Phillips' 1970 endeavor.

As earlier, the setting was twentieth century, a world of health salons, cocktail bars, and Mafia chieftains. And again there was a marked physical contrast between Valentine, an amateur boxer, and a less-athletic Proteus.

In 1970 Mel Shapiro and John Guare adapted *Two Gentlemen* as a musical comedy; Guare wrote the lyrics, and Galt MacDermot composed the melodies. They were, in a sense, participating in the same impulse that had led Frederick Reynolds to set the play to music a century and a half earlier. The watchword of the late sixties and early seventies, however, was "relevance," and the adapters pursued this with a vengeance. The urban flavor of the production reflected its genesis in the New York Shakespeare Festival; the play toured all five boroughs of the city. And when it played at the open-air Delacorte Theater in Central Park, the set consisted of a three-tiered scaffold, suggesting the multistory buildings of the city just beyond the trees. The characters, moreover, made topical remarks (allusions to Vietnam, for instance), and their speeches contained numerous colloquialisms. Befitting the nature of New York, the cast was interracial: Proteus and Julia were Puerto Rican; Valentine and Silvia were black; and Launce had a Yiddish accent. The music reflected this ethnic diversity: Hispanics sang to a Caribbean beat, while the blacks performed in Motown style. This was a joyous production, and Joseph Papp moved it to Broadway, where it had 627 performances (and where the play lost the definite article in its title).

In 1981 the Royal Shakespeare Company decided to present *Two Gentlemen* alongside *Titus Andronicus,* both plays to be part of the same evening's entertainment. Necessarily, the two had to undergo major surgery; 850 lines were cut from *Titus,* 515 from *Two Gentlemen.* The point of this cutting and coupling was to enforce differences, thereby heightening the theatrical impact of each play. Although the scheme had a dubious premise—that the tragedy "looks to the past" whereas the comedy looks to "Shakespeare's future"—John Barton managed to intensify the comedy of *Two Gentlemen* both by the sharp contrast in mood between the two plays and by the specific recollection in *Two Gentlemen* of particular moments in the tragedy, still fresh in the minds of the audience. For example, Patrick Stewart's Eglamour, attired in armor, recalled his portrayal of the armed Titus; Sheila Hancock, who played Tamora in the tragedy, played the leader of the outlaws in the comedy; and the forest inhabited by the outlaws consisted of the same prop trees that served as forest in *Titus*. Perhaps never in its theatrical history had *Two Gentlemen* been presented in a stranger context, and the result was controversial; one reviewer called it an abomination. But the yoking of not so mighty opposites had the virtue of demonstrating Shakespeare's diversity at an early point in his career.

Unlike some better-known Shakespearean plays, *Two Gentlemen* has never been made into a movie, but it became part of the BBC television series in 1983. The keynote of this production was its interpretation of Proteus. Tyler Butterworth's character was a troubled man, full of second thoughts and self-doubts. During his soliloquy at the end of 2.4, the camera moved in for a closeup, revealing the face of a man in torment. As Proteus spoke of forsaking Julia and betraying Valentine, thunder was heard in the background; the sky darkened and the wind sprang up. Clearly, the storm without mirrored the storm within. His soliloquy in 4.2 was heartfelt too, and the result was to engender sympathy for the character even as he was pursuing a reprehensible course. There was, however, no glossing over of Proteus' attempted rape of Silvia: he violently ripped off the face mask that she had donned when she entered the forest. And when confronted by Valentine, the guilty Proteus wept, apparently out of shame. In his direction, Don Taylor adopted a tone altogether more serious than those of previous productions. If this TV adaptation sacrificed comic effect, it did so to achieve a psychologically explicable portrait of Proteus.

What we gain from a production like Taylor's is an enhanced appreciation of the pain that lies just beneath and, at times, on the very surface of the action. What we may lose is the sheer delight that a Shakespearean comedy can offer. Directors, of course, do not need to make either-or choices. Indeed, those productions that have accommodated the serious action most successfully have been those that exploited comic effect most exuberantly.

Bibliographic Note: Shakespeare Quarterly and *Shakespeare Survey* contain reviews of Shakespeare productions each year. In addition, readers may find short accounts of *Two Gentlemen* productions and references to reviews in the following books: William Babula, *Shakespeare in Production, 1935–1978: A Selective Catalogue* (New York and London: Garland, 1981); Samuel Leiter, ed., *Shakespeare Around the Globe: A Guide to Notable Postwar Revivals* (New York, Westport, Conn., and London: Greenwood Press, 1986). Many university libraries contain the BBC videotaped production of *Two Gentlemen*.

Addendum: The Last Decades of the Twentieth Century and the First of the Twenty-first

A 1984 production at Stratford, Ontario, directed by Leon Rubin, used contemporary dress, but not quite what the audience was wearing: The young lovers wore punk attire, with colored hair and metal accessories, and the adults wore suits. Valentine's servant, Speed, wore a black suit with white lapels and what seemed to be a somewhat crushed top hat; in the scene when Proteus parts from Julia, Proteus wore—well, not much of anything (the two were in bed—something unthinkable on the Elizabethan stage). Another production at Stratford, Canada, this one in 1991 and directed by

Richard Rose, also used modern dress: The opening scene was a photo shoot of a hockey team, with Proteus and Valentine wearing the appropriate gear.

Occasionally a director forgoes modern dress. Stuart Vaughan, who in 1957 directed a highly successful production at the New York Shakespeare Festival in Central Park (see above), in 1987 directed another successful production of *Two Gentlemen* in Central Park, this one using dress of the early seventeenth century. Vaughan thus avoided a museum-theater production, i.e., something that seemed to be an attempt to duplicate the original staging, and yet the old-fashioned costumes distanced the play from the present. Playgoers are so accustomed to seeing Shakespeare done in modern dress that they may not realize how unconventional Vaughan's decision was. One can indeed ask what is gained by using modern dress for this play, a play that draws so heavily on a convention of friendship that today's audiences can only wonder at or try to explain in erotic terms. In an interview in the *New York Times,* July 26, 1987, Vaughan said that he close "old-timey" costumes "because people didn't think the same way, or say the same things. I think we have to be very careful what period we put the play in so we're not contradicting their emotional content for the intelligent in the audience." It is all very well for us to insist that a play by Shakespeare is a classic—even if it is an early work—and that a classic is contemporary in every age, but we should also remember, in the words of L. P. Hartley's *The Go-Between,* that: "The past is a foreign country; they do things differently there." Vaughan in the interview continued: "I'm not really interested in the new for its own sake. . . . I think a work of art of any time has its own integrity. And if you can penetrate to the heart of the experience it's almost inevitably something nobody's seen before. That's why I don't strain myself too much hunting for strange and unexplored resonances that have to do with physical production. I feel my search should be elsewhere."

The production of the play at the new Globe, directed by Jack Shepherd in the "prologue season" of 1996, using modern dress (jeans, baseball caps, sunglasses) was notable chiefly for Mark Rylance's Proteus, played as a skulking stage villain. In 1998 Edward Hall directed the play at Stratford-upon-Avon, also in modern dress; judging from the reviews, it was relatively dark, emphasizing the thuggish nature of most of the characters to such an extent that audiences were hardly aware that the play is a comedy. Far more successful was David Thacker's 1991–92 production, also at Stratford-upon-Avon and later at the Barbican in London. Set in the 1930s (white flannels, cocktail dresses, wicker furniture, golf clubs, a cigarette case, big-band music), it effectively used songs by the Gershwins, Cole Porter, Irving Berlin and others. Thacker's production is discussed in this volume at some length by Peter Holland.

Given the play's thin stage history for four centuries, it is not surprising that productions do not abound in the early years of the twenty-first century. Only one production has aroused more than routine interest. Directed by Rachel Kavanaugh in 2003, the play was staged in London's Regent's Park. The greenery and the Gainsborough-like costumes pleased the eye (boots and ankle-length coats for the men, opulent frocks and piled-up hair for the women), and Proteus's stage villainy evoked good-natured boos from the audience. Add two excellent clowns and a very satisfactory dog, and the result was—for the average theatergoer if not for the professional Shakespearean—a most satisfying evening.

Bibliographic Note: Shakespeare Bulletin, Shakespeare Quarterly, and *Shakespeare Survey* contain reviews of productions. For useful short histories of the play on the stage, consult the editions of *Two Gentlemen of Verona* by Kurt Schlueter (1990) and William C. Carroll (2004). See also

Michael D. Friedman, *"The world must be peopled": Shakespeare's Comedies of Forgiveness* (2002), and Carol J. Carlisle and Patty S. Derrick, "The Two Gentlemen of Verona on Stage; Protean Problems and Protean Solutions," in *Shakespeare's Sweet Thunder: Essays on the Early Comedies,* ed. Michael J. Collins (1997), pp. 126–54, rptd. in *Shakespearean Criticism* 63: 361–73. Thirteen reviews of productions from 1821 to 1991 are reprinted in *Two Gentlemen of Verona: Critical Essays* (1996), ed. June Schlueter.

—SYLVAN BARNET

Suggested References

The number of possible references is vast and grows alarmingly. (The *Shakespeare Quarterly* devotes one issue each year to a list of the previous year's work, and *Shakespeare Survey*—an annual publication—includes a substantial review of biographical, critical, and textual studies, as well as a survey of performances.) The vast bibliography is best approached through James Harner, *The World Shakespeare Bibliography on CD-Rom: 1900–Present.* The first release, in 1996, included more than 12,000 annotated items from 1990–93, plus references to several thousand book reviews, productions, films, and audio recordings. The plan is to update the publication annually, moving forward one year and backward three years. Thus, the second issue (1997), with 24,700 entries, and another 35,000 or so references to reviews, newspaper pieces, and so on, covered 1987–94.

For guidance to the immense amount that has been written, consult Larry S. Champion, *The Essential Shakespeare: An Annotated Bibliography of Major Modern Studies,* 2nd ed. (1993), which comments briefly on 1,800 publications.

Though no works are indispensable, those listed below have been found especially helpful. The arrangement is as follows:

1. Shakespeare's Times
2. Shakespeare's Life
3. Shakespeare's Theater
4. Shakespeare on Stage and Screen
5. Miscellaneous Reference Works
6. Shakespeare's Plays: General Studies
7. The Comedies
8. The Romances

9. The Tragedies
10. The Histories

11. *The Two Gentlemen of Verona*

The titles in the first five sections are accompanied by brief explanatory annotations.

1. Shakespeare's Times

Andrews, John F., ed. *William Shakespeare: His World, His Work, His Influence,* 3 vols. (1985). Sixty articles, dealing not only with such subjects as "The State," "The Church," "Law," "Science, Magic, and Folklore," but also with the plays and poems themselves and Shakespeare's influence (e.g., translations, films, reputation).

Byrne, Muriel St. Clare. *Elizabethan Life in Town and Country* (8th ed., 1970). Chapters on manners, beliefs, education, etc., with illustrations.

Dollimore, John, and Alan Sinfield, eds. *Political Shakespeare: New Essays in Cultural Materialism* (1985). Essays on such topics as the subordination of women and colonialism, presented in connection with some of Shakespeare's plays.

Greenblatt, Stephen. *Representing the English Renaissance* (1988). New Historicist essays, especially on connections between political and aesthetic matters, statecraft and stagecraft.

Joseph, B. L. *Shakespeare's Eden: the Commonwealth of England 1558–1629* (1971). An account of the social, political, economic, and cultural life of England.

Kernan, Alvin. *Shakespeare, the King's Playwright: Theater in the Stuart Court 1603–1613* (1995). The social setting and the politics of the court of James I, in relation to *Hamlet, Measure for Measure, Macbeth, King Lear, Antony and Cleopatra, Coriolanus,* and *The Tempest.*

Montrose, Louis. *The Purpose of Playing: Shakespeare and the Cultural Politics of the Elizabethan Theatre* (1996). A poststructuralist view, discussing the professional theater "within the ideological and material frameworks of Elizabethan culture and society," with an extended analysis of *A Midsummer Night's Dream.*

Mullaney, Steven. *The Place of the Stage: License, Play, and Power in Renaissance England* (1988). New Historicist analysis, arguing that popular drama became a cultural institution "only by . . . taking up a place on the margins of society."

Schoenbaum, S. *Shakespeare: The Globe and the World* (1979). A readable, abundantly illustrated introductory book on the world of the Elizabethans.

Shakespeare's England, 2 vols. (1916). A large collection of scholarly essays on a wide variety of topics, e.g., astrology, costume, gardening, horsemanship, with special attention to Shakespeare's references to these topics.

2. Shakespeare's Life

Andrews, John F., ed. *William Shakespeare: His World, His Work, His Influence,* 3 vols. (1985). See the description above.

Bentley, Gerald E. *Shakespeare: A Biographical Handbook* (1961). The facts about Shakespeare, with virtually no conjecture intermingled.

Chambers, E. K. *William Shakespeare: A Study of Facts and Problems,* 2 vols. (1930). The fullest collection of data.

Fraser, Russell. *Young Shakespeare* (1988). A highly readable account that simultaneously considers Shakespeare's life and Shakespeare's art.

———. *Shakespeare: The Later Years* (1992).

Schoenbaum, S. *Shakespeare's Lives* (1970). A review of the evidence and an examination of many biographies, including those of Baconians and other heretics.

———. *William Shakespeare: A Compact Documentary Life* (1977). An abbreviated version, in a smaller format, of the next title. The compact version reproduces some fifty documents in reduced form. A readable presentation of all that the documents tell us about Shakespeare.

———.꞉ *William Shakespeare: A Documentary Life* (1975). A large-format book setting forth the biography with facsimiles of more than two hundred documents, and with transcriptions and commentaries.

3. Shakespeare's Theater

Astington, John H., ed. *The Development of Shakespeare's Theater* (1992). Eight specialized essays on theatrical companies, playing spaces, and performance.

Beckerman, Bernard. *Shakespeare at the Globe, 1599–1609* (1962). On the playhouse and on Elizabethan dramaturgy, acting, and staging.

Bentley, Gerald E. *The Profession of Dramatist in Shakespeare's Time* (1971). An account of the dramatist's status in the Elizabethan period.

———. *The Profession of Player in Shakespeare's Time, 1590–1642* (1984). An account of the status of members of London companies (sharers, hired men, apprentices, managers) and a discussion of conditions when they toured.

Berry, Herbert. *Shakespeare's Playhouses* (1987). Usefully emphasizes how little we know about the construction of Elizabethan theaters.

Brown, John Russell. *Shakespeare's Plays in Performance* (1966). A speculative and practical analysis relevant to all of the plays, but with emphasis on *The Merchant of Venice*, *Richard II*, *Hamlet*, *Romeo and Juliet*, and *Twelfth Night*.

———. *William Shakespeare: Writing for Performance* (1996). A discussion aimed at helping readers to develop theatrically conscious habits of reading.

Chambers, E. K. *The Elizabethan Stage*, 4 vols. (1945). A major reference work on theaters, theatrical companies, and staging at court.

Cook, Ann Jennalie. *The Privileged Playgoers of Shakespeare's London, 1576–1642* (1981). Sees Shakespeare's audience as wealthier, more middle-class, and more intellectual than Harbage (below) does.

Dessen, Alan C. *Elizabethan Drama and the Viewer's Eye* (1977). On how certain scenes may have looked to spectators in an Elizabethan theater.

Gurr, Andrew. *Playgoing in Shakespeare's London* (1987). Something of a middle ground between Cook (above) and Harbage (below).

———. *The Shakespearean Stage, 1579–1642* (3rd ed., 1992). On the acting companies, the actors, the playhouses, the stages, and the audiences.

———, and Mariko Ichikawa. *Staging in Shakespeare's Theatres* (2000). Like Alan C. Dessen's book, cited above, a careful analysis of what the Elizabethans saw on the stage.

Harbage, Alfred. *Shakespeare's Audience* (1941). A study of the size and nature of the theatrical public, emphasizing the representativeness of its working-class and middle-class audience.

Hodges, C. Walter. *The Globe Restored* (1968). A conjectural restoration, with lucid drawings.

Hosley, Richard. "The Playhouses," in *The Revels History of Drama in English*, vol. 3, general editors Clifford Leech and T. W. Craik (1975). An essay of a hundred pages on the physical aspects of the playhouses.

Howard, Jane E. "Crossdressing, the Theatre, and Gender Struggle in Early Modern England," *Shakespeare Quarterly* 39 (1988): 418–40. Judicious comments on the effects of boys playing female roles.

Orrell, John. *The Human Stage: English Theatre Design, 1567–1640* (1988). Argues that the public, private, and court playhouses are less indebted to popular structures (e.g., innyards and bear-baiting pits) than to banqueting halls and to Renaissance conceptions of Roman amphitheaters.

Slater, Ann Pasternak. *Shakespeare the Director* (1982). An analysis of theatrical effects (e.g., kissing, kneeling) in stage directions and dialogue.

Styan, J. L. *Shakespeare's Stagecraft* (1967). An introduction to Shakespeare's visual and aural stagecraft, with chapters on such topics as acting conventions, stage groupings, and speech.

Thompson, Peter. *Shakespeare's Professional Career* (1992). An examination of patronage and related theatrical conditions.

———. *Shakespeare's Theatre* (1983). A discussion of how plays were staged in Shakespeare's time.

4. Shakespeare on Stage and Screen

Bate, Jonathan, and Russell Jackson, eds. *Shakespeare: An Illustrated Stage History* (1996). Highly readable essays on stage productions from the Renaissance to the present.

Berry, Ralph. *Changing Styles in Shakespeare* (1981). Discusses productions of six plays (*Coriolanus*, *Hamlet*, *Henry V*, *Measure for Measure*, *The Tempest*, and *Twelfth Night*) on the English stage, chiefly 1950–1980.

———. *On Directing Shakespeare: Interviews with Contemporary Directors* (1989). An enlarged edition of a book first published in 1977, this version includes the seven interviews from the early 1970s and adds five interviews conducted in 1988.

Brockbank, Philip, ed. *Players of Shakespeare: Essays in Shakespearean Performance* (1985). Comments by twelve actors, reporting their experiences with roles. See also the entry for Russell Jackson (below).

Bulman, J. C., and H. R. Coursen, eds. *Shakespeare on Television* (1988). An anthology of general and theoretical essays, essays on individual productions, and shorter reviews, with a bibliography and a videography listing cassettes that may be rented.

Coursen, H. P. *Watching Shakespeare on Television* (1993).

Analyses not only of TV versions but also of films and videotapes of stage presentations that are shown on television.

Davies, Anthony, and Stanley Wells, eds. *Shakespeare and the Moving Image: The Plays on Film and Television* (1994). General essays (e.g., on the comedies) as well as essays devoted entirely to *Hamlet, King Lear,* and *Macbeth.*

Dawson, Anthony B. *Watching Shakespeare: A Playgoer's Guide* (1988). About half of the plays are discussed, chiefly in terms of decisions that actors and directors make in putting the works onto the stage.

Dessen, Alan C. *Elizabethan Stage Conventions and Modern Interpretations* (1984). On interpreting conventions such as the representation of light and darkness and stage violence (duels, battles).

Donaldson, Peter. *Shakespearean Films/Shakespearean Directors* (1990). Postmodernist analyses, drawing on Freudianism, Feminism, Deconstruction, and Queer Theory.

Jackson, Russell, and Robert Smallwood, eds. *Players of Shakespeare 2: Further Essays in Shakespearean Performance by Players with the Royal Shakespeare Company* (1988). Fourteen actors discuss their roles in productions between 1982 and 1987.

———. *Players of Shakespeare 3: Further Essays in Shakespearean Performance by Players with the Royal Shakespeare Company* (1993). Comments by thirteen performers.

Jorgens, Jack. *Shakespeare on Film* (1977). Fairly detailed studies of eighteen films, preceded by an introductory chapter addressing such issues as music, and whether to "open" the play by including scenes of landscape.

Kennedy, Dennis. *Looking at Shakespeare: A Visual History of Twentieth-Century Performance* (1993). Lucid descriptions (with 170 photographs) of European, British, and American performances.

Leiter, Samuel L. *Shakespeare Around the Globe: A Guide to Notable Postwar Revivals* (1986). For each play there are about two pages of introductory comments, then discussions (about five hundred words per production) of ten or so productions, and finally bibliographic references.

McMurty, Jo. *Shakespeare Films in the Classroom* (1994). Useful evaluations of the chief films most likely to be shown in undergraduate courses.

Rothwell, Kenneth, and Annabelle Henkin Melzer. *Shakespeare on Screen: An International Filmography and Videography* (1990). A reference guide to several hundred films and videos produced between 1899 and 1989, including spinoffs such as musicals and dance versions.

Smallwood, Robert. *Players of Shakespeare 4* (1998). Like the volumes by Brockbank and Jackson, listed above, contains remarks by contemporary performers.

Sprague, Arthur Colby. *Shakespeare and the Actors* (1944). Detailed discussions of stage business (gestures, etc.) over the years.

Willis, Susan. *The BBC Shakespeare Plays: Making the Televised Canon* (1991). A history of the series, with interviews and production diaries for some plays.

5. Miscellaneous Reference Works

Abbott, E. A. *A Shakespearean Grammar* (new edition, 1877). An examination of differences between Elizabethan and modern grammar.

Allen, Michael J. B., and Kenneth Muir, eds. *Shakespeare's Plays in Quarto* (1981). One volume containing facsimiles of the plays issued in small format before they were collected in the First Folio of 1623.

Blake, Norman. *Shakespeare's Language: An Introduction* (1983). On vocabulary, parts of speech, and word order.

Bullough, Geoffrey. *Narrative and Dramatic Sources of Shakespeare*, 8 vols. (1957–75). A collection of many of the books Shakespeare drew on, with judicious comments.

Campbell, Oscar James, and Edward G. Quinn, eds. *The*

Reader's Encyclopedia of Shakespeare (1966). Old, and in some ways superseded by Michael Dobson's *Oxford Companion* (see below), but still highly valuable.

Cercignani, Fausto. *Shakespeare's Works and Elizabethan Pronunciation* (1981). Considered the best work on the topic, but remains controversial.

Champion, Larry S. *The Essential Shakespeare: An Annotated Bibliography of Major Modern Studies* (2nd ed., 1993). An invaluable guide to 1,800 writings about Shakespeare.

Dent, R. W. *Shakespeare's Proverbial Language: An Index* (1981). An index of proverbs, with an introduction concerning a form Shakespeare frequently drew on.

Dobson, Michael, ed. *The Oxford Companion to Shakespeare* (2001). Probably the single most useful reference work for information (arranged alphabetically) about Shakespeare and his works.

Greg, W. W. *The Shakespeare First Folio* (1955). A detailed yet readable history of the first collection (1623) of Shakespeare's plays.

Harner, James. *The World Shakespeare Bibliography.* See headnote to Suggested References.

Hosley, Richard. *Shakespeare's Holinshed* (1968). Valuable presentation of one of Shakespeare's major sources.

Kökeritz, Helge. *Shakespeare's Names* (1959). A guide to pronouncing some 1,800 names appearing in Shakespeare.

———. *Shakespeare's Pronunciation* (1953). Contains much information about puns and rhymes, but see Cercignani (above).

Muir, Kenneth. *The Sources of Shakespeare's Plays* (1978). An account of Shakespeare's use of his reading. It covers all the plays, in chronological order.

Miriam Joseph, Sister. *Shakespeare's Use of the Arts of Language* (1947). A study of Shakespeare's use of rhetorical devices, reprinted in part as *Rhetoric in Shakespeare's Time* (1962).

The Norton Facsimile: The First Folio of Shakespeare's

Plays (1968). A handsome and accurate facsimile of the first collection (1623) of Shakespeare's plays, with a valuable introduction by Charlton Hinman.

Onions, C. T. *A Shakespeare Glossary*, rev. and enlarged by R. D. Eagleson (1986). Definitions of words (or senses of words) now obsolete.

Partridge, Eric. *Shakespeare's Bawdy*, rev. ed. (1955). Relatively brief dictionary of bawdy words; useful, but see Williams, below.

Shakespeare Quarterly. See headnote to Suggested References.

Shakespeare Survey. See headnote to Suggested References.

Spevack, Marvin. *The Harvard Concordance to Shakespeare* (1973). An index to Shakespeare's words.

Vickers, Brian. *Appropriating Shakespeare: Contemporary Critical Quarrels* (1993). A survey—chiefly hostile—of recent schools of criticism.

Wells, Stanley, ed. *Shakespeare: A Bibliographical Guide* (new edition, 1990). Nineteen chapters (some devoted to single plays, others devoted to groups of related plays) on recent scholarship on the life and all of the works.

Williams, Gordon. *A Dictionary of Sexual Language and Imagery in Shakespearean and Stuart Literature*, 3 vols. (1994). Extended discussions of words and passages; much fuller than Partridge, cited above.

6. Shakespeare's Plays: General Studies

Bamber, Linda. *Comic Women, Tragic Men: A Study of Gender and Genre in Shakespeare* (1982).

Barnet, Sylvan. *A Short Guide to Shakespeare* (1974).

Callaghan, Dympna, Lorraine Helms, and Jyotsna Singh. *The Weyward Sisters: Shakespeare and Feminist Politics* (1994).

Clemen, Wolfgang H. *The Development of Shakespeare's Imagery* (1951).

Cook, Ann Jennalie. *Making a Match: Courtship in Shakespeare and His Society* (1991).

Dollimore, Jonathan, and Alan Sinfield, eds. *Political Shakespeare: New Essays in Cultural Materialism* (1985).

Dusinberre, Juliet. *Shakespeare and the Nature of Women* (1975).

Granville-Barker, Harley. *Prefaces to Shakespeare*, 2 vols. (1946–47; volume 1 contains essays on *Hamlet, King Lear, Merchant of Venice, Antony and Cleopatra,* and *Cymbeline*; volume 2 contains essays on *Othello, Coriolanus, Julius Caesar, Romeo and Juliet, Love's Labor's Lost*).

———. *More Prefaces to Shakespeare* (1974; essays on *Twelfth Night, A Midsummer Night's Dream, The Winter's Tale, Macbeth*).

Harbage, Alfred. *William Shakespeare: A Reader's Guide* (1963).

Howard, Jean E. *Shakespeare's Art of Orchestration: Stage Technique and Audience Response* (1984).

Jones, Emrys. *Scenic Form in Shakespeare* (1971).

Lenz, Carolyn Ruth Swift, Gayle Greene, and Carol Thomas Neely, eds. *The Woman's Part: Feminist Criticism of Shakespeare* (1980).

Novy, Marianne. *Love's Argument: Gender Relations in Shakespeare* (1984).

Rose, Mark. *Shakespearean Design* (1972).

Scragg, Leah. *Discovering Shakespeare's Meaning* (1994).

———. *Shakespeare's "Mouldy Tales": Recurrent Plot Motifs in Shakespearean Drama* (1992).

Traub, Valerie. *Desire and Anxiety: Circulations of Sexuality in Shakespearean Drama* (1992).

Traversi, D. A. *An Approach to Shakespeare,* 2 vols. (3rd rev. ed, 1968–69).

Vickers, Brian. *The Artistry of Shakespeare's Prose* (1968).

Wells, Stanley. *Shakespeare: A Dramatic Life* (1994).

Wright, George T. *Shakespeare's Metrical Art* (1988).

7. The Comedies

Barber, C. L. *Shakespeare's Festive Comedy* (1959; discusses *Love's Labor's Lost, A Midsummer Night's Dream, The Merchant of Venice, As You Like It, Twelfth Night*).

Barton, Anne. *The Names of Comedy* (1990).

Berry, Ralph. *Shakespeare's Comedy: Explorations in Form* (1972).

Bradbury, Malcolm, and David Palmer, eds. *Shakespearean Comedy* (1972).

Bryant, J. A., Jr. *Shakespeare and the Uses of Comedy* (1986).

Carroll, William. *The Metamorphoses of Shakespearean Comedy* (1985).

Champion, Larry S. *The Evolution of Shakespeare's Comedy* (1970).

Evans, Bertrand. *Shakespeare's Comedies* (1960).

Frye, Northrop. *Shakespearean Comedy and Romance* (1965).

Leggatt, Alexander. *Shakespeare's Comedy of Love* (1974).

Miola, Robert S. *Shakespeare and Classical Comedy: The Influence of Plautus and Terence* (1994).

Nevo, Ruth. *Comic Transformations in Shakespeare* (1980).

Ornstein, Robert. *Shakespeare's Comedies: From Roman Farce to Romantic Mystery* (1986).

Richman, David. *Laughter, Pain, and Wonder: Shakespeare's Comedies and the Audience in the Theater* (1990).

Salingar, Leo. *Shakespeare and the Traditions of Comedy* (1974).

Slights, Camille Wells. *Shakespeare's Comic Commonwealths* (1993).

Waller, Gary, ed. *Shakespeare's Comedies* (1991).

Westlund, Joseph. *Shakespeare's Reparative Comedies: A Psychoanalytic View of the Middle Plays* (1984).

Williamson, Marilyn. *The Patriarchy of Shakespeare's Comedies* (1986).

8. The Romances (*Pericles, Cymbeline, The Winter's Tale, The Tempest, The Two Noble Kinsmen*)

Adams, Robert M. *Shakespeare: The Four Romances* (1989).

Felperin, Howard. *Shakespearean Romance* (1972).

Frye, Northrop. *A Natural Perspective: The Development of Shakespearean Comedy and Romance* (1965).

Mowat, Barbara. *The Dramaturgy of Shakespeare's Romances* (1976).

Warren, Roger. *Staging Shakespeare's Late Plays* (1990).

Young, David. *The Heart's Forest: A Study of Shakespeare's Pastoral Plays* (1972).

9. The Tragedies

Bradley, A. C. *Shakespearean Tragedy* (1904).

Brooke, Nicholas. *Shakespeare's Early Tragedies* (1968).

Champion, Larry S. *Shakespeare's Tragic Perspective* (1976).

Drakakis, John, ed. *Shakespearean Tragedy* (1992).

Evans, Bertrand. *Shakespeare's Tragic Practice* (1979).

Everett, Barbara. *Young Hamlet: Essays on Shakespeare's Tragedies* (1989).

Foakes, R. A. *Hamlet versus Lear: Cultural Politics and Shakespeare's Art* (1993).

Frye, Northrop. *Fools of Time: Studies in Shakespearean Tragedy* (1967).

Harbage, Alfred, ed. *Shakespeare: The Tragedies* (1964).

Mack, Maynard. *Everybody's Shakespeare: Reflections Chiefly on the Tragedies* (1993).

McAlindon, T. *Shakespeare's Tragic Cosmos* (1991).

Miola, Robert S. *Shakespeare and Classical Tragedy: The Influence of Seneca* (1992).

———. *Shakespeare's Rome* (1983).

Nevo, Ruth. *Tragic Form in Shakespeare* (1972).

Rackin, Phyllis. *Shakespeare's Tragedies* (1978).

Rose, Mark, ed. *Shakespeare's Early Tragedies: A Collection of Critical Essays* (1995).

Rosen, William. *Shakespeare and the Craft of Tragedy* (1960).

Snyder, Susan. *The Comic Matrix of Shakespeare's Tragedies* (1979).

Wofford, Susanne. *Shakespeare's Late Tragedies: A Collection of Critical Essays* (1996).

Young, David. *The Action to the Word: Structure and Style in Shakespearean Tragedy* (1990).

———. *Shakespeare's Middle Tragedies: A Collection of Critical Essays* (1993).

10. The Histories

Blanpied, John W. *Time and the Artist in Shakespeare's English Histories* (1983).

Campbell, Lily B. *Shakespeare's "Histories": Mirrors of Elizabethan Policy* (1947).

Champion, Larry S. *Perspective in Shakespeare's English Histories* (1980).

Grene, Nicholas. *Shakespeare's Serial History Plays* (2002).

Hodgdon, Barbara. *The End Crowns All: Closure and Contradiction in Shakespeare's History* (1991).

Holderness, Graham. *Shakespeare Recycled: The Making of Historical Drama* (1992).

———, ed. *Shakespeare's History Plays: "Richard II" to "Henry V"* (1992).

Jones, Robert C. *Those Valiant Dead: Reviving the Past in Shakespeare's Histories* (1991).

Knowles, Ronald. *Shakespeare's Arguments with History* (2002).

Leggatt, Alexander. *Shakespeare's Political Drama: The History Plays and the Roman Plays* (1988).

Levine, Nina S. *Women's Matters: Politics, Gender, and Nation in Shakespeare's Early History Plays* (1998).

Ornstein, Robert. *A Kingdom for a Stage: The Achievement of Shakespeare's History Plays* (1972).

Pugliatti, Paola. *Shakespeare the Historian* (1996).

Rackin, Phyllis. *Stages of History: Shakespeare's English Chronicles* (1990).

Reese, Max Meredith. *The Cease of Majesty: A Study of Shakespeare's History Plays* (1961).

Ribner, Irving. *The English History Play in the Age of Shakespeare* (rev. ed., 1965).

Saccio, Peter. *Shakespeare's English Kings* (2nd ed., 1999).

Spiekerman, Tim. *Shakespeare's Political Realism* (2001).

Tillyard, E.M.W. *Shakespeare's History Plays* (1944).

Velz, John W., ed. *Shakespeare's English Histories: A Quest for Form and Genre* (1996).

11. *The Two Gentlemen of Verona*

Useful scholarly editions of *Two Gentlemen of Verona* have been prepared by Kurt Schlueter (1990) and William C. Carroll (2004). The edition by Rex Gibson and Susan Leach (1999), in the Cambridge School Series, includes much apparatus that will help inexperienced readers.

For a collection of essays on the play (some reprinted, some newly commissioned) see the volume by June Schlueter listed below. Essays on all aspects of the play are reprinted in volumes 6, 12, 40, 54, and 63 of *Shakespearean Criticism*.

For the play on the stage, see the references on pages 185 and 187, at the end of *The Two Gentlemen of Verona* on Stage and Screen. For the play in the context of Shakespeare's other comedies, see above, Section 7 (page 200). In addition to those titles, the following titles are especially recommended.

Brooks, Harold F. "Two Clowns in a Comedy (to Say Nothing of the Dog): Speed, Launce (and Crab), in *The Two Gentlemen of Verona,*" *Essays and Studies,* New Series 16 (1963): 91–100. Rptd. in June Schlueter: 71–78.

Ewbank, Inga-Stina. " 'Were Man but Constant, He Were Perfect': Constancy and Consistency in *The Two Gentlemen of Verona.*" In *Shakespearean Comedy,* ed. Malcolm Bradbury and David Palmer. *Stratford-upon-Avon Studies* 14 (1972): 31–57. Rptd. in June Schlueter: 91–114.

Girard, René. "Love Delights in Praises: A Reading of *The Two Gentlemen of Verona.*" *Philosophy and Literature* 13 (Oct. 1989): 231–47.

Hallett, Charles A. " 'Metamorphosing' Proteus: Reversal Strategies in *The Two Gentlemen of Verona.*" First published in June Schlueter: 153–77.

Kiefer, Frederick. "Love Letters in *The Two Gentlemen of Verona.*" *Shakespeare Studies* 18 (1986): 65–85. Rptd. in June Schlueter: 133–52.

Schleiner, Louise. "Voice, Ideology, and Gendered Subjects: The Case of *As You Like It* and *Two Gentlemen.*" *Shakespeare Quarterly* 50 (1999): 285–309.

Schlueter, June, ed. *Two Gentlemen of Verona: Critical Essays* (1996).

Slights, Camille Wells. *Shakespeare's Comic Commonwealths* (1993). A very slightly different version is given in June Schlueter: 115–32.

Timpane, John. " 'I am but a foole, looke you': Launce and the Social Functions of Humor." First published in June Schlueter: 189–211.

READ THE TOP 20 SIGNET CLASSICS